THOMSON

━━ RSE TECHNOLOGY ™

sional ■ Trade ■ Reference

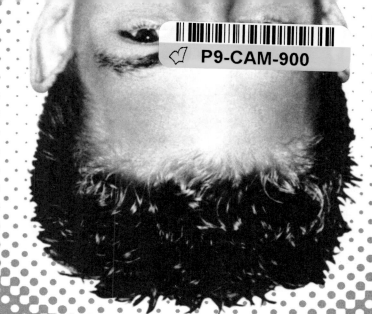

BLOGGING

For Teens

John Gosney

THOMSON
⋆
RSE TECHNOLOGY

sional ■ Trade ■ Reference

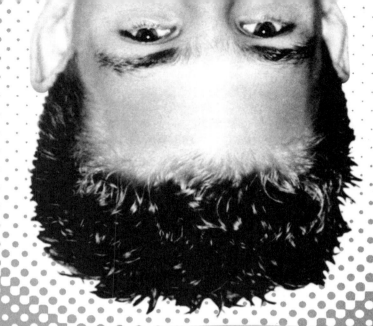

BLOGGING

For Teens

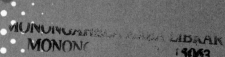

John Gosney

SVP, Thomson Course Technology PTR: Andy Shafran

Publisher/Acquisitions Editor: Stacy L. Hiquet

Senior Marketing Manager: Sarah O'Donnell

Marketing Manager: Heather Hurley

Manager of Editorial Services: Heather Talbot

Associate Marketing Managers: Kristin Eisenzopf and Sarah Dubois

Project/Copy Editor: Karen A. Gill

Technical Reviewer: Arlie Hartman

Thomson Course Technology PTR Market Coordinator: Amanda Weaver

Interior Layout Tech: Bill Hartman

Cover Designer: Mike Tanamachi

Indexer: Kelly Talbot

Proofreader: Sean Medlock

Teen Reviewer: Genna Kae Gosney

ISBN: 1-59200-476-8

Library of Congress Catalog Card Number: 2004108009

Printed in the United States of America

04 05 06 07 08 BH 10 9 8 7 6 5 4 3 2 1

THOMSON

COURSE TECHNOLOGY

Professional ■ Trade ■ Reference

Thomson Course Technology PTR, a division of Course Technology
25 Thomson Place ■ Boston, MA 02210 ■ http://www.courseptr.com

To Genna Kae, who will soon discover the wonder and magic of being a teenager. Never be afraid to find your true self, or to let people know who you really are and what you think. Your dad is very proud of you, and loves you very, very much!

Acknowledgments

This book was truly a labor of love, but it was certainly not a one-man show. Many very talented people contributed to the production of this book and the ideas that appear within its pages.

Right off the top, I'd like to thank my terrific project editor, Karen Gill. Karen has the unique ability to keep an author honest about meeting his deadlines while retaining a great sense of humor and appreciation for the difficulties that writing a book can present. She also has a great eye for detail and suggested many wonderful ideas for improving this book's content. In short, Karen is the real thing, and this book would not have been the pleasure it was to write without her involvement.

Many other talented people also made invaluable contributions. Arlie Hartman ensured the technical accuracy of the book, and—in many places—helped me to clarify simply and efficiently what would otherwise be long, rambling technical descriptions. Sean Medlock, Kelly Talbot, and Bill Hartman also played key roles in the production and editing process and deserve thanks for their fine efforts.

Special thanks, as always, are due to Stacy Hiquet. This book certainly would not have evolved the way it did without the great privilege and pleasure I consistently have in being able to discuss ideas with her. So thanks again, Stacy, for allowing me the opportunity to write for you, and I look forward to future collaborations.

Finally, I'd like to thank my family—Melissa, Genna, Jackson, and George—who always completely and unselfishly support my professional goals and interests. Your encouragement and love are what make everything possible, and I could not imagine my life without you.

About the Author

John Gosney has been working with technology for several years, as an author of computer books, a programmer, and a teacher. However, his real interest in technology is not so much in how it works but in how people use it to express their creativity and individuality. Not surprisingly, John is passionate about blogging because it is one of the best ways for people to express their creativity and individuality through technology. What he finds especially interesting about blogging is how people of all ages use blogs as "electronic thought processes" to link to other areas of interest. The focus of his blog (http://www.my-15minutes.com) is on why popular music can be such an important element in someone's life. John also likes to write about the sometimes hidden relationships between the ideas expressed in popular music and other areas.

John is a graduate of Purdue and Butler universities and serves as an instructor and technology director at the Indianapolis campus of Indiana University. John enjoys sports, reading, listening to music, and spending time with his family.

Contents at a Glance

Contents

Chapter 5
Planning Your Blog. 61

Chapter 6
Choosing Your Blog Hosting Service 73

Chapter 7
Building Your Blog with Angelfire, Part I. 87

Chapter 8
Building Your Blog with Angelfire, Part II 107

Chapter 9
Advanced Blog Design with Microsoft FrontPage. . . . 131

Introduction

More than likely, you have lots of interests. You like to watch movies, listen to music, hang out with your friends, and play sports. And, if you are like other teenagers, you like to talk about the things that interest you. You probably spend quite a bit of time thinking about and talking about school.

So, what if you had a place where you could write about your ideas and in turn have other people respond to you about those ideas? Better yet, what if you could link to other things that you think are related to your ideas or that help to better explain what you are thinking or feeling?

If you have opinions and ideas that are important to you, you have more than enough reason to be interested in blogging. A blog can help you make sense of your ideas and give you a way to express yourself to a potentially wide audience. It is possible that anyone who has access to the Web can, if you choose, have access to your blog. Keeping a blog can also help you to become a better student because you'll learn how to organize and write about your ideas—two skills that can benefit you in every class that you take. But most of all, keeping a blog can be great fun. You can use your blog to keep in touch with your friends, make new friends, and most importantly, learn about yourself.

You have interests, opinions, and ideas that are important to you. Why not use a blog so that you can share and express them? That is what *Blogging for Teens* is all about!

Know Yourself, Have Fun, Learn to Blog

So you've just been assigned another big term paper assignment, and you are wondering how you are going to come up with 10 pages of original stuff about a topic you are—how shall we say it?—really not that interested in. To top it off, you have to write three of these papers in the next three weeks, and you have to find time to do all this writing in between your other classes, baseball practice, getting tickets for Ozzfest, hanging out with your friends… the list goes on. Why would you want to take the time, which you don't really have, to write a blog when you don't like to write in the first place?

Probably the biggest misconception about blogging is that you have to write a lot to make it a real blog. This just isn't true. In fact, some of the best blogs are those that have short daily or weekly postings. Also, remember that the best blogs are those that are a genuine reflection of the person writing them. You might have heard the old saying that to be a good writer you should write about what you know. Now, this isn't always practical when it comes to school assignments. After all, the point of writing papers for school is to go out and do some research so that you can learn about things you don't know. Admittedly, this can sometimes be a painful process and not something you look forward to, but then again, I don't think anyone has loved every homework assignment he had to do. But you definitely should *not* think of blogging as homework! Rather, you should think of blogging as a way of writing about the things you know the most about—or want to know the most about—and that is you.

Finding Your "Cool Self"

How do you know yourself? That probably sounds like way too serious of a question for anything that could possibly be fun, right? In fact, that sounds like something your guidance counselor asks you, and we all know how much fun talking to a guidance counselor can be, right? I don't mean to give guidance counselors a hard time—they do important work. But it isn't always easy to explain what you are feeling or what you want to do when you grow up. In fact, the answers to those questions don't really get any easier the older you get (although they do get more interesting)!

The really cool thing about blogging, though, is that you can know yourself just by exploring and writing about the things you are really interested in. For example, one of my big interests and hobbies is music, and I mean all kinds of music, from Rage Against the Machine and Superjoint Ritual to Jason Mraz and Fountains of Wayne to Dr. Dre and Outkast. I like it all. (Yes, even a little country music, too.) I've been seriously collecting music since I was 10 and have more than 1,100 CDs in my collection, with more being added all the time. Music has always been important in my life. It helps me through the bad times and makes the good times that much more special. I also like to read and write about music because I'm fascinated by how other people think of music as an important part of their lives.

That's why it should come as no surprise that when I started to develop my own blog, I decided that music was going to be its focus. But even after my first few postings, I started to realize something:

- When I would sit down to make a quick posting about music, I would often end up not writing about music at all. Or maybe a better way of saying it would be that the music inspired me to think about and write about something else.

- As I would make postings and read them later, I started to understand that I did in fact have a strong opinion about ideas and issues that, prior to keeping a blog, I wasn't sure how I felt about. That is, I would read back over my posts and see the same idea and opinion coming out in my writing, just expressed in a different way, and usually expressed through a reference to a song or artist that I was listening to at the time.

- As my blog started to grow, the number of links I made to other blogs and outside sources started to grow, too. And the links I was making from my blog often didn't have anything to do with music. But again, when I read back over my posts and could put those links in the context of what I was writing about, it all made sense.

- Finally, I realized that what other people posted about my ideas were just as interesting as my own, and those postings often gave me ideas and thoughts that I had never even considered on my own.

A common theme runs through all these points: Although you can have a subject for your blog, you will find that the subject will quickly grow much larger and probably more interesting than you had initially thought. Over time, you will find that as you make your posts, a pattern will start to develop in how you express your ideas, opinions, and thoughts. It might be expressed differently, but that is what makes blogging such a unique pastime. Take my blog, for example. I can describe a bad day by making a reference to Sepultura just as easily as I can to a Kenny Chesney song. Granted, those are two pretty extreme opposites in terms of kinds of music. But if the reference makes sense to me—because of the way I've written about it or linked other blogs or Web sites to my posting—and it makes sense to other people, this is where the magic and fun of blogging really becomes evident. I call these types of wild, varied postings finding your "cool self," because you are finding all the cool things that interest you. And, when other people comment to these postings, I like to refer to that as "the collective cool," because your postings are a reflection of how other people can relate to and comment on what you have to say.

How This Book Is Arranged

So do you want to find your cool self? Do you want to be part of the collective cool? Do you want to have a tremendous amount of fun? And, oh yeah, just for good measure, do you want to become a better student as you become a better reader and writer?

You can accomplish all of these things by reading this book. But before you start, let me tell you how this book is arranged so that you can have some idea of what your journey to blogging will look like:

- ◆ **Finding Your Voice.** Chapters 1–5 focus on the idea of discovering ways to express your interests and using blogging as a way to make those expressions available to a wider audience. You'll see how you can draw on your interests to help discover your unique voice and how to put that voice on a blog for others to enjoy and discover. These chapters make connections to all kinds of varied sources, from music to movies to books (including two teen favorites: *The Perks of Being a Wallflower* and *Catcher in the Rye*), all in an effort to help you build on what you are already interested in so that you can write about these things in your blog.

- ◆ **Building Your Blog.** After you know what and how to write, you need to know how to actually build a blog. Chapters 6–10 show you in step-by-step examples how to register and build your own blog. You'll learn how to work with hyperlinks and all kinds of exciting Web technologies to make your blog fun and easy to use. You'll also get some advice on how to integrate your blog into your life so that you don't feel like you have to spend hours working with it every night to make it a good blog or to have fun with it.

- ◆ **Blogging Examples.** After you've found your voice and know how to build a blog, you'll probably want some examples to get you started. Chapters 11 and 12 look at two specific blogs (including my own) that use different voices, styles, and Web design techniques to express their ideas.

Although you don't really need to read the book in order from Chapter 1 to Chapter 12, you will find that the book's content builds on each chapter, so it might be to your advantage to read the chapters in sequential order. Also, as described in the next section regarding the special "blogger70" element, there is a narrative running through the entire book, so as you learn about blogging and start to think about your own blog, you'll get to see how a fictitious but realistic teenager develops his ideas, too.

Special Elements Used in This Book

Throughout this book, you will see special elements that touch on all elements of blogging. Some of these elements let you know techie stuff about blogging, such as how blogging software works. However, much of this special material offers comments on the entire blogging experience from a teenage perspective. Following are these special elements:

 These special elements provide a more personal, insider's guide to the book's content. You'll find these comments sprinkled throughout the book, so think of them as proof that what you are reading is applicable to the real world, especially the real world as it is perceived by teenagers like you.

 Look to these elements for quick additional information on the subject being discussed, especially for ways to help you do whatever is being discussed faster or more efficiently.

 Although everything about blogs is fun, there are some things you need to be on the lookout for so that your fun is not compromised. These special elements will give you the lowdown on what to avoid, or at least what to keep a special eye on.

 Look to Notes for extra information that's not critical to your understanding of the text but can give you additional ideas or point you in new directions.

 *At the end of every chapter, you will see a special posting from blogger70. These fictitious but realistic blog postings are meant to convey a sense of how you can use the ideas presented in these chapters as inspiration for creating your own blog postings. These 12 postings tell a story that you can get ideas from, as blogger70 begins a new school year and a new blog. That story—and the voice and methods that blogger70 utilizes—can serve as your guide. Think of this special element as a blog in a book about blogging!*

Chapter 1
The Perks of Being a Wallblogger

You wanna learn to blog? You've come to the right place! You've got something to say, and you want to say it to as many people as possible. Or, maybe you have just a few close friends who you want to read your blog. Regardless of whether your intended audience is big or small, there are some real advantages to blogging that you need to know about, as well as some basic terminology and concepts that you should be familiar with before you start your own blog or pay money to subscribe to a blog hosting service.

I know you're anxious to get blogging, but take a few minutes to chill out with your favorite beverage and read through this chapter to be sure we're straight on a few blogging basics. This chapter also introduces you to a few blogging deficiencies—things you might be able to do better by utilizing other Web communication tools.

In a nutshell, this chapter will

- ◆ Talk about the needs and desires of people who think blogging is a fun and important thing to do in the first place
- ◆ Describe the differences between a blog and a regular Web page
- ◆ Describe the differences between keeping a blog and using instant messaging and e-mail

> **tip** In addition to giving you strategies for writing and maintaining your blog, this book will also show you the technical components for creating your blog. In the process, you'll learn some fairly advanced HTML (short for Hypertext Markup Language, which is a set of tags from which Web pages are built), as well as how to work with a Web page editor such as Microsoft FrontPage. But don't worry about this stuff just yet—there will be plenty of time for that a bit later in this book (Chapters 6, 7, 8, and 9, to be exact).

Why Blog in the First Place?

Do you like to read? I'm assuming you probably do if you are interested in blogs because they ask you to do quite a bit of reading and writing.

Maybe you like to read novels or short stories. Or maybe you like to read magazines and newspapers. Then again, maybe you just like to read other blogs. Whatever and wherever you like to read, the point is that you are engaging in a high-energy activity when you take time to read.

Wait a minute. When did reading become a "high-energy" activity? Taking your neighbor on in a game of one-on-one hoops is pretty high energy. Arguing with your little brother or sister can be pretty stressful, too. But *reading*? That's something you do when you want to relax, not get all fired up.

Wait another minute, though. Think about the last thing you read that really stuck in your head. How did you feel after you read it? Were you excited? Did reading whatever it was give you new ideas of your own, or make you rethink something that you were pretty sure you had a good handle on?

When you read something that really engages you—or put another way, when you read something that really makes you *think*—you are most definitely taking part in a high-energy activity. When you read something good, it makes your brain get moving with all kinds of new ideas and thoughts. And thinking is probably the most high-energy activity there is, because the right thought at the right time can change the world.

Figures 1.1, 1.2, and 1.3 show some examples of blogs, the same kind that you'll be able to create, publish, and maintain after reading this book.

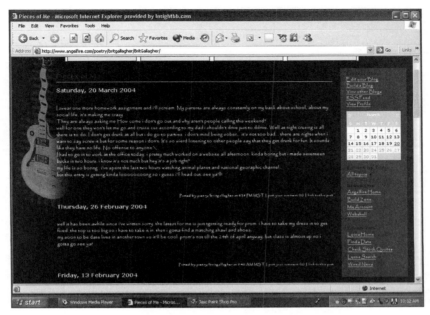

FIGURE 1.1 *Many of the blog hosting services allow you to use design templates to give your blog a certain look and feel.*

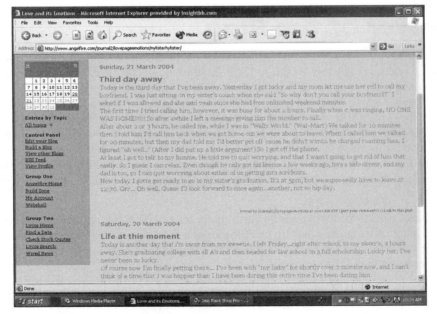

FIGURE 1.2 *Most blogs will have some kind of calendar so that you can read the specific posting for any given day.*

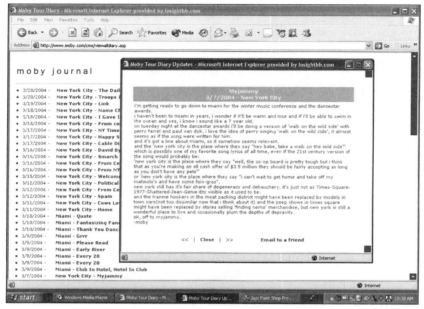

FIGURE 1.3 *Many celebrities keep blogs. Here's a blog posting kept by the musician Moby.*

The Power of the Blog

Now, if you agree with me about the power of thinking, think for a minute about the power of a really great blog. Better yet, think about the really great blog that you will know how to write when you finish this book. You are diligent in posting to your blog on a regular basis—maybe not every day, but often enough that you keep the information current. You wouldn't keep a blog if you didn't have something to say, but let's assume you are just keeping a blog of the things that are happening in your life. More specifically, a few of your close friends have started their own blogs, and you use your blogs to record the events and experiences that are going on in your lives. You learn a lot about your friends, you become a better writer and reader, and... oh yeah... you have a ton of fun.

But one day, because you've opened your blog up for public viewing (that is, you haven't restricted it to your "buddy list"), your blog happens to be read by someone you don't know. Let's call this person by his screen alias WhiteStripe50, which he picked because his favorite band is the White Stripes.

You don't know it, but WhiteStripe50 has been having a hard time lately. He has just moved to a new school and has had a hard time fitting in. To make things worse, he is shy, and even though he really wants to make new friends, he can't seem to find the right words when meeting new people. He usually ends up feeling like a dork when he tries to talk to anyone.

One afternoon, however, WhiteStripe50 just happens to find your blog on Angelfire because he likes the title of your site, which you've decided to call "Life and Times at Greendale High School." As he reads through the postings between you and your friends, he learns a lot about what is happening at your school. Better yet, he finds that you and your friends share the same interests that he does. As it turns out, you all like music and going to concerts.

 tip Angelfire is one of many blog hosting services. You'll learn about these services and how to use them later in this book.

And then, an amazing thing happens: WhiteStripe50 doesn't just read your blog entries—he decides to *post a reply*, too. In your most recent entry, you and your friends were arguing about the best song on *Elephant* (the latest White Stripes CD). All your friends think that "Seven Nation Army" is the best, but you think that "The Hardest Button to Button" is the best. Well, in his posting, WhiteStripe50 takes your side and says that although all the songs on that CD are great, "The Hardest Button to Button" is definitely the best.

The next day after school when you sit down to update your blog, you notice a new posting from someone you don't know. As you read WhiteStripe50's posting, you find yourself smiling and laughing because he was so cool and funny in his response to your friends. Then, another even more amazing thing happens: You link over to WhiteStripe50's blog (he left his address in his posting), you click on his profile (where you see his name and where he lives), and you find out that WhiteStripe50 goes to your school and might even have a few classes with you.

The next day at lunch, you notice WhiteStripe50 (real name: Ben Roberts) sitting alone. You go over and introduce yourself, and you end up having a great conversation about your posting. Your friends wander in for lunch, too, and you introduce them to Ben. Not surprisingly, all of you immediately find out that you have lots of things in common. Even cooler, Ben's sister works at a record store and has the inside scoop on getting good seats for an upcoming concert. As the lunch bell rings and it's time to go back to class, all of you eagerly make plans to meet up that weekend and get tickets for the big concert.

You've made a new friend because of your blog and helped that new friend fit in at his new school. You might have met Ben anyway eventually, but having a well-written, updated blog allowed you to meet him even faster. And you just might end up getting front-row seats to the best concert of the year! What could be better than that?

 You can learn so much about your friends by reading what they have to say in their blogs.. You can make new friends, too, by letting other people know about your blog and then having them reply to your postings.

 The story I've told here is fictitious, and as far as I know, there is no WhiteStripe50 (or if there is, I don't think that his real name is Ben Roberts). Although this kind of story happens all the time—and is evidence of what a cool and powerful communication tool blogs can be—you should always use caution when giving out any identifying information about yourself in your blog postings or your blog profile. We'll talk more about safe blogging later in this book.

Wielding Your Blog Power Wisely

The story I told in the previous section was fictitious. Still, it points out several of the really great advantages of blogging:

◆ Keeping a blog along with your friends is a great way not only of communicating with each other, but also keeping a record of that communication. As you'll see later in the chapter when we compare blogging to instant messaging, this "permanent record" is a real benefit of blogging. Not only can you go back and read your blog later, but other people also can read your postings (if you open your blog to public viewing).

◆ A well-written blog is going to give you an outlet for your ideas, and it's also going to let other people comment on those ideas. Best of all, it doesn't matter what you write about on your blog. From a discussion about the history of mathematics (yes, there are such blogs) to your favorite kind of ice cream (yep, there are blogs about that, too!), you will get new ideas if you take time to write your own blog *and* read what other people say in the blogs they keep.

◆ Last but certainly not least, a well-written, updated blog might take you in directions you never thought possible. Although you need to be careful about the amount of personal information you give out over the Web (whether it's in a blog, an instant message, or a Web site), there is nothing wrong with meeting new people and making new friends through the power of the blog. In fact, that is one of the best things about keeping a blog. And even though you might never get to physically meet the new friends you make online (they could live thousands of miles away from you, in a different country!), you can still learn from them and enjoy them.

Keeping all these things in mind, then, you have to be sure to wield your blog power wisely.

What do I mean by that? Let's think back to our earlier story involving WhiteStripe50. Imagine that, after reading Ben's posting, you immediately replied with something like, "Hey, WhiteStripe50 or whoever you are. This is a *private* conversation and you are *not* invited."

Although responding like that is certainly within your power, it's not a good idea. First, it's not polite. Second, you would lose out on a new online friend (and in this case, a real-world friend, too). Finally, you should be aware of the general structure of blogs and the rules of the game, so to speak. For example, if you only want your friends to be able to view and respond to your blog, you should set those options in your blog management. (Again, you'll learn more on these types of issues in Chapters 6–9.)

What I'm trying to say here is that a blog is a powerful tool because it has the power to communicate ideas, and there are few things in this world that are more powerful than a well-communicated idea. Unfortunately, not all blogs or Web pages communicate good ideas. There are a lot of… well… ugly blogs out there, and I don't just mean those with bad color designs. For example, some blogs proclaim all kinds of racist/bigoted viewpoints. As you travel around the Web reading and responding to blogs, remember that not everyone will agree with what you have to say and that you might find yourself disagreeing with what someone else might have to say. If you feel you must respond to someone's blog with a comment, always respond intelligently. In other words, take time to engage in that high-energy activity of thinking to be sure you are saying what you really want to say, in the words you really want to use.

---

tip Whenever I write something I feel really emotional about (either good or bad), I save a draft of it. Then I go away and think about it for a day before doing anything with it, such as sending it in an e-mail. If, after a day, I can come back to the writing and still feel just as emotional about it, then I go ahead and send it.

Why do I do this? Well, as I'm sure you know, when you feel really strongly about something, your emotions can cloud your thinking. Have you ever said/written something to someone, and then a few hours later thought to yourself, "Jeez, I wish I hadn't said that"? You don't get that kind of after-the-fact perspective until, well, after the fact.

The same holds true for posting to blogs. You might read a posting on someone's blog that absolutely burns you up, but rather than fire off a nasty reply (or to use a Web term, before you *flame* the author of the blog), take some time to think about your reply. Make sure you are saying what you really want to say, and that it's an honest reflection of how you really feel.

Why Blog Instead of Keeping a Web Site, Instant Messaging, or E-Mailing?

Blogging really is a unique way of communicating, and as such, it has developed its own set of protocols, tricks and traps, and so on. Indeed, blogging is so different from other Web-based forms of communication that it deserves to be treated as its own unique medium, which is why there was a need for a book like this.

Still, you might be thinking at this point that a blog is too much work compared to a regular Web page, Instant Messaging (IM), or e-mail. But, in reality, a blog doesn't have to be any more time-consuming than these other ways of communicating. In fact, a blog might take even less time than these other tools and be more productive and fun in the long run, too.

What I'd like to do in the next few sections of the book is to compare the blog to the traditional Web page, IM, and e-mail and look at the pros and cons of working with each. Take some time to be honest with yourself as you read through these sections. Ask yourself how you use your computer now. If you end up thinking that some parts of blogging just aren't for you, and that a good old-fashioned e-mail would do the trick, more power to you. The point of this book is not to convince you that blogging is the greatest thing since sliced bread (or the digitally remastered 5.1 audio surround-sound Led Zeppelin DVD box set). However, I do want to make sure you see the full spectrum of what it means to blog. If that results in your starting your own blog, you should understand why to keep a blog, how to build it, and how to care for and feed it.

Blog Versus Web Page

There are some real similarities between a blog and a typical Web page. You can access both of them through a specific URL (such as www.my-15minutes.com, which is similar to the address of a typical Web site). In addition, you can employ HTML and other Web design tools, such as cascading style sheets. Finally, you can access (with many blog hosting services) your blog through Microsoft FrontPage or some other type of HTML editor.

You could say that a blog is just a type of Web site. Although that is technically true, blogs are in fact very different from Web pages, both in terms of their design and their purpose:

◆ **Web sites are made up of multiple pages.** Although you can have blogs that are composed of several pages, you probably won't see many blogs with menu systems or site maps. The great thing about a blog is that everything is there to see on the front page: a way of navigating through the messages and links to other sites of interest. Web sites have these things, too, but because of their design, you usually have to click through a few pages to get to the discussion section. So, generally speaking, blogs are easier to navigate, because everything you are looking for is usually right there when the blog first loads in your Web browser.

◆ **Web sites are hosted differently from blogs.** Let's say that you're really interested in music. Actually, let's make it more specific and say that you're really interested in hip hop music. You could go a Web search engine like Yahoo! or Google and type in "hip hop," but you would be presented with a general listing of sites and categories, as shown in Figure 1.4.

Now, compare Figure 1.4 with a blog hosting service, as shown in Figure 1.5, where, upon first glance, you can easily see different categories of interest neatly organized. This makes it easier to start your search and find the information you're looking for.

 I'm not saying that you can go to any blog hosting service and instantly find the perfect blog to match your interest. But, generally speaking, you might have better (and faster) luck finding a blog that matches your specific interest than trying to find a random Web page that really matches it.

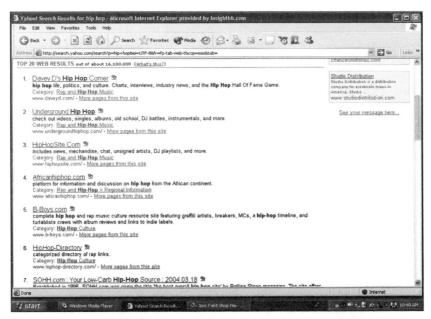

FIGURE 1.4 *The Web contains a lot of cool information. Finding exactly what you are looking for, though, can take quite a bit of digging through lots and lots of Web sites.*

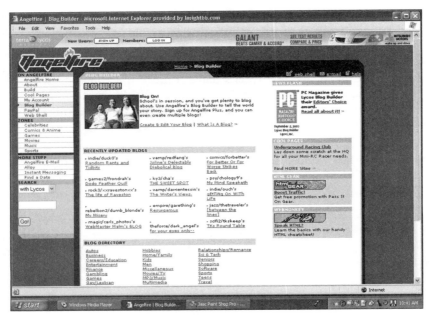

FIGURE 1.5 *Blog hosting services offer straightforward organization of blogs, so you can more quickly find what you are looking for.*

◆ **Blogs are designed to be more "active" than traditional Web sites.** Remember that perhaps the key difference between a blog and a Web site is that a Web site is designed to be more "static" than a blog. A Web site can be designed, have content placed on it, and be perceived as being a "good" Web site for many months (or years) without having either its design or content changed. Think about it: Let's say there is some company that wants to establish a *Web presence* so that customers can go to the site and find the store location, its hours of operation, and so on. A Web site like that would be pretty boring, but as long as it gave the customers the information they were looking for, it would have to be considered a successful Web site.

Compare that to a blog, though. If you went to a blog and found that the last entry was a month ago or more, you'd probably think the owner of the blog either gave up on making entries or just wasn't that interested in keeping a good blog. The really cool thing about blogs is that they capitalize on the immediate nature of the Web. When something happens in your life that you want to write about, you can log in to your blog, write about the experience, and within minutes, that experience is available for others to see. Although you could do the same thing with a Web site, it is generally harder and more time consuming to update a Web site. This is because if you change information on one page, it likely needs to be changed on other pages of the site, too.

 Many people who used to have a Web site often find that the part of the site they were using the most was the message section, where they would post comments and other people would read and respond to them. Although other parts of a Web site can be useful, you can often do the same thing with a blog. That way, you can focus on what you really want to do, which is talk about different topics and have other people respond.

Blog Versus IM

If you use IM very often, you know the great benefit of using it: It is fast. You are online with your friends, and the only things limiting your conversation are how fast you can type and how fast your connection speed is. There is no doubt about it: IM is the fastest way to talk via the Web. The only faster way to communicate is to pick up the phone and call someone.

I'm not going to try to convince you to give up IM. It is too much fun and too easy to use for me to argue against its benefits. But because this is a book about blogging, I do want you to think about a few things in regard to IM:

◆ **IM sessions usually aren't recorded.** When you are IMing with your friends, you are doing so "in the moment." You are communicating as fast as you can type. But, unless you are keeping a text log of your conversation, you don't have a record of everything you say. Now, sometimes this is a good thing. Not all conversations should be recorded for the ages! On the other hand, how many times have you been instant messaging for hours, and then later wished you could read back through some of these conversations? If you could, some would probably make you laugh, whereas others might make you upset. The point here is that when you're comparing blogs to IM, blogs give you a record of your postings (your own and those who respond to you), and you can review and edit them "after the fact."

◆ **It is harder (if not impossible) to link to other items of interest in an IM session.** Imagine that you and your friends are talking about a new movie. Earlier in the day (maybe during computer lab, when you should have been listening to your teacher, but got bored and started surfing the Web), you checked out the Web site for the movie and found all kinds of cool stuff, such as interviews with the actors. Now it's later in the evening and you are in an IM session with your friends. You mention the Web site in your message, but if your friends want to visit it, they probably have to quit your IM session (or in the best case, launch another browser window) to check it out. If you were keeping a blog, you could just place a link to the movie's Web site in your list of links so that your friends could go and check it out whenever they wanted.

◆ **You can't "take time" for your ideas in an IM session.** If you keep a diary, you know that you can take your time when you put your ideas down on paper. The same thing holds true for a blog. When you are posting to your blog, you can write and then review your posting before you put it out there for the world to see. With IM, you have to post responses quickly.

Let's face it: IM is pretty great and—just like a phone conversation—there are times when you just want to talk and not worry about saying just the right thing or recording every idea you have. But keep the previous list in mind when you are thinking about ideas you want to write about in your blog—and the benefits of writing those ideas in your blog in the first place.

Blog Versus E-Mail

Compared to blogging and IM, e-mail is the granddaddy of Web-based communication. It's hard to argue with e-mail, even when half (or more) of the e-mail you get is probably spam or just a bunch of junk you don't want to read. Let's compare blogging to e-mail, just as we compared blogging to IM:

◆ **An e-mail conversation can be hard to follow.** Not everyone has his e-mail client set up in the same way. That is, when some people reply to an e-mail, they don't include the original message in their response. Think about that compared to IM or a blog. In both of those, you can see the other remarks that have come before. With e-mail, you sometimes only get the latest remark, and all the comments that have come before it are erased.

◆ **Usually, e-mails are supposed to be short and sweet.** Okay, maybe you've written the world's longest e-mail. (I know I have, from time to time.) Usually, though, e-mails are short and to the point. In fact, lots of people don't like to get long, rambling e-mails because it takes too long to read them. A blog, on the other hand, is the exact opposite. As I said earlier, a blog gives you space to stretch out and develop your ideas. And, when people read your blog, they're usually interested and have more time to read through those thoughts. This is not to say that your blog postings can't be short, but—as compared to e-mail and definitely IM—you can feel more confident in writing longer blog postings, knowing people will read through them.

◆ **E-mail can be hard to organize.** Maybe the coolest thing about a blog—at least compared to IM and e-mail—is that you can organize your postings pretty neatly. Most blog templates give you a calendar option so that you or one of your readers can click on a date on the calendar and immediately go to that day's postings. Although you can archive e-mail by subject or date, it is a lot harder to find that special e-mail when you are really looking for it.

> **tip** Don't feel like you have to pick between blogs, IM, and e-mail. Each has benefits and drawbacks, and, depending on your mood, how much time you have, and what you have to say, one might be better than the other. The real key is to know the advantages and disadvantages of each one so that you can recognize during your conversation/posting that you might want to use another of the three to get your message across in the most efficient way possible.

SATURDAY, AUGUST 23

MOOD: DEPRESSED

TOPIC: THINKING ABOUT A BLOG

Things are getting crazy. Chris (my brother) has gone back to college for his sophomore year, and I am alone again with the parental units. I thought that watching some old John Hughes movies would help me get over my depressed frame of mind, but about halfway through The Breakfast Club *I started wondering how old Molly Ringwald is now. I mean, weren't those movies made like 20 years ago? I just couldn't stand to watch the whole thing, even the part where Bender hooks up with her at the end, 'cause all I could think about was the two of them being about 40 years old, and then I started to think they were as old as my parents, and I then got a really nasty vision of my parents making out and that, as they say, was the end of that!*

I tried to go down to the park and shoot hoops, but the only game was with a bunch of guys who were much better than me, and having my butt kicked in a game when I was already feeling depressed did not strike me as a particularly fun thing to do. Of course, all of these joyous feelings were compounded by the thought of having to go back to school in a week. I can't believe the summer is almost over. But at least I'm a sophomore now, and maybe I'll be able to blend into the fold a little more, instead of being that pimply, dorked-out freshman I was (still am?) just a few months ago.

If you want to know the truth, about the only thing I can think about these days is getting my license, but I soooo hope my parents either (a) develop a totally different personality and trade in that mini-van for a Corvette or (b) somehow become aware of my terribly uncool predicament and buy me a decent car. I guess the old family truckster mini-van is still better than nothing, but blasting Outkast from the van makes me think I won't score any points with the ladies (especially Jessica Reynolds, who I keep thinking about even though she is a year older than me and probably doesn't know I exist).

So, here I am: depressed, carless, still slightly nauseous from that image of my parents making out, and wondering what this year is going to be like. At least my best friend

> *Kickstart got me into the blogging thing a few weeks ago, and I have a place to record all my twisted thoughts. I still don't really know how all this works. Yes, I admit it: I'm a bit out of the Web/computer thing. I mean, I e-mail and all, and I had to use PowerPoint for Mr. Park's speech class last year, but I don't know how to place links and work with graphics and do all the stuff Kickstart told me was so easy to do. But I guess I'll figure it out as I go along.*
>
> *So, I'm going to sign off for now. Maybe in my next posting I will thrill you with my description of my first day of school. Hopefully I'll survive it. At least that would be a good start to the year.*

Summary

Think you are ready to start blogging? I hope this chapter has gotten you excited about starting a blog and all the neat things you can do with one.

At this point, you know what a blog is and what a powerful communication tool it can be. Reading about WhiteStripe50 has taught you the different ways you can reach out to people by keeping a well-written, updated blog. You've also learned to be careful with the kinds of personal contact information you give out on your blog.

This chapter showed you the differences between blogging and keeping a traditional Web site, using instant messaging, and sending e-mail. You learned the advantages and disadvantages of using each one, especially when compared to blogging. You don't need to decide on just one kind of Web-based communication tool, though. Some days you feel like a blog... some days you don't. Remember: The real message of blogging is to have fun. Whatever you do, don't let your blog stress you out.

Let's move on to Chapter 2, where you'll learn how to find your own voice and decide the best way to represent who you are with your blog.

Chapter 2

Reaching Out and Finding Your Own Voice

Things are happening in your life that are important to you in terms of how you define yourself as a person. Some of those things might seem pretty silly to other people (and maybe even to you sometimes!). Nevertheless, they are important in terms of how you think about yourself; how you relate to your friends, parents, and family; and how you make sense of the world you live in.

The great thing about keeping a blog is that it is a place where you can describe and record these experiences so that you (and others) can read them and maybe discuss them even more. Remember in Chapter 1 when I talked about the differences between blogs and other Web-based communication tools, such as instant messaging and e-mail? Well, in this chapter, you are really going to see those differences come to light. A blog—by being a tool that can help you record your experiences and make sense out of them—allows you define yourself and find your own voice in a much more powerful way than any of these other tools.

So, think of this chapter as your "strategy guide" to finding your blog voice, and in turn how to make sure you are using that voice to its best advantage. To help you in this process, this chapter will

◆ Give you the confidence to find your own voice by showing you ways that you can talk about yourself and your interests and experiences through a blog.

◆ Show you how to make your voice an original one. We'll look at strategies for writing and using the format of the Web to help get your ideas across.

◆ Describe, through an example blog, how you can use the ideas presented in this chapter when you sit down to start work on your own blog.

> **note** Still not sure about the technical side of blogging, in terms of how to construct a blog and how to let other people see it? Don't worry about that just yet; you will get all the information you need to actually place your blog on the Web in Chapters 6–9. For now, though, use the information in these chapters as your guide to start thinking about what you want to say in your blog and how you are doing to say it.

You've Got Something to Say, Right?

Even if you don't have any interest in blogging, the answer to that question is absolutely, totally, without a doubt, a big YES!

Your thoughts, ideas, and experiences are important, and other people want to hear them. So, although you can express yourself in lots of different ways, blogs (a) just happen to be the topic of this book and (b) are a great, fun way of getting your ideas out to a potentially large audience. That's pretty exciting, and for good reason: If the Web is anything, it is about allowing everyone a voice and an easy way to make sure that voice is heard.

In this section, you're going to look at how a blog compares to a typical diary as a way of expressing your own voice. You are also going to explore how to consider all the things that shape your own thoughts (books, movies, television, music, friends, parents, and teachers, to name just a few) when you start to define your own voice. Let's face it: Many things influence us. That influence is okay as long as you can find ways to merge it with your own ideas so that you can produce something uniquely your own.

Don't worry—finding your own voice isn't as difficult as I might have made it sound. Actually, the most important thing I should say here is that finding your own voice—rather than being heard—can be lots of fun and can help you become a better communicator, as well as a better student. Yes, blogging can actually help you in your schoolwork, but don't let that make you think it isn't a really fun and cool thing to do!

Blogging and Diaries: What's the Difference?

If you think that a blog is sort of like an online diary, well… you are right. Actually, you are only partially right. A blog is in many ways like a diary and in many ways different from a diary. Think about the following when comparing a blog to a typical diary:

◆ **Both blogs and diaries give you a space to express your thoughts.** That sounds like a pretty obvious statement, but think about that phrase, "give you a space to express your thoughts." That's a powerful statement when you really stop to think about it. In school, you spend most of your time listening to what your teachers have to say. At home, your parents are the ones who often spend most of the time talking because they want to give you structure and guidance for living your life. Aside from your teachers and parents, you spend a great deal of time listening to your friends talk. Although all this listening to other people is important, you need time—and a place of your own—to listen to yourself and figure out what you think about these ideas. Obviously, you are going to consider the ideas and opinions of your teachers, parents, and friends, but you need a place to call your own where you can express yourself. A diary or a blog is a great way to do this.

◆ **A blog lets you express yourself to (potentially) a very wide audience.** I placed the word "potentially" in parentheses because even though your blog is on the Web, that doesn't mean you have to let everyone read your ideas. Maybe you only want to share your ideas with a few of your best friends, or maybe you don't want to share them with anyone at all. There is no wrong way to use your blog; however, if you choose to open your blog to a wider readership, you can also open it to some of the more useful and fun tools that the Web has to offer. One of those tools is linking to sites that interest you. I'll talk much more about hyperlinks later in the chapter, but for now, know that you can use hyperlinks to help frame your ideas and to show the things you are interested in, instead of just writing about them. For example, if you have a posting about your favorite movie, you can provide a link to the movie's Web site.

◆ **A blog can be a "two-way" diary, where other people comment on what you write.** This is perhaps the biggest difference between a blog and a regular diary, and it's also the biggest advantage of a blog. A paper diary is something that, in most cases, is kept in a single place and doesn't have room for other people to comment. Also, most paper diaries aren't intended for other people to read. So again, although you might let your best friend read your entries, she isn't going to have much space to provide written comments about them. Also, because a traditional diary is usually handwritten, it would be hard to organize all those back-and-forth comments. On the other hand, a blog can give your readers a virtually unlimited amount of space to respond to your ideas, as well as a way to organize all this communication so that it can be read easily. Indeed, this two-way communication is the real benefit of blogging, and you should not forget it when deciding whether to keep a traditional diary or a blog.

> **tip** Remember that your readers can use all the same functionality in responding to your blog that you can use when making the initial postings. For example, if a reader is commenting on one of your postings and wants to reference a Web site that talks more about his ideas, he can include a link to that site right within his posting. This is without a doubt one of the coolest features of the Web in general because it allows all kinds of different ways of thinking about ideas. One link leads to another link, that link leads to other links, and so on.

Again, I'm assuming that because you're reading this book, you are indeed interested in blogging. But it's important to take some time to think about the similarities and differences between diaries and blogs as ways of expressing yourself. If you've been keeping a regular diary for many years, there's no reason that you can't keep writing in it, even if you decide to start a blog, too. Maybe there are some things you want to keep to yourself in your diary, and other things you want to comment about to wider audience. Any way you want to use a blog/diary combo is absolutely fine—there are no rules here, and there is no "right way" or "wrong way." The important thing is that you are writing and taking time to capture your ideas. As you will see, writing is time well spent that can help you in ways that you might not even be able to imagine right now.

Considering Other People's Ideas

Even though I've just finished telling you that there's nothing wrong with keeping a traditional diary versus a blog, I have to admit I tend to lean more toward the blog.

Why? Well, as I noted earlier, the really awesome thing about blogging is that it allows for that powerful two-way communication between you and your readers. And it is through this type of communication that the really great benefits and fun of having a blog start to shine.

But maybe we should ask a simple question at this point: Why care about other people's ideas? I mean, if people have been keeping regular diaries for hundreds (thousands?) of years with only themselves as the readers, why suddenly open up your personal thoughts to anyone who has a connection to the Web?

That is a good question, and the answer is evidence of just what a big impact blogs have made on the way we communicate in today's world. Less than 10 years ago, few people had access to the Web. And if they did, using it was definitely not the same experience that it is today. There weren't useful search tools to find what you were looking for, and trying to post something yourself—although it was possible—was much more difficult than today because there weren't easy tools (such as Microsoft FrontPage) to help you get your ideas online.

But around 1996, the Web as we know it began to explode, and everyone was online with a Web page of his own. Suddenly, instead of keeping ideas private, everyone wanted to express those ideas to the world at large. Overnight, the idea of personal communication changed, and with it, the way we define ourselves through our online or e-personalities changed.

"Okay," you say. "All these people have placed their ideas on the Web, but the question remains: Why should I care about what they have to say?" That's a good question, especially in the context of blogging. To answer that question, I'd like to turn to good old-fashioned books, as well as movies. For both books and movies, I want to focus on those that you are probably familiar with and that are popular with adolescent and teen readers. When looking at them, I want you to consider two things: why you like them, and what ideas you've taken from them. Then we'll talk about how you can use books and movies (or music, or art, or conversations with your friends, or any other format where other people express their ideas) to find your voice when you sit down to write your blog postings.

Finding Your Voice in Books

You do remember what a book is, right? You know, they're those things with a bunch of pages bound together that you don't need a computer to read? Seriously, I'm assuming that you still like to read from time to time, and that at least a few books have stuck with you and influenced you in some way.

As it turns out, several adolescent and teen-focused books have some strong similarities to blogs. What do I mean by that? Well, several of the best books for teenagers are written from a first-person perspective, and using a teenage voice. Before I start sounding too much like an English teacher, a simpler way of saying this is that the books are written in a diary format. You can easily think of these books as "bound blogs." They're a great place to get ideas and inspiration for the style and voice of your own blog.

The first of these books is one that is still considered a classic among teen readers even though it was written more than 50 years ago: *The Catcher in the Rye*, by J.D. Salinger. This book details a weekend in the life of Holden Caulfield, an incredibly smart 15-year-old who has trouble staying in various preparatory schools because of what he believes is the rampant "phoniness" of all the people around him. If Holden were a real person living today, and he had access to a computer, it would be easy to imagine his narrative being told through a blog. What is interesting about Holden is that his blog entries would tell as much about the people he interacts with as they would tell about him.

Indeed, Holden's focus is on the characters he is interacting with. Actually, that has been one of the major reasons the book has remained so popular with teen readers over the years. It is easy to compare the comments Holden makes about other people to the way you—as a teen reader—view the people you interact with. As a result, *Catcher* is a neat book to think of in blog terms, but with a twist: Holden is really describing himself when he describes other people. This is another interesting way to think about expressing yourself through your blog and, as you'll read about in more detail, it's a good way to think about using things that interest you (music, books, and so on) to help define your own voice.

The second book that is easy to think about as a blog is more contemporary than *Catcher in the Rye*, but it has often been compared to it: *The Perks of Being a Wallflower*, by Stephen Chbosky. This book revolves around a young teenager named Charlie and his struggle to define himself in a world filled with situations and people that he doesn't really understand. Unlike *Catcher*, Charlie's writings take a more diary-style approach. Instead of chapters, the book is divided into dated diary entries and is told in sequential order. The entries run from August to August, encompassing a year in Charlie's life.

Given that Charlie's entries cover a much greater period of time than those of Holden, there are more experiences and situations described in *Perks* than there are in *Catcher*. And, since Charlie makes references to all kinds of other things that are important in his life (television, books—including *The Catcher in the Rye*—and especially music), it makes it even easier to imagine Charlie's blog. He would have his regular postings and then links to the things that were important in his life. For example, Charlie likes to make mix tapes for himself and his friends. These tapes consist of favorite songs that Charlie puts together to try to define (and remember) certain moods and situations that he experiences. Now, imagine if Charlie's entries were on a blog instead of in a paper diary. Instead of just listing the songs he puts on his tape, he could provide links to the Web sites of the bands that sing those songs. He could also place links on his blog to sites that discuss the authors of the books that he reads.

I really like to think of *Perks* in blog terms for two specific reasons:

◆ **The book is told in a short diary entry/dated-posting format**. Even though a great blog doesn't have to be like an online diary, there is something to be said about using this approach. That's not so much because of the style, but because you can say a lot with just a small amount of writing. This is important to think about because you might want to keep a blog but feel like you don't have the time to write pages and pages for each posting. In looking at the "chapters" in *Perks*, Charlie's entries are often short, but because he is telling things from his own perspective and being honest in expressing how he really feels, he doesn't have to write very much to make his writing powerful and interesting.

◆ **Charlie uses other items of interest (books, music, and so on) to help bring out the real meaning of what he is trying to say.** Haven't there been times when a favorite song can say as much about how you feel as pages and pages of writing or a long conversation with a friend? That is the great thing about music, of course, in that it gives us a way of expressing feelings that words just can't seem to capture. Obviously, because *Perks* is a book, it uses words to convey its meaning. But the references that Charlie makes (again, especially to music) are just as important to understanding what he is saying—and the feelings he is experiencing—as the words he chooses. This is also a great point to take away from the book when using it as a guide for your blog. The tools of the Web—especially the ability to link to other sites—can be just as powerful and effective as your words. In fact, you could have a blog that was nothing but hyperlinks, and if those links were well organized, they could tell your story perhaps just as well as lots of writing on your part. Although I wouldn't recommend a blog consisting of just links, it is something to think about as you consider all the Web tools at your disposal in finding your voice.

These books are just two examples of how you can look to literature for inspiration in writing your blog, as well as the format in which to present it. Although both *Catcher* and *Perks* are told from the perspective of a teenager, you should be open to finding inspiration in other kinds of books, as well as other types of writing, such as poetry and non-fiction. You can't be a good writer unless you are a good reader, so keep your eyes open to wherever the written word might provide inspiration!

BUT... AREN'T THOSE BOOKS ABOUT TROUBLED TEENS?

I should probably mention something about the two books listed here, especially if you have read them. Both Charlie and Holden (the protagonists of *Perks* and *Catcher*, respectively) require some serious counseling at some point in their stories. Given that fact, you might be asking yourself why I picked these two books as "inspiration" for your blogs. After all, couldn't I have chosen some more upbeat, happier examples to give you guidance in your writing?

Well, the truth of the matter is that both of these books, although they deal with some pretty serious issues, are realistic as to the questions, issues, and problems that a typical teenager will face. (Although *Catcher* is 50 years old, it remains just as fresh and current as when it was first published.) Also, I really like these books as inspiration for your blogs because, in addition to being realistic, they are funny. Humor—or more specifically, the ability to see the lighter, positive side of your experiences—is a critical ingredient in the best blogs. Although there is nothing wrong with writing a serious blog, you will find that if you have the courage to laugh at yourself, your writing will take on a richer meaning.

I am certainly not saying that you should demean yourself or your experiences just for the sake of a laugh, but it is important to remember that even the most serious experiences often have a humorous quality, if you give yourself a little perspective when thinking about them. What I mean is that any experience—depending on who is viewing it and under what context—can be funny, sad, terrifying, enlightening… any emotion you can think of. After all, you might be the best writer in the world and be able to really detail an experience so that your readers feel as if they had the same experience, too. But, depending on the background of your readers, the personal experiences they have had, and the mood they are in when they read your blog, they might view your postings in a different way from how you intended them.

So again, that is why *Perks* and *Catcher* are such great examples from which to draw inspiration for your blog. Yes, the characters within them might have some serious troubles, but it is up to you—as the reader—to actually perceive those troubles. And it is what you—as the reader—take away from them that is most important.

Keep this in mind when writing your own blog, too: Your postings might help another reader work through a problem and feel less alone. Or your serious postings might strike another reader as the funniest thing they've ever read. Blogging is in the eye of the beholder, but that is usually a good characteristic and should not deter you from writing what you feel.

Finding Your Voice in Music

Okay, so maybe you don't read that many books. If you do, congratulations! Reading is an activity that's well worth your time. But if you don't like to read or don't have time, you can find lots of ideas in other things, including two of the more popular ways of spending your time: listening to music and watching movies.

Imagine the following situation:

It's late August, and the summer is almost over. Actually, summer is over because the new school year begins tomorrow. It's a Sunday afternoon, and you are driving home after spending some last-minute vacation time with your best friend. Although you are looking forward to the start of your senior year, you're feeling just a little depressed, not just that the summer is ending (always a bummer), but that this is your last year of school. It will be cool to be a senior, but you start to wonder about where you'll be next year at this time. Colleges start the fall semester earlier than high schools (or at least the college does that you hope to attend), so you have less than a year left before you'll pack your bags and head off to college and a totally different life. You are scared, excited, depressed… actually, you are feeling about 20 different emotions.

As you are thinking about all this stuff in your car, a song comes on the radio. It could be a song you know, or one you've never heard. But the lyrics and the music perfectly match your mood and somehow manage to express how you are feeling. When you get home, the song reminds you of other songs, so you decide to put together a CD of all those songs and call the finished disc "End of Summer Driving Music." Although the individual songs don't have much in common, when put together on one disc, they define and express all kinds of thoughts and emotions that you're having, from excitement about your senior year to being scared about growing up and going to college.

I'm guessing that even though you might not have directly experienced the previous situation, you probably have had many experiences in which music somehow managed to express your mood where words just couldn't. That is, of course, the great thing about music and why it remains such a powerful form of communication.

Still, what does this have to do with blogging? Well, imagine that you have gone through the situation just described, and you want to make a posting about it to your blog. You could try to describe how you felt driving in your car, but—for the same reasons that the song on the radio made such perfect sense—you can't seem to find the words to express how you feel. So instead, you list the songs that you put on your "End of Summer Driving Music" CD, and give a brief description of the lyrics of each song. When your posting is finished, you've managed to describe your emotions by referencing the songs on your CD. Maybe you've also provided links to other blogs, discussion forums, and band Web sites about the songs, so you've found a way of expressing yourself (in other words, you've found your voice!) by talking about the music that has influenced you.

 The example here might lead you think, "You know, a really cool posting would be not only to describe the songs, but also to upload them to my blog so that other readers could hear them and really understand why I picked those songs." That would indeed be a cool posting, but you would be breaking several copyright laws because you don't have permission to distribute commercially recorded music. This holds true for any copyrighted material, so as you develop your blog, keep this issue in mind.

Finding Your Voice in Movies

Like music, you can also use movies to help express your ideas. I'm sure you can think of favorite movie characters that somehow speak for you through their dialogue or the way they deal with a given situation. If you are like me, you probably have a few favorite movies that you know by heart and that you always enjoy returning to because they so perfectly match a specific feeling that you've experienced.

If you have movies like this, I would encourage you to think about why you really like them. As a matter of fact, you might try the following little exercise and see where it leads you in thinking not only about the movie, but also about other things you're interested in. That way, you can refer to them when you make postings to your blog. Jot your answers down to each of the following questions so that you have something to refer to:

1. Pick a movie that has made a big impact on you, or just one that you really like. Don't think too hard—it can be any movie. And don't worry if you think the movie is "stupid" or "cheesy." The important thing here is to start thinking about how you describe things, regardless of what those things happen to be.

2. Try to remember where you were and who you were with when you saw the movie. If you can't remember that, try to remember the last time you saw the movie, where you were, and who you were with. Are you still in touch with those people? Do you still visit that place where you saw the movie? (If it was a friend's house, do you still talk to that friend?)

3. What characters in the movie do you like the most, and why do you like them? Is it something about the way they talk? A way they deal with a particular situation? If you just like the plot of the movie, why do you like it? Does it make you laugh? Does it remind you of events in your own life, people you know, or something you wish would happen (or would not happen) to you?

4. Finally, if you can remember the last time you saw the movie, why did you happen to pick that movie? This is especially important if it's a movie you've seen many times. What caused you to watch the movie again? If you were just "in the mood to watch it," see if you can remember what was going on in your life that perhaps caused you to think about watching the movie again.

After you have some things written down about the movie, think about how you might turn that into a posting for your blog. Maybe you just want to post a description of the movie because you like it. If so, that's perfectly fine. But take a minute and think about some of the ways that you might use your answers—and as a result, the movie—to help find your voice about a variety of different topics.

For example, think about the answers you wrote down for question 2. Now, let's say the last place you saw the movie was with your cousin who lives on the other side of the country from you. When you watched the movie with your cousin, it was when you and your family were visiting them last summer. During that vacation, your cousin took you to a basketball game at his school, and after the game, you went to a party with him and some of his friends. You found your cousin's friends to be cool, and all of you got along and had a great time. In fact, someone you met at the party you found... how should we say... interesting(!), and you continue to keep in touch with her. As a matter of fact, you just found out that this person has a summer internship working for a company that isn't far from where you live, so you'll be able to spend a lot of time with her this summer.

Now, think about writing about this person on your blog. How would you start your posting? How would you try to convey in your posting how you met this girl, what you were feeling when you met her, and how you feel about her? Well, what if the movie reminds you in some way of that vacation when you first met her? You could use the movie and its characters, plot, and scenes to help describe your feelings. Just like the music example in the previous section, you could talk about the elements of the movie (and maybe provide links to Web sites about the movie) as a way of framing your experiences that you want to write about.

The point about using movies and music in this way is that although not very many people will be familiar with your specific experiences, there is a good chance that many people will be familiar with the music and movies you are using to give meaning to those personal experiences. You can use these resources to express your feelings to a wide audience, just like you used them to understand those same feelings for yourself.

> **tip** What about finding your voice in other stuff, including other blogs? As I wrote earlier in this chapter, you can't be a good writer unless you're a good reader. Don't just read other blogs, but be aware of all kinds of things, from current events to things that interest you, such as music and movies. In the next chapter, you'll learn different strategies and ways of thinking about this "other stuff" so that you can use them to find ideas and your own voice.

Being Original and Finding Your Own Voice

We've talked about finding your voice in books, music, and movies. Actually, you can find your voice in just about anything, especially if you are a good reader and take the time to explore different areas of interest. And, like the little exercise I asked you to do when thinking about a favorite movie, I've given you some ideas about how to take those things you are interested in and use them to help express your own ideas. Even though someone else might not have experienced a situation in the same way you have, that person might know the song, movie, poem, or other blog that you are using to help frame your experience.

In the next chapter, we'll talk more about finding your own voice and putting it into practice, as we learn to read and review other blogs. Although you don't necessarily have to read lots of blogs to write your own, it's good practice to see what other people are doing and how they are communicating their ideas. And, as we've been talking about with books, music, and movies in this chapter, reading other blogs is a great place to find inspiration for how to express your own thoughts on your own blog.

Before we get to the next chapter, though, let's take a quick look at two additional items you should consider as you find your own voice.

The Collective Cool: Linking Your Voice to Others

I've mentioned throughout this chapter that you can link to other blogs and sites to further express your ideas. As you will see when we start to build your blog in Chapters 6–9, most (all?) blog hosting services give you a space on your blog where you can provide links to things you're interested in.

Although there is nothing wrong with just giving links to other sites and blogs, you might consider using links to help further define what you are trying to say. Remember the mix CD example from earlier in this chapter? By giving links to more information about the bands and the songs you are referencing, you allow your readers to better understand the songs and, more importantly, why those songs are so important to you and how you use them to give meaning to your emotions and feelings.

Using hyperlinks on your blog is also a great way to develop "the collective cool" of the Web. As you place links within your blog—and in turn, other people link to your blog—you will, over time, develop a "web" of connections. Taken individually, link A to link B might not appear to have anything in common. However, if you look at all the links on your blog as a whole, you will see that these links do a great job of describing who you are. They highlight not only your interests, but how you see those interests interacting with each other.

We'll talk more about using links within your blog in later chapters, but don't overlook how important they can be. You might even say that a link is worth a thousand words if it's used to highlight or give more information on the topic of your posting.

Developing Your "Universal Appeal"

Imagine that you came across the following posting on a blog:

> *Note to all passengers:*
>
> *Mr. B indicates that the coast is clear. Meet at the gas station, where we'll stock up on necessary supplies. Mr. W: Did you find out your grade in school today? We'll leave on Tuesday. Bring that CD!*

Doesn't make a lot of sense, does it? Of course, if you knew the "secret code," this might make all kinds of sense.

You will find this type of secret writing on many blogs. There's nothing wrong with it, assuming you are one of the few who are in the know and can decipher it, but the emphasis here is on the phrase "one of the few." If you want your blog to be read by only a select few, that's your choice. However, you will be missing out on the real fun and power of blogging: allowing your postings to be read, understood, and commented on by other people—especially people you don't know. Why take all the time to write in a cryptic language when you could just as easily pick up the phone and call whomever it is you want to communicate with?

So, along with the collective cool of blogging, another term I like to use is developing your "universal appeal." Simply put, if you are going to keep a blog, you should strive to make it as widely accessible and understood as possible. As I wrote in the earlier sections of this chapter about using universal or widely known points of reference in finding your voice (movies, books, music that people have seen, read, or heard), it is in your interest to keep your blog accessible—or at the very least, intelligible—to anyone who might find it. You never know when someone who has similar interests to yours might find your blog and give you a new perspective on whatever it is you are writing about.

Of course, the only way others can do this is if they understand what you are writing about. Therefore, although you should use as many different sources as possible, both to clarify what you are saying and to highlight all your interests, you should also keep in mind this "universal appeal" factor to ensure that your blog has the best chance of being read by as many people as possible.

 tip Even though it is a cool idea to pretend your blog is being read by a large number of people, playing the numbers game should not be your overriding concern when you sit down to make a posting to your blog. If you get caught up in wondering how many people are reading your posts, your writing will probably start to suffer because you will be trying to please your readers before you please yourself. If you are going to take the time to keep a blog, the primary person you should be worried about is you! If you do that, you will write honestly and have an engaging, interesting, and entertaining blog. And if that happens, people will find your blog by themselves.

 **WEDNESDAY, SEPTEMBER 3**

MOOD: INTERESTED

TOPIC: BACK TO SCHOOL

Back in school. Much to my surprise, the year has started off pretty well. Although my parents didn't come through with the Corvette, they did mention the possibility of getting me a newer car. I'm not sure what "newer car" means, but it has to be better than the mini-van or one of many alternatives I can think of. I guess we'll see how things develop...

Kickstart, Jessica, and I all scored tickets to the White Stripes concert, which is less than two weeks away. Hopefully the show will be as good as when I saw them in the spring. Well, let me rephrase that: I hope the show is as good, but maybe, ah, a little less "eventful" than the one in the spring. I don't know how much Jessica would approve of me giving out too many details, but let's just say that maybe next time she should make sure she has enough gasoline in the car before she heads out to a show, as running out of gas on the interstate at 2:00 a.m. is not a good situation to be in. Okay, I admit it, I did laugh (a little bit...) at the image of her freaking out when the car ran out of gas, and her thinking that we would never get home. I wasn't that thrilled about having to walk nearly a mile to the nearest gas station, and we could have gotten killed walking along the interstate. But it was a warm night, and we made the best of it. Actually, I seem to remember having a really good time. We all felt so free, being out in the world, just walking and talking about everything we could think of, so we wouldn't start to wonder if there even was a gas station within walking distance.

In computer lab today, we started to work on building Web sites. I didn't think I'd be that interested in it, really, but I can start to see how I can use this stuff to express myself. Well, "express myself" probably sounds lame, but the more I think about it, I do have some fairly crazy thoughts from time to time, and it might be interesting just to write them down. Just the other night, I was riding around town with Jessica, and this Tool song came on the radio. I don't know what the deal was, but I had this thought suddenly pop into my head about the "meaning of life" and how important a serious relationship is to finding it. I asked Jessica if she ever thought of stuff like that when she heard the song, but she doesn't even really like Tool and didn't have much to say. Jessica is more into the "classic rock" thing: You know, Pink Floyd, Led Zeppelin, and stuff like that. My brother likes those bands and said that if I really wanted to be cool, I had to listen to Led Zeppelin. So, I went out and bought the "untitled" CD (the one with "Stairway to Heaven"). It's pretty good, and I can see why everyone likes that song and all, but it just doesn't do much for me, if you want to know the truth.

Anyway, getting back to the Web stuff, we started learning today about linking our pages to other Web sites, and I wondered if I could put links to stuff I was interested in on my blog. I asked Kickstart about it, and he said it all worked the same way, and that if my blog service provider used FrontPage extensions, I could do all kinds of other stuff, too. I'm still not exactly sure what that means, although we've started working with FrontPage in our class. Jessica has her own blog, and she said she would come over this weekend and help me put some more stuff on mine, like links and other stuff. She asked me what I was going to write about on my blog, and I said I didn't know yet.

And then she said, "Well, you could always write about how much you like me," and I laughed and jokingly said, "No, no...I actually want people to be interested in what I write about!" She laughed, but there was something in the way she looked at me when she said that. I don't know... just a feeling I got that maybe she was trying to tell me something, and that maybe I hurt her feelings when I blew her off with that comment.

Anyway, I'm probably hallucinating because I haven't had anything to eat all day. I'm starting to wonder if my recent postings have anything to do with, well, anything, but Jessica tells me I should just write what I feel, and if I mention other things to put links to them, and that will help everything fit together and make more sense. I sort of like that idea, that I can use links to other sites to tell a story about my own life. When Jessica comes over this weekend, I'll be sure and ask her about it.

Summary

This chapter gave you some ideas about how to find that all-important ingredient of a great blog: your own personal voice. Call it your own style, your e-personality, or just how you communicate, but writing honestly and expressing how you really feel is one of the greatest perks of keeping a blog. This chapter also gave you some strategies and ideas for finding your voice in other things you are interested in, such as books, movies, and music, and how you can use these other sources to help clarify what you are writing about and to give the best overall representation of who you are. Finally, you were asked to keep your universal appeal and collective cool in mind as you start to think about your blog so that it has the best chance of being read, understood, and enjoyed by the widest possible audience.

Chapter 3

The Daily Report: Reading Other Blogs

Have you ever been talking with your friends and had the subject turn to movies or music and suddenly realized that a particular CD or movie has been released that you didn't even know about? Or, have you ever been talking about an event and realized that you haven't heard nearly as much about it as the rest of your friends? We all have situations where it seems like we are the last to know. Sometimes this is just because, well, we are really the last to know!

In case you haven't noticed, there is a ton of information on the Web. Some of it is good and useful, some of it is bad and worthless, but most of it is somewhere in between. The same carries over to blogs: With millions of blogs published and more being added to the Web every day, it is impossible to keep current with all of them. Now, even if you could, you probably wouldn't want to read every blog, but imagine for a minute if that were possible. How would you distinguish the good from the bad, and make sure you were always "in the know" about the most exciting and relevant blogs?

In case you were drifting off for a moment, welcome back to reality. There is, of course, no way you can stay current with all the blogs being published. However, if you know some tricks and strategies for reading critically, you can read and enjoy more of the best blogs. And that is what this chapter just happens to be about.

Thinking About What You Read

Do you ever find yourself reading something but not really understanding it, or worse still, forgetting it the second after you read it? We all have this happen from time to time. Usually when this happens, we are either tired, bored, or a combination of the two. When this happens, it is best to walk away from that reading material and go do something else. I mean, why spend time just looking at words if you are not going to think about, remember, or enjoy whatever it is you are reading?

On the other hand, think about what it's like to read something that is really exciting and that interests you. You hang on every word, thinking about the ideas being presented and what is going to happen next. You probably will relate what you are reading to your own life, as you imagine yourself in the situation being described, or think about how you would react to the events being experienced by the people you are reading about. When reading is this exciting, it can't be beat. That's why people like to read in the first place!

But these types of moments aren't limited just to reading. For example, think about what it's like to listen to your favorite band or CD. What do you think about when you listen to really good music? When I listen to my favorite group (which just happens to be R.E.M), I often find myself thinking about all of the following:

◆ **The first time I heard the music.** When I first heard R.E.M., I was a junior in high school. At that time, not many people knew about the band (at least not at the level they are known now). I liked mainstream rock groups, but there was something special about R.E.M., and I can remember feeling like I was part of a special club that only a few people knew about. Even though R.E.M. is now a huge band that everyone knows about, I can still hear some of their earlier CDs and remember what it was like to listen to them when hardly anyone else even knew who they were.

◆ **My friends who also were fans of the music.** My best friend in high school introduced me to R.E.M., along with many other great bands. Even today when I listen to their music, I often think about my friend and the other people we would hang out with, and all the good times we had. If music can be a soundtrack to your life, then I definitely have a few CDs that represent growing up and being a teenager. Of course, the most important parts of this soundtrack were my friends who shared those experiences with me.

◆ **How I'm feeling.** You probably have music that you listen to when you are sad, and other music that you like to rock out to when you are in a good mood. Because the music of R.E.M. was a part of so many different experiences in my life, I often equate specific songs with different moods that I am in.

So what does thinking about your favorite music have to do with reading? Well, when you listen to music you really enjoy, it is an *active* process. Your foot taps to the beat, you sing (hopefully better than I do), and you find yourself thinking about things that you relate to the music, from memories of when you first heard it to how the music relates to how you are feeling. Although you probably don't tap your foot or sing when you read something really interesting, you can still go through these same thought processes. Indeed, if you replace the phrase "to listen" with "to read" in the earlier descriptions, and replace your favorite band with your favorite book, you can easily see the similarities between listening to music and reading in this active thinking process.

Okay, so we've established that reading and listening to music can be similar in terms of the active thinking process. But what does this have to do with blogs?

Remember what I said at the beginning of the chapter about how it is difficult to keep up with your favorite blogs, let alone all the new blogs that are being published every day? There really is no practical way to read all the blogs you want to read, and you are going to miss some stuff that you might find cool and interesting. Unfortunately, that's the way it goes.

But if the thought of missing that one great blog depresses you, cheer up, because I have some good news for you. The truth is, you don't have to read everything that is out there. And as I've said a few times already in this chapter, you wouldn't want to read *everything* that is out there. However, if you know how to *actively* read your favorite blogs, you will not only get more out of them, but you'll have a lot more fun reading them. Remember: Blogging should be first and foremost about fun.

 I'm going to assume for a minute that you spend more time listening to music than you do reading. Even if you do spend a good deal of time reading blogs, books, and homework, there's a good chance that you have **note** music playing in the background. I could be mistaken by this assumption, but I know how important music was to me as a teenager, and I know how important it remains to me now. Whether I'm at home, at work, or in my car, I *always* have music close by. It's an essential and critical part of my day.

So, if music is a way of demonstrating an active thinking process, we can use that same process to *critically* think about the blogs we read. Best of all, if we know how to critically think about what we read, we don't have to worry about reading everything that is out there because we will enjoy and get more out of the blogs that we *do* read.

Ready to think critically? Don't let that phrase scare you. We're going to return to our music example throughout this chapter, as a way of highlighting the active thought process that is so important to being an active reader. And don't forget: If you become an active and critical reader, you will become a better writer, in your blog postings as well as everything else that you write.

Becoming a Critical Reader

Critical reading sounds pretty boring, doesn't it?

I'll admit it: When my teachers would ask me to read something critically, I never really looked forward to the assignment. To me, this always meant that I was going to have to study what I was reading, and that I would spend so much time worrying about the details and facts that I wouldn't have a chance to actually enjoy what I was reading. And if you can't enjoy what you read, you're missing out on the whole point of reading in the first place! Although you might not always think this is the case, reading should be an *enjoyable* way to spend your time.

But allow me to let you in on a little secret. When you read stuff you enjoy—from newspapers and magazines to blogs and e-mails from your friends—you are practicing critical reading whether you realize it or not. What exactly constitutes critical reading? It is made up of three major elements:

◆ **What's the point?** Probably the most important question on your mind is, "What's the point of this material that I'm reading?" Is the author trying to persuade you? Or, is he trying to inform you of certain facts? When we read (or listen to music—more on this in a bit), we always want to know what the main idea is, to help us understand the larger ideas of what we are reading.

◆ **How is the author achieving his goals?** Is the author using humor to try to get his point across? Is he trying to use metaphors to make his point more valid and interesting? Writing on the Web can use these things, too, of course, but authors can also use hyperlinks, graphics, animation, and other types of special devices to get the point across. We'll talk more about how to read these special Web elements later in the chapter.

◆ **What effect does the writing have on you, the reader?** If "What's the point?" is the most important question on your mind when you read, the most important factor to your reading is to ask yourself, "What effect is this having on me?" The ways that reading as an active process can shape how we think are what make it such an important activity. When it comes to blogging and the effect that reading a blog has on you, the issue becomes even more important because so many blogs detail personal experiences and opinions of the author. If you, as the reader, take these experiences and opinions and make them your own, you are helping to make blogging the truly magic tool that it can be.

The rest of this chapter will be devoted to looking at the three aspects of critical reading. As we discuss each one, we'll highlight how you can think about it in regards not only to reading blogs, but listening to music, too.

> **tip** Remember in Chapter 2 when I suggested that a good way to express your feelings was to use other resources (movies, music, books) as a way of writing about how you feel in a more universally understood way? If you'll recall from that chapter, I mentioned that although not many people will understand your exact personal experience, many people will be able to relate to a popular CD or movie. Therefore, if you can relate your experiences to these more widely known media, you can find your voice. The same is true when you are reading: When you are reading a blog that uses such a reference to highlight the feelings of the writer, take time to think about your own reaction to the reference in question. For example, if the writer says that some movie is a perfect representation of a personal experience he had, don't just take his word for it, but also take time to think about how you feel about the movie. Then compare your thoughts about the movie to what the author is saying. By making this comparison, you are critically reading as you try to understand the author's point of view—but *in conjunction* with how you feel, too.

Critical Reading, Step 1: What's the Point?

Here's a scenario for you: You are sitting in class, listening to your teacher give a lecture. You know that what she is saying is important, and you know that the information is probably going to be on your next big test. But even though you know all of this is true, and you are listening intently to what she says and taking good notes, you still find yourself asking the same question:

What's the real point of this?

The point of this book is not to convince you that every homework assignment or lecture you have to sit through is going to be as good as your favorite movie. Let's face it: Sometimes school can be pretty boring. No offense to any teachers, of course, but even they get bored.

So how do you deal with these kinds of situations, where you know you have to pay attention but you just can't seem to find the main point of the lecture? Well, it's the same thing you need to do when you sit down to read something that you really want to understand: You have to find the point of what is being said.

Fortunately, this is not as difficult as you might think it is. In fact, finding the point can be quite easy if you allow yourself to react to what you are reading. What do I mean by that? Put simply, if you are going to find the main point of the story, article, or blog you happen to be reading, you need to be aware of how it is affecting you.

Think about the last thing you read that really made a big impact on you. For this example, imagine that, in your favorite magazine, you've just read a horrible review of the latest CD by your favorite band. This is the band that you've worshipped since you first heard them, and their new CD hasn't left your player since the day it came out. Basically, you think it is the greatest music ever made.

But in a magazine that you read all the time and that you always agree with, the music editor thinks this CD—your favorite CD—is the worst music ever recorded. In fact, the reviewer says that he'd rather listen to stray cats wailing in the night than have to listen to this CD one more time.

Think about how this makes you feel. Better yet, think about the emotional roller coaster you would go through as you read the article:

◆ You get home from school to find the latest copy of the magazine in your mailbox, and you're excited to see your favorite band on the cover. You grab a soda and quickly head to the sofa, excited to read what you are sure is a great review of the CD that you think is the best one yet.

◆ The opening paragraph is fairly nondescriptive. You quickly focus in on the article, savoring every word, waiting for what you are sure is going to be a great review.

◆ And then it happens: The review turns ugly. The writer says listening to one track in particular (your favorite song on the CD) made him sick to his stomach. He goes on to say the entire CD is terrible, and that it should be avoided at all costs.

◆ The review ends by slamming the group one more time. You sit on the couch, stunned by what you've read. You're angry. You head to your computer to make a posting on your blog about how the review is totally wrong, and to mention that you're canceling your subscription to what is obviously a seriously flawed magazine.

In situations like this, you don't have any problem identifying the point of what you are reading. In fact, you can probably recite the entire article, section by section, word for word. Granted, this is an extreme example, but the important thing to take notice of here—especially from a "what's the point?" perspective—is that the reason you have no problem finding the point is that you are having a real emotional reaction to what you are reading. Basically, you are *actively* seeking the point.

You won't have this kind of reaction to everything you read, but you should always be open to allowing the article/textbook/blog to have an effect on you. When you open yourself up to what you are reading, you are going to engage yourself in conversation. That is, you will start asking yourself questions about what you are reading, and when you do that, you will have no problem finding the main point.

Critical Reading, Step 2: How Is the Point Being Made?

Let's return once again to the previous example. I want you to imagine the method that the review writer utilized to get his point across.

What do I mean by "method"? Again, think about the last thing you read that really made an impact on you. Chances are, it made such an impact not just because it was something you were interested in, but also because of the words, style, and references the writer used to get his point across. The method refers to the way the writer says what he has to say.

So, getting back to our bad review example, consider the following method that the writer might have used to get his point across:

♦ **The writing style.** Compare these two sentences:

> The CD attempts to strike a balance between egotistical rantings and introspective cries for help. Unfortunately, the balance tips far much to the egotistical, with the only cries being that of the listener, wishing the disc would come to a quick end.
>
> The music is like a cross between Metallica having a bad day and a 20-car pileup on the interstate. Put simply, it's like chalk being scraped across a blackboard, amplified to ear-splitting levels.

There's quite a difference between the two, right? A writer's style is important to how he gets his point across. It will often reflect his interest, mood, and opinions.

♦ **The choice of words.** Similar to style (actually, an essential part of style) are the words a writer chooses to express his point. There can be a big difference between "nice" and "exquisite," or "big" and "gargantuan."

♦ **The writing format.** An article that appears in *Seventeen* is going to have a different format than an article that appears in a scientific magazine. The science article might utilize charts and graphs to help illustrate some new findings or data, whereas the *Seventeen* article might have pictures of the new spring clothing line being introduced. More than just being about the content, the format of the writing has an effect on how the larger point is made. Obviously, you need to read an article with lots of charts and graphs differently from an article with lots of pictures.

What is interesting about this list is how it is applied to writing that appears on the Web, and especially blogs. Given that blogs often have writing of a personal nature, the style, word choice, and format can have an effect on how you, the reader, relate to the blog. Also, as we talked about in the previous section, the style, word choice, and format can affect your ability to find the main point.

Think about the previous list in relation to a blog:

1. If the writing on most blogs is of a personal nature, style becomes an important issue. You might think of "blog style" as the mood the writer is in when he writes a specific posting. If you are in a good mood, your writing style is probably going

to be different than if you are in a bad mood. For example, when you are happy, you might be more inclined to elaborate on what you are saying (in other words, write more). Compare that to when you are in a bad mood. Unless you are really angry, when you are in a bad mood, you usually write short, quick sentences. Keeping a "critical eye" out for the mood of a blog writer—as reflected by the writer's style of writing—can be an important clue as to the larger point the writer is trying to make.

2. Word choice is also key when writing your blog, just as it is with any writing that you do. Imagine that you are angry about some topic, and you want to make sure your opinion is understood. Actually, let's again use our example of the magazine writing a bad review of your favorite CD. If you were really upset, you probably wouldn't just say, "I don't think the magazine is right about the CD not being any good." If you *really* wanted to get your point across, you'd say something like this: "If not knowing what you are talking about is a crime, that magazine should be punished to the full extent of the law, because they don't have a clue about what good music is." It's the same idea, but one expressed in a different style.

 Have you ever been so angry with someone that you wanted to cuss him out? I know, I know. . the thought of using any kind of bad word has never entered your head. Seriously, we all have those moments when our mouths get ahead of our brains. You don't have to read many blogs to realize quickly that many of them are chock-full of profanities. I'm not going to tell you I haven't spoken or written some words that, ah, let's say, you don't hear in church. But that being said, you might think about how much profanity you want to use in your blog postings. Sometimes, such language really gets the point across. But most of the time, profanity can be distracting to what you really have to say and can make you look kind of stupid. So, as you consider your own style and word choice, keep this issue in mind.

3. Finally, the format of a blog is one of the more interesting aspects of writing in a Web-based format. What I mean by "format" is that you can use all the tools of the Web (especially hyperlinks) to help in furthering your point. For example, you could provide a direct hyperlink to a band's Web site within the posting where you were talking about the band's latest CD. Also, blogs are organized so that you can easily see and respond to different postings, which affects the overall format. It allows you to read a much larger discussion of an issue all at once, as compared to reading an article in a magazine and then having to wait until the next issue is published to read the "Letters to the Editor" and see what other people have to say.

tip We'll start looking at blog formatting in Chapter 5, and then move into a more complete discussion when we look at the blog examples in Chapters 11 and 12.

Critical Reading, Step 3: Deep Impact!

I've made the point several times in this chapter that allowing what you read to have an effect on you is important, not just in helping you to identify the main idea of the writing, but in recognizing how that idea is being made. I'd like to make that point one more time in this section.

In addition to working with technology, I am an English teacher. One of my favorite things to teach—especially to younger students—is poetry. Maybe you love poetry. If you do, I congratulate you. I happen to think that poetry is terrific and fun to read. But I know that many young people aren't fans of poetry. As a matter of fact, they hate it.

What is interesting, though, is the reason many young people hate it. The number one reason is that they don't understand it. "Okay," I tell my students, "I can appreciate that. But is it that you don't understand the words?"

Usually the answer to that question is, "No, we understand the words, but it's how they are put together that we don't understand." I usually follow that with, "But you like music, right? Many popular songs have words that are put together in weird ways, so that they don't really make any sense. But you still like them. Why is that?"

The answer to that question is always, "But the music makes you feel a certain way, so it gives the words meaning that we can understand." And it is here that I make the point I've been making throughout this chapter: The key word here is "feel." What do you do when you feel something? You let whatever it is have an impact on you and your state of mind. So, to get my students to understand poetry, I ask them to read it out loud, so they can hear the rhythm of the words and the way those words are put together. Basically, I do this so they can feel the words, and when that happens, they start to look at the poet's style and word choice. And when that process starts to take shape, they are well on their way to understanding—and enjoying—poetry.

My intention here is not to convince you to go out and buy a book of poetry. This is, after all, a book on blogging! However, it's important for you to think about how writing can influence your emotional state. It is especially important because most blogs are emotional in nature. And the best blogs are going to combine that emotion with a certain style and word choice so that the main idea is not only going to be clear, but powerful and influential, too.

So, in summarizing all these critical reading tips, remember these three questions:

◆ **"What's the point?"** It's a basic question, but it's always a good one. No matter what you read, always be on the lookout for the main idea of the writing and, in the process, be aware of how that point is making you feel. Again, think about our "bad review" example and how, if you are actively engaged in what the author is saying, you will pay closer attention to what you are reading.

◆ **"How is the point being made?"** What special style, word choice, and format is the author using? Is he being funny? Serious? Ironic? When it come to blogs, which special Web elements (hyperlinks, general layout of the blog page) is the author using to get his point across? What mood is the author in, and how is that mood being communicated?

◆ **"How is this making me feel?"** This is perhaps the most important question of all. There will be times when you read something that doesn't really make you feel one way or another. Admit it: You probably aren't going to get overly excited reading your math book. But we're not talking about math here. We're talking about blogs, and blogs usually consist of emotional, personal writing. That being said, you should allow that writing to have an impact on how you feel, all the while keeping in mind the larger point the writer is making and his method of making that point.

A Blog-Reading Example: Moby.com

Let's put your critical reading skills to the test by looking at one of the more interesting and frequently updated celebrity blogs. It's the blog kept by the musician Moby. Figure 3.1 highlights the blog section of his larger Web site.

Moby has one of the better celebrity blogs, in that it is updated on a regular basis. Also, as you can see in Figure 3.1, the updates are neatly organized by date, so you can quickly get to the latest posting.

Let's look at some of the postings on this blog, and see if we can apply our critical reading skills to the postings. Whether you like Moby's music or you've never heard of him, you can use the same strategies to find the main point of his blog and how it's designed to influence you.

Reading the Blog: What's the Point?

Figure 3.2 highlights a typical posting on the Moby blog.

This posting is characteristic of what you will find on Moby's blog. If you are familiar with Moby and his music, you know that he is opinionated and comments on all kinds of different political and social issues. In fact, if you dig into the blog and look through several postings, you will see him commenting on everything from the horrors of war to the benefits of being a vegetarian.

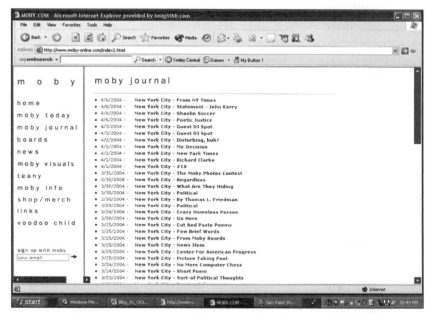

FIGURE 3.1 *The blog section of Moby's Web site. Access the site at http://www.moby-online.com.*

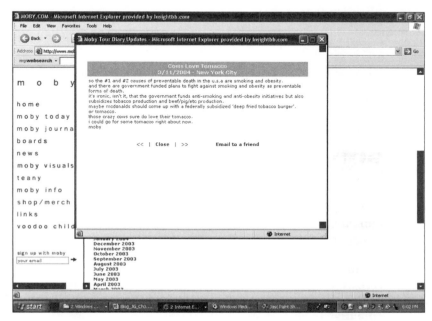

FIGURE 3.2 *A typical Moby posting that mixes some humor with a larger, more serious point.*

In looking at this posting, you can probably tell that it addresses some pretty serious issues (obesity, the dangers of smoking), but it makes the point using humor, or more specifically, satire. The use of the word "tomacco" is a great example of using language that, although perhaps funny and made-up, is still understandable to anyone who reads it. Remember from Chapter 2 that we talked about keeping your appeal universal so that any potential reader can understand your postings and will want to visit your blog on a frequent basis. Well, this posting is a good example of that appeal. Moby is relying on some funny language, but he's doing so in a way that everyone can understand (even if not all people agree with what he is saying).

GET YOUR CELEBRITY BLOGS HERE!
Celebrity blogs can be fun, and in some cases—like the Moby blog we are investigating in this chapter—well written. Depending on your interests, you might want to check out one or more of these celebrity blogs. This is not the definitive list of celebrity blogs, but it should provide enough variety to get you started.

- **Margaret Cho** (comedienne): http://www.margaretcho.net/blog/blog.htm
- **Madonna** (musician): http://home.madonna.com/
- **Hilary Duff** (musician/actress): http://www.hilaryduff.com
- **Marilyn Manson** (musician): http://www.marilynmanson.com
- **Anne Rice** (author): http://www.annerice.com
- **Bill Maher** (comedian): http://www.safesearching.com/billmaher/blog/
- **William Gibson** (author): http://www.williamgibsonbooks.com/blog/archive.asp
- **Anna Kournikova** (athlete): http://www.kournikova.com/journal/
- **Flea** (musician): http://www.redhotchilipeppers.com/fleamail/index.html

---

Reading the Blog: How Is the Point Made?

Moby's posting shown in Figure 3.2 uses humor to make a point. If you look through more of his blog postings, you will find that he often uses humor.

Aside from humor, notice the larger Web site and the way it is presented (especially the links to other things that are present). Look at Figure 3.3, which highlights links that Moby has placed to other Web sites.

If you quickly scan through this list, you can see that there are links to some political and social activist organizations (Greenpeace, PETA). Why these particular links? Well, if you read through just a few of Moby's blog postings, you will quickly see that Moby has an opinion on many social issues, including the preservation of the environment

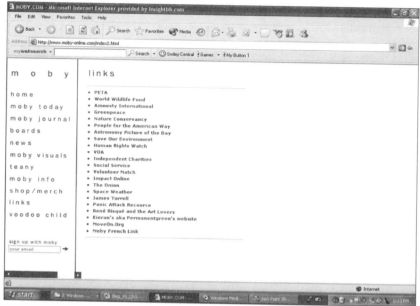

FIGURE 3.3 *More than random links, this list represents the larger interests of Moby.*

(link to Greenpeace) and the ethical treatment of animals (link to PETA). Remember from our discussion earlier in the chapter, as well as in Chapter 2, that as you read a blog, you should take notice not only of the number of links that are presented, but what those links are pointing to. If you read closely, you can often discover the larger interests of the blog author by the types of links they provide on their blog. Moby's blog is no exception.

Another interesting thing about this blog is that Moby also provides links to extended writings, or essays. Figure 3.4 shows the Essays page, with its associated links.

Why are these postings important? Well, they further highlight the opinions and ideas of Moby, and they give some background to the ideas and style of his regular blog postings. Although these essays aren't much different from the blog postings, they provide important clues to the focus of the blog.

Reading the Blog: How Does It Make You Feel?

Again, Moby's blog can be pretty controversial, depending on your opinions on a range of topics. If you agree with Moby on a specific issue, you are probably going to read his posting(s) and be glad that someone else—especially a celebrity—is reflecting what you feel is the right opinion.

FIGURE 3.4 *You can think of these essays as extended blog postings.*

But what if you don't agree with what he says? Although Moby's is a celebrity blog, there is a good chance that you also will read postings on "regular" blogs that you really don't agree with. How do you read those blogs without getting so upset that you either miss the author's point entirely or move on to a different blog before you finish reading the postings?

I'm not saying that you should continue to read stuff that really makes you angry. However, just because someone has a different opinion doesn't mean that what that person has to say isn't important or well written. Remember our example from earlier in the chapter, about the bad CD review? Assuming for a minute that the review really did exist and that it dissed your favorite band, such a review would probably make you angry. But again, that doesn't mean the review is poorly written or isn't important. To be a critical reader, you have to be on the lookout for writing that expresses ideas and opinions that are different from your own.

Rather than discard those opinions you don't agree with, you should read them to determine (a) what point the author is trying to make and (b) how the author is making his point. Once again, let's imagine our bad review example. Let's say that the writer compared your favorite band to another group that he thought was really good. He used this other group as an example of what great music is, and said that your favorite band was nowhere close to making the same kind of music. This is what I mean by reading for specific detail and to determine how the point is being made. Although you probably still disagree with the review, if you read it critically, you can at least understand why the author is making his point. That way, when you write your scathing response on your blog, you can do so intelligently and answer the reviewer's comments, perhaps by writing a review of that other band that the reviewer thinks is so great.

Think about this "bad review" example for another minute, and specifically the idea that, in responding to the bad review, you write your own review of the band that the review writer thinks is so good. Imagine that you are not familiar with this band, and because the review author used the band to slam your favorite band, you put this other's group CD in your car stereo, already thinking that you are going to hate them before you even hear a note. But what happens if you really like it? This is one of the *great* benefits not only of reading and responding critically to a piece of writing, but of keeping a blog in the first place. You might broaden your horizons by taking the time to think critically about something that, at first glance, you either disagree with or just plain hate. Again, I'm not saying that a blog that makes you angry is suddenly going to be your virtual best friend, but if you read critically, you might be surprised at what you find.

Friday, September 12

Mood: Confused

Topic: The Other Guy's Opinion

Jessica did come over last weekend, and we were talking about links to other cool stuff to place on our blogs. Anyway, she said that I just had to put a link to this guy named Sergeant Fields. I guess he's this kid who is like 17 or 18, and everyone says he writes the best reviews and has the best opinions of all the new stuff that comes out, especially movies and music. Jessica really thinks he is cool, and I have heard other people talk about him, so I decided to check out his blog.

Well, after reading about two paragraphs, I nearly threw up. What an idiot! I mean, the guy is just totally wrong about EVERYTHING. Here's a good example: He said that the Beatles were the greatest band ever, and that no music being made today even comes close to what the Beatles did. Okay, for starters, welcome to the twenty-first century, Sergeant Fields, or whatever your name is. In case you haven't noticed, the Beatles aren't really a group that is popular right now. I mean, I don't really know anything about them, but I asked my mom about it, and she said they were popular when she was a kid, and that was quite a few years ago (sorry, Mom…). Then Sergeant Fields said no decent movie has been made in the past 10 years.

I told Jessica about what I thought of this guy and his postings, and that there was no way I was going to put a link to this on my blog. I don't want to give anyone the idea that I think this guy is right, or that I think his opinion is valid. But then Jessica and I got in this big argument about it, and she said I didn't have an "open mind" and that I needed to at least think about what this guy says before I make judgments on his opinions. So, I asked my mom if she could recommend what she thought was the best Beatles CD, and she told me to check out their CD Abbey Road.

Okay, I admit it. It's a pretty cool CD. Lots of good songs and some wild lyrics. So, to appease Jessica and make her think I do, in fact, have an open mind, I went back to Sergeant Fields blog to see what he had to say about this CD. As it so happened, I saw that he made a link to a blog about Outkast (one of my favorite bands, by the way). I thought that was a pretty weird link, but when I checked it out, there was a great quote from Andre 3000 saying how he thought the Beatles were one of the greatest and most influential bands ever.

So anyway, I've been listening to the Beatles quite a bit, and although I don't think they are as good as everyone says they are, I guess they are pretty cool. So maybe Jessica was right (as usual) about taking time to read stuff before I fly off the handle and say that it's not any good. More on this later, as I read more of Sergeant Field's postings… that is, if I can put up with his ridiculous ramblings (just kidding).

Summary

This chapter gave you some advice on how to closely read other people's writings and intelligently think about what they are trying to say and how they make you feel. Along the way, we consistently returned to the example of finding a bad review of your favorite band's new CD, and how you could do a close reading of that review to see if you could understand (but not necessarily agree!) with the opinion of the writer. We then used this example to highlight the types of reactions and experiences you will have when reading other blogs, especially those that you might not agree with. To further illustrate the point of how to do a critical reading of a blog, we looked at one of the better celebrity blogs (www.moby-online.com) and how you can apply the tips you learned in this chapter to reading such a blog so that you can (a) understand the main point, (b) understand how that point is being made, and (c) understand how the blog postings make you feel.

Chapter 4

Beyond the Blog: Expanding Your Voice

After reading the first three chapters of this book, you might be starting to think that blogging is a singular activity—something you only do when you are lonely, depressed, or otherwise not in the best of moods. Admittedly, a lot of blogs out there are devoted to the trials and tribulations that life can throw at you. And let's face it: When you are a teenager, life's little curveballs can be, well, not so little. I mean, one day everything is going great and then—wham!—three or four things happen at once and you're left feeling like you just got run over by a truck.

There's no doubt that using a blog to chart your way through these dark teen waters is a great thing. Too often, teenagers—or anyone of any age, for that matter—don't take the time to express what they are feeling, and as a result just get more and more depressed. For that reason alone, blogs are a great outlet and a great way to feel like there are others out there going through the same things you are.

You can use your blog to interact with other people in all kinds of ways, beyond just making regular postings and having others read them. And when I say "other people," I am not just talking about the friends you meet in cyberspace. I'm also talking about your friends at school, your teachers, and yes—believe it not—those weird people who live in the same house as you do. (Yeah, I'm talking about your family here!) This chapter will look at ways you can go "beyond the blog"—in the personal, singular sense that has been the focus of the first three chapters—as well as using your blog to interact with people in even more exciting ways. Specifically, we're going to look at how you can use your blog to

◆ Communicate with—gasp!—your parents in new and dare I say fun ways so that you can actually get them to understand what you are talking about. I know, I know… It's hard to believe that this a possibility, but with a blog, it just might be!

◆ Document your family history and events. Think about it: What if you could use your blog not only to talk about yourself but also as a way to write about unique experiences your family is going through? You might think of this as your family's electronic scrapbook, but again—because we're talking about blogs here— there's a lot more to it.

◆ Step in the realm of video and turn your blog into a video blog (*vlog* for short). With some inexpensive hardware and software, you can bring your unique visual appeal to your blog.

 note Not interested in any of the topics you see presented in this list? That's cool—you don't have to be. It is perfectly fine to think of your blog as something personal and unique only to you, and you shouldn't feel like you need to "integrate" it with other people or things to make it a great blog. But, if you're interested, you can expand your voice and go "beyond the blog" by connecting your blog to other people's experiences, too, and in turn using it to communicate with those people in ways you might not have thought possible.

 tip If you find, after reading this chapter, that you want to learn more about the topics presented here, be sure to look at Chapters 9 and 10. They talk about advanced features of blogging, as well as different ways you can use your blog to communicate.

Blogging with the Parental Units

So you're a few chapters into this book, and you're getting all these great ideas for how to express yourself on a blog. We've talked about drawing from your own experiences, as well as talking about your favorite movies, books, and music to help develop your own voice as you build and make postings to your blog.

Now that you have all these great ideas, though, here's a little question for you: Have you thought about your parents reading your blog? I know—it's a scary thought. I mean, after all, you spend all this time devoting your blog to descriptions of your personal experiences. What happens if your parents happen to read your blog?

Although there are ways to restrict who can read your blog, I want you to take a minute to consider what might seem like a crazy idea: What if allowing—or even asking—your parents to read your blog was a good thing? What if it were something that could help you communicate with your parents in new and better ways?

I'm not going to pretend that a blog is the magic answer to that age-old question of how to get teenagers and parents to communicate. But more and more teenagers are using technology as a primary method of communicating. From blogs to e-mail to instant messaging, every teenager I know spends a great deal of time online. If you are one of those teens—and undoubtedly you are, given that you are reading this book—why not consider using that technology as a way of communicating better with your parents?

The Blog-to-Bedroom-Wall Connection

While I have your attention about this idea, I'd like you to compare how you express yourself on your blog to what is still—even in the age of technology—the classic mechanism of teenage expression: your bedroom door and walls. Do you have posters of your favorite band or movie stars hanging up in your bedroom? Maybe you have paintings or drawings that you've done, or perhaps your bedroom walls are covered with pictures of special times shared between you and your friends or family.

If you've decorated your bedroom walls like I've described, think about how and why you chose to decorate in that way. More than likely, you didn't just pick any poster of your favorite band to hang on your wall; rather, you found just the right one that you thought was the coolest of all. Or, if you have picture collages covering the paint, chances are good that you spent some time organizing and picking out only the best pictures to include.

The central question here is this: Why do you plaster stuff all over your bedroom door and walls? After all, what's wrong with just simple painted walls? The answer is easy, of course: Your room is your sanctuary, the one place you can go to recharge your mental batteries. To make your room even more comfortable and an expression of who you are, you deck the walls with stuff you like and things you use to define yourself.

Be honest, though. Do you really hang all that stuff on your walls only for your benefit? While it's great to head to your room after a long day and be surrounded by stuff that you think is cool, you probably like the idea of other people seeing your room and the stuff you have decided to display. Otherwise, why go to so much trouble and money putting it together in the first place? And aside from your friends, who probably sees all this stuff more than anyone else? That's right—your parents and other family members!

At this point, think about the way you decorate your bedroom in the context of how you will "decorate" your blog. In other words, you are using your blog to express your interests and individuality, just as you do with the stuff you put up on your bedroom walls. And assuming you let your parents into your room from time to time, why not "decorate" your blog and let your parents "visit" that, too?

> **tip** If your room is your real sanctuary, you might think of your blog as your "virtual sanctuary," and you might not like the idea of having just anyone snooping around. When we move into later chapters (6–9) and talk about choosing a blog hosting service and actually building your blog, you'll learn about ways to limit who can visit your blog or make replies to your postings.

Turning Your Bedroom Walls into Hyperlinks!

Obviously, you're not going to want to spend all your free time hanging out in your room with your parents. (I'm making a wild assumption with that statement, but I feel pretty safe that it's the truth.) The same thing goes for your blog. More than likely, you are not going to the effort of building a blog just for your parents to read. Actually, the thought of having them read any part of it might give you the creeps.

Still, if you think of how you've decorated your bedroom as a metaphor for your blog, some interesting things come to mind, not only about using your blog to communicate with your parents and others, but also how using a blog to express your individually and interests is just plain cool:

◆ **Make that "poster" a hyperlink!** Imagine that you have a poster of your favorite band hanging on your wall. Chances are quite good that if one of your friends or family touches that poster, no magic voice will start talking, explaining why you think the band is so great and what special connection the band has to your life. But, think in blog terms: You could easily make a picture of your band a hyperlink so that when visitors click it, they are taken to a Web site that talks more about the band.

◆ **Turn four physical walls into 40 or more virtual walls.** You might be lucky enough to have a big bedroom and plenty of wall space to decorate with posters and pictures. But even the largest wall space is limited because you can only hang so many posters or pictures before you run out of space to put more stuff. With a blog, though, you don't really have that problem. Your "virtual walls" are limited only by how much space your hosting service provides you, and that is usually more than sufficient.

◆ **Comment on your "virtual decorations."** Again, with a blog, you are not limited just to displaying an item of interest, whatever that item of interest happens to be. You can post that item and then comment on it through a regular set of postings or as a combination of links to related Web sites about the item.

So, what's the point of all this? Well, it's really pretty simple: Although you can feel happy about blogging just for the sake of sorting out your own ideas, blogging's real magic comes when other people read your ideas and comment on them. Thinking about your blog as a "virtual room" might be a bit over the top, but on the other hand, it shouldn't surprise you to find that the same stuff you are "decorating" your blog with is what you have hanging on your bedroom walls. And assuming that your parents—among other people—are viewing and wondering about what you have on those real walls, why not extend that to your "virtual walls," to further expand your individuality and in the process use the power of the Web to define and make that individuality known?

The Family (Blog) Tree

One of the most popular pastimes on the Web is genealogy, or tracking your ancestors. Given that the Web is such a powerful communication tool, and that anyone sitting in his own home with a Web connection has access to such a wealth of information, it's not surprising that lots of people are digging through this information to find people they are related to.

Again, what does this have to do with blogging? Well, if you happen to be interested in genealogy or uncovering some new limbs on your family tree, a blog is a great way to track your extended family and let them know you are interested in finding out more about them. Figure 4.1 highlights one of the many blog hosting services devoted to online family trees.

But this isn't really what I have in mind here. Rather, I'm talking about using your blog as a kind of electronic family scrapbook to document the experiences your family is going through. What do I mean by "experiences"? Well, for starters, think about how you might use your blog to talk about the following:

◆ **Your move to a new city.** You haven't made new friends yet, and your family is starting from the beginning with nearly everything. Using a blog to talk about your new experiences is a great way not only to keep in touch with those you left behind but also to meet people in your new surroundings.

◆ **Your new baby brother or sister.** You can use your blog to post pictures of your new sibling and to keep distant friends and relatives up to date with all the changes that having a baby in the house brings with it. In fact, these "baby blogs" are becoming increasingly more common.

◆ **Updates with other family members.** Again, although the idea of having family members read your blog might be frightening, it can be a great way to express how you feel about certain situations and for others to get to know you better.

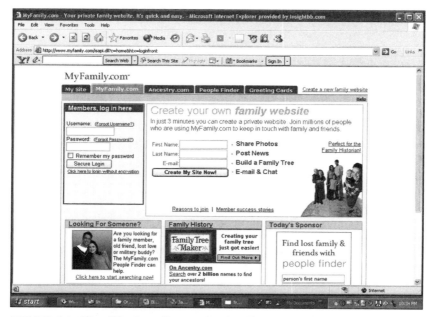

FIGURE 4.1 *Sites like http://www.MyFamily.com are geared toward building blogs for an entire family.*

You might not be comfortable with the idea of having your family take much of a focus on your blog. But if you could link your blog to a larger family site (as illustrated in Figure 4.1) or comment on your blog about experiences that your family is going through, you could use blogging not only to better define yourself, but also to give others a better picture of what your self-definition is all about. If you make postings about these topics, and your family (or other people interested in your family) can read and enjoy them, your blog will have risen to a whole new level of communication.

Here's the bottom line: Don't be afraid to link or otherwise use your blog to post about these subjects. You just might find that in doing so you open up a new channel talking about difficult subjects with your family and bringing your family closer together. That might be asking a lot for a blog, but it can happen!

Vlog: The Video Blog

The last "expanding your voice" blogging topic I want to discuss in this chapter is one that is growing more popular by the minute: adding video to your blog to create a vlog.

What is a vlog? You can think of it as the next evolution in blogging, where you begin to move beyond text and graphics information to video streaming. In many ways, the vlog is the fulfillment of the ultimate promise of a blog, which has given people a way of documenting what is going on in their lives. From political rallies to family reunions, if you can add video to your online diary, you bring a whole new level of personalization and power to your blogging.

Why would you want to build a vlog? Before I answer that question, I should probably tell you what you need to actually build a vlog.

The first thing you need is a way of capturing on video the events you want to record. Although digital video cameras are becoming more popular and less expensive, chances are good that you still have an analog video camera, or one that is designed to work with your typical VCR. By purchasing a video capture device, you can easily transfer your analog video onto your computer, where you can edit it and prepare it for posting to your vlog.

Hardware and Software Vlog Requirements

There are three technical components to building a vlog: an analog or digital video camera, a capture device to transfer the video onto your computer, and some type of video editing software to make your captured video the best it can be.

Although it is beyond the scope of this book to go too far into detail on how to capture and manipulate video on your computer, I do want to give you some general information on the hardware and software requirements, especially if you are using an analog video camera.

In terms of hardware, you need a video camera and a way of placing that video on your computer. Although digital video capture is easier (you just plug your digital video camera into your computer, typically through some type of USB connection), what do you do if you are using a nondigital video camera? In that case, you need a capture device, or something to convert your analog video into a signal that your computer can recognize.

Several capture devices are available, and many of them don't require you to open up your computer to install. (That is, they plug in externally to your computer.) Figures 4.2, 4.3, and 4.4 illustrate some of these different devices, as shown on the manufacturer's Web sites.

note If you look at some of these products in more detail, you will notice that a lot of them talk about converting VHS home video to DVD. This is a popular topic now, as more and more people want to convert their old VHS home movies to DVD. But even if you aren't interested in that topic, you can still use these capture devices to convert your analog videos into a digital format that you can place on your vlog.

FIGURE 4.2 *ADS Instant DVD 2.0.*

FIGURE 4.3 *Belkin USB VideoBus II. Unlike the other devices illustrated here, this is a simple cable connection from your video camera to your computer.*

FIGURE 4.4 *Dazzle Digital Video Creator 80.*

You can purchase most of these capture devices for less than $200. Before you buy, though, keep the following issues in mind:

◆ **Is the device compatible with the type of hardware interface your computer supports (USB 1.1, 2.0, or Firewire)?** "Hardware interface" in this case means the type of connection you will use to plug the capture device into your computer. If you purchased your computer before August 2003, it likely uses USB 1.1 as its hardware interface. Some of these capture devices only work with USB 2.0 (which is much faster), so before you buy one, see if it is backward compatible with USB 1.1.

◆ **Is the device dependent on a specific version of operating system?** Are you running Windows XP? Windows 2000? Maybe even Windows 98? Many of these devices will work across the different versions of Windows, but be sure to confirm this before you make the purchase.

◆ **What software is supported in working with the device?** You will find that the vast majority of the video conversion devices come with software to help you edit and prepare your converted video.

Just as there are a variety of capture devices available, there are many video editing software packages to choose from. Applications like Ulead Video Studio, VideoWave, WinDVD Creator, MyDVD, and Final Cut Pro are all popular choices. As I mentioned earlier, many of these applications come bundled with video capture devices. Although many of the devices claim they are for converting your home movies to a DVD, you don't have to actually take that final step (converting to DVD) to get the video from your analog video camera onto your computer, where you can edit it with one of the applications in the previous list and then send it to your vlog for others to view.

Special Considerations with Vlogs

If you've never worked with video files on your computer before, there are a few things you should know. The first and perhaps most important thing is that it is incredibly easy to get existing video onto your computer using a capture device like I talked about a minute ago. And, by using one of the editing applications, it is easy and fun to do all kinds of neat things with that video, such as adding special effects and audio backing tracks.

But this fun doesn't come without a price. And when it comes to video, the price isn't really about money; many of the good video capture devices are less than $100. The price comes down to the amount of space that video files take up on your computer's hard drive. Depending on the speed of your computer and the type of interface you are using (the USB 1.1, 2.0 issue again), transferring the video from your video camera to your computer can be slow.

The good news is that you can add more storage space to your computer for very little money, and you can upgrade the type of hardware interface pretty cheaply, too. You should be aware, though, that even though it's not rocket science to open up your computer to add new stuff, it's definitely not something you should do without previous experience. You can seriously damage your computer and the data it contains if you aren't careful.

When you upload your video files to your vlog, here are some things to keep in mind:

◆ As you'll see in Chapter 6 when we talk about choosing your hosting service, you usually get a certain amount of disk space on the hosting service's computer to store all the files and text that compose your blog. It doesn't take long for video files to become big, and it's not unusual for a video file that is only a few minutes long to be several hundred megabytes in size. Your hosting service will probably charge you a fee to accommodate these big files.

◆ The speed issue will be a factor when it's time to place the video files on your vlog. If you are using a dial-up service to connect to the Web (that is, you are using your regular phone line), uploading big video files is going to be slow—painfully slow. Having a cable or high-speed connection to the Web certainly helps this issue, but even then it can take you several minutes to upload large video files.

◆ Finally, the issue of bandwidth could be a factor when working with a vlog. Put simply, bandwidth is the amount of connection space your vlog is allowed to use on the hosting service's computer. If you only have a few people visiting your vlog at one time, bandwidth won't be an issue. But if you have tens or hundreds of people trying to view your vlog at the same time, all that video you are sending over the Web might max out your bandwidth and result in some of your visitors being denied access. Think of this in terms of going to a concert: If the band decides to play in the middle of a cornfield, and there is only one access road, lots of people aren't going to make it in time to see the group play. On the other hand, if the show is right off a major highway, the flow of people is more easily accommodated. I'll talk more about this in Chapter 6. Many hosting services allow you to get additional bandwidth for a fee.

Examples of Vlogs

Now that we've talked so much about vlogs, you probably want to see a few, right? Read on!

Compared to regular blogs, vlogs are still fairly uncommon. But as it becomes easier and cheaper to work with video on your computer and to put that video on the Web, the number of vlogs is probably going to explode. That old saying about how a picture says a thousand words is definitely true with vlogs, because you can convey more information with a video file. And it's just plain cool and fun to work with video on your computer.

Okay, so where do you go for some vlog examples? A good place to check out a general listing of vlogs is http://www.vidblogs.com, which is shown in Figure 4.5.

Ultimately, vlogs can be seen as the next step in the evolution of blogs. And if you look at some of the examples on vidblogs.com, you can see that they are really like mini movies about the individual's life or specific interests. Many of them are really funny, too.

Video blog? Vlog? Vidblog? Lots of terms are being used to describe these things, although it seems that vlog is the one that is gaining the most acceptance and popularity.

Vlogs and blogs aren't just for fun—they also make great school assignments. If you have the chance to do some extra credit work in one of your classes or to work on a special term project, you might think about building a vlog. It would be more fun than writing a big paper!

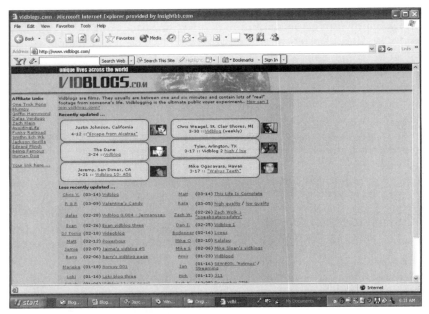

FIGURE 4.5   *The Vidblogs home page, where you can see an organized list of recently updated vlogs.*

FRIDAY, SEPTEMBER 19

MOOD: DELIRIOUS (WITH LAUGHTER)

TOPIC: KICKSTART'S VIDEO BLOG

There are few things in life that really crack me up. But I have to say I've just added another item to my list, and that is Kickstart's vlog.

Jessica and I were hanging out in the computer lab today during lunch, working on a project for class, when she happened to ask me if I had seen Kickstart's vlog. I didn't know what, exactly, she was talking about at first. But when Jessica started laughing just describing this thing to me, I knew I had to check it out.

Sorry for writing this, K, as I know you are going to read it later, but all I can say is: What were you thinking when you decided to make that video available to the whole world? We all realize that your secret dream is to be the lead singer in some cheesy band, but don't you think you need a few voice lessons first? Again, sorry for writing this, my friend, but seeing you in that tuxedo shirt singing "The Way You Move" is just too funny. I hope OutKast doesn't see that. They might put a hit out on you!

I have to admit that watching Kickstart's feeble audition for American Idol did get me thinking about how to use some video on my blog. Since I've been listening to some different music (those Beatles songs are sort of stuck in my head), I've been thinking about how cool it would be to use some of those songs and make a video about my life. Not any big retrospective or anything like that, but maybe something funny that... I don't know... tries to explain how I feel about something. There is this one Beatles song called "Blackbird" that is pretty cool. The lyrics are really good; they talk about how you wait your whole life for one moment to finally arrive. I'm not sure exactly what the song is saying. You know, when that moment arrives, what happens? And is that "moment" a good thing or a bad thing? Is it something that you are dreading or really looking forward to? I've been thinking about one of those moments: the homecoming dance. I'm not really a dancer (you could say I dance about as well as Kickstart sings), but there is someone I've been thinking a lot about lately and would really like to ask to the dance. But... well... I'm not sure that going to a dance and all is really my thing. I mean, it would be cool to go with this person because I really like her and we have a lot in common, but I'm not sure how she would feel about it. You know—if it would weird her out.

Anyway, I thought I could maybe add some kind of video to my blog and use that song as a backing track. At the very least, I think "Blackbird" is a cool song, and it really does express a lot of things that I am feeling right now. The other thing, too, is that my mom wants to start a family "e-scrapbook" on the Web so that all of our family who lives out of state can get the latest news on what is going on in our lives. She asked me if I thought we could put some video of everyone on the site, and I told her yes, so that's making me think about the video idea even more, too. More later...

Summary

This chapter introduced you to different ways of thinking about your blog and how you can use it to communicate who you are and what makes you tick to your family and friends. From thinking of your blog as your "virtual bedroom wall" to using it to talk about family experiences, the focus of the chapter was on viewing the blog not only as a way of defining yourself but really sharing that definition with all kinds of people. The chapter also talked about the "next evolution in blogging," which is the video blog, or vlog. With some inexpensive hardware and software, you can add video to your blog and use it to define and express yourself in new ways. Although there are some technology concerns you need to be aware of when working with video files (such as the size of the files, the speed of your computer, and the amount of space you have to post video files on your blog), it is easy and fun to work with video. You can usually overcome the technology issues pretty cheaply and easily if you have a little experience with working on your computer.

Chapter 5

Planning Your Blog

The time has come to start thinking seriously about your blog!

After reading the first four chapters of this book, you should have all kinds of ideas about how you want to present yourself and your ideas on a blog. You've read how to find and express your unique voice by relating your interests and experiences to things such as movies and books, and you've learned how to critically read what others are saying and incorporate those ideas into your own postings. In Chapter 4, you got a glimpse of how to expand your voice even more by using a vlog.

Yep, you should have some pretty good ideas at this point about what you want to write. (But even if you don't, that's fine. Getting a blog going isn't a race, and you can always read through the early chapters as many times as you like.) Now it's time to organize all those ideas and thoughts into an outline for your blog. Think of this chapter, then, as the final step before you start placing your ideas on the Web. From here on out, the focus will be on actually building and publishing your blog, from choosing a hosting service to working with specific blogging tools.

So, as this final step in the planning process, this chapter will

- ◆ Quickly review the major ideas of the first four chapters to help you get your thoughts and ideas organized

- ◆ Work through a blog outline template so that you can "fill in the blanks" for the initial design and content of your blog

- ◆ Present an example of this planning process

Reviewing and Organizing Your Ideas

We've covered quite a bit of ground in the first four chapters. From convincing you that you have something to say to helping you think of ways to say it, a blog can be a personal, powerful communication tool.

Again, now that you have all these ideas, you need to organize them so that you can start to seriously plan how you want to put them on your blog. The following sections are a review of some of the major headings in the previous chapters (especially Chapters 1–3). As you read through each one, jot down some ideas so that when you get to the section "A Blog Planning Example," you will have some ideas to work with.

 tip Don't worry if you can't think of something for every topic. Some of the topics are general and are intended only to give you advice as to a certain kind of writing style you might want to follow. On the other hand, if you have an idea—no matter how crazy it might sound right now—definitely write it down! Some of those crazy ideas turn out to be the best ones, and they can lead to different ideas, especially when other people begin to read them.

Also, for each of the following sections, I will talk about my own blog in regard to each topic. For example, in the next section, "Why Blog in the First Place?", I will give you some background on why I became interested in blogging. Although I'm certainly not saying that all my ideas are the greatest, I hope they will give you some ideas on how to organize ideas for your own blog.

Why Blog in the First Place?

To blog or not to blog: That is the question. If you've gotten this far into the book, I'm assuming you are definitely interested in blogging!

Think back to Chapter 1 when you were first introduced to the concept of blogging. Can you remember some of the first ideas that ran through your mind about the things you might talk about on your blog?

Well, even if you can't remember all those first thoughts, take a few moments now to answer the question being presented here: Why blog in the first place? If you suddenly find yourself stumped for ideas, think about some of the following reasons why people enjoy blogging:

◆ **It's a great outlet for expressing your ideas and feelings.** This is the primary reason that most people blog. Perhaps no other technology allows people to express themselves to a potentially huge audience so quickly and easily. Best of all, you can think of a blog as an online diary, but one that, while allowing you to write in a personal voice, also allows you to share your thoughts with a world-wide audience. All kinds of books and research are being written and performed on that very contradiction (that is, how a blog allows you to keep your private, personal voice but potentially share it with the world). Although that apparent contradiction is interesting, the important thing to take away at this point is that blogging gives you such a great way to express yourself.

◆ **It's a great way to make new friends.** You can have a successful blog without other people commenting on what you say, but one of the really great benefits of blogging is that other people can comment back to you on your thoughts and ideas. As this process continues, you will undoubtedly begin to develop friend-ships with the people who read—and comment—on your blog postings.

---

tip You really can have a great blog without having people commenting on your postings. Remember that the first real benefit of blogging is that it gives you a dynamic outlet for expressing yourself. Who cares if you are the only one reading your postings? After all, if you can read through your own postings to make better sense of how you feel, how to deal more effectively with a given situation, or just simply to have fun, you have a successful blog. We'll talk more about this idea in Chapter 10, but don't get hung up on the idea that unless people post to your blog, it's no good. Nothing could be further from the truth!

◆ **It's a fun, interesting way to become a more critical reader and thinker.** I've said many times throughout these early chapters that blogging can make you a better student. That's true, but you will only be a student for a small per-centage of your life. However, as we discussed in Chapter 3, you will always need to be a critical reader and thinker, to be able to listen to/read/watch some-thing and find "the point," and to distinguish between ideas that are well devel-oped and those that are, well, just this side of half-baked. By keeping a blog and reading and responding intelligently to other blogs, you will build this ability to read and write critically.

You don't need your own specific answers to these benefits of blogging. As long as you can understand these benefits and see why blogging is something that is growing in pop-ularity among teens, that's enough for now. Think of these points as evidence you can use to support your interest in blogging when other people ask you about it.

Picking Your "Personal Style"

You might remember from Chapter 1 that blogging can open your eyes to all kinds of new ideas and opinions that you might otherwise not have considered. As you start to think seriously about your blog, now is the time to also think about the tone and style of how you are going to write and to play devil's advocate against your ideas and opinions that you are interested in posting on your blog.

What do I mean by playing devil's advocate with yourself? Put simply, I mean thinking about how other people might view your ideas and opinions differently than you do. The best writers, speakers, and thinkers have always been able to do this. By understanding how other people might not agree with what you are saying, you can better argue your own ideas. There's an old saying that says "Keep your friends close and your enemies closer." I'm not implying here that you should think of people who don't agree with you as your enemies. Still, as you prepare your blog and think about how you are going to express your ideas, consider how other people will react to them. In turn, you can adjust your postings to consider the other guy's viewpoint, which will make you a much better thinker and writer.

At this point, you should also be thinking about who you hope will read your blog. Again, there is absolutely nothing wrong with keeping a blog just for yourself or for a few close friends. But if you write in such a style that only a few close friends will understand or you decide to restrict the viewing of your blog to just a few people, you might be missing out on the real fun and power of the blog as a communication and learning tool. The choice is up to you, though.

Selecting the Best Web Communication Method

Another important planning issue to consider is how your blog will fit in with and complement other ways of communicating on the Web, especially via traditional Web pages, instant messaging (IM), and e-mail.

Let's face it: Just because you have a blog doesn't mean you are going to suddenly stop using e-mail and instant messaging your friends. As a matter of fact, your use of these other technologies will probably grow as your friends comment on your blog postings. So, as you plan your blog, think about how you will use these other methods of communication to enhance your blog and your enjoyment of it. We'll talk more about this issue in Chapter 10 when the discussion focuses on how to integrate your blog into your life.

Finding Your Voice

I devoted Chapter 2 to giving you ideas for how to find your voice so that you can express your thoughts and ideas in the most effective and fun way.

In that chapter, I asked you to think about finding your voice by thinking about your favorite music, movies, and books. I also asked you to think about your personal experiences and how you can draw from them as a way of defining who you are and expressing your individuality.

There is no right or wrong way to express yourself. The important thing to keep in mind is that if you are having trouble finding something to write about on your blog, you're thinking too much. Just write! Have you ever had an English class where your teacher instructed you to take out a piece of paper and just start writing the first thing that pops into your head? Or, perhaps you've done that classic exercise where you write a few sentences of a story and then pass what you've written to someone else, who then writes a few sentences building on what you wrote and passes on the story to someone else. The point of this exercise is not to write a funny story (although that is usually the result) but rather to show that taking your initial idea and allowing others to comment on it can result in something that none of you had ever considered.

The same holds true for finding your voice and posting to your blog. If you are having trouble thinking about what to write about, picking a topic that interests you can be a great way to get a conversation going. You might remember from our discussion in Chapter 2 about how a favorite movie, book, or song can be a great "universal" way of expressing your ideas.

For example, if you think the movie *Mean Girls* best sums up your opinion of high school cliques, you might express your opinion by making a posting that says, "I think the movie *Mean Girls* is the best representation of a day in the life of a typical high school." Again, chances are good that many people will have seen this popular movie and can relate to it in the same way you are. As people post to your blog or you make more postings about what the movie means to you, you will quickly find that your voice is taking on a life of its own. And, more than likely, as the postings begin to grow in numbers, so will your ideas, not just about the first topic but others, too.

 There is something to be said for being popular, as anyone would probably tell you. Popular people are usually that way for a reason. The point here is that blogs that are immediately popular are also that way for a reason—usually because they are well designed, have postings that are well developed and interesting, or simply because the author is well known. So, although you can certainly start your blog with a simple posting on something you are interested in, don't be surprised if other blogs that are more intricately designed—either in regard to what they are saying, how they look, or both—get more immediate attention. Still, don't get discouraged if your blog doesn't get much attention right from the start. These things can take time, and once again, if you are getting enjoyment from keeping a blog, that is all that ultimately matters.

Reading for Ideas

Last but certainly not least, we've talked quite a bit about how blogging can make you a better critical reader and thinker. But, as we discussed in Chapter 3, you can also use your critical reading skills to find ideas for your blog.

How can you do this? It's easy. If you'll recall from Chapter 3, I suggested you keep in mind three simple questions when reading other blogs, especially when you are looking for ideas:

◆ What's the point?

◆ How is the point being made?

◆ How is the point making you feel?

In addition to these simple questions, don't limit yourself too much on what you define as "reading." Too often, when people say they like to read, others interpret that as meaning they like to read *books*. This is not always the case. Don't limit yourself in where you think you can find ideas, or to reading only books. You can actually use all that stuff you are learning in school in the real world, so don't forget to apply your reading and thinking skills when you are planning your blog.

> **tip** When you think about reading, consider all the things you read on a daily basis—you never know where you'll get your ideas. For example, the booklets that come with CDs (that is, the ones with song lyrics, comments from the band, and so on) can be pretty extensive and give you lots of ideas.

A Blog Planning Example

Up to this point, the chapter has pretty much been a review of what you've seen in Chapters 1-4, with a few additional ideas for you to consider. Now it's time to take all this information and put it into a planning perspective. I want to show that you can successfully plan your blog before you make even one posting.

> **tip** Once again, if you are reading this far into the chapter, I'm assuming you are interested in the topic. But in case your interest is starting to wane a bit, stay with me just a little longer. Taking even a short time to plan can save you lots of time later, not only in what you post on your blog but in how you post it.

The remaining sections in this chapter illustrate how planning can help you organize your ideas and get a better handle on what you have to say. As an example, I will go through the planning steps I took in preparing my own blog, which will be discussed in Chapter 12.

Purpose of the Blog

I've always been interested in music. When I was a little kid, I used to do Elvis impersonations for my family, and somewhere (I'm sure) there are pictures of me striking my best Elvis pose.

To fuel my musical interests, I had the great benefit of two older sisters. Why was this such an advantage? Well, for one, I got their hand-me-down stereo equipment and their hand-me-down records. Yes, I do mean "records" in that these were the days before CDs, and definitely before MP3s and other technologies of today. But don't peg me as being too ancient. I got my first CD player when I was 14, after all!

Anyway, as my CD collection started to grow, so did my interest not just in the music itself, but also in how people thought about the music they listened to and what music meant in their lives. For example, I remember when the U2 album *The Joshua Tree* first came out—before the band was the corporation that it is today. That album had a huge impact on a lot of people. Not only was the music great, but the ideas being presented in the music and the causes and organizations the band supported also were relevant and engaging. I was 17 when that record hit the airwaves, and it made a huge impact on me. Put simply, it was some of the first music I had heard that made me think.

From that point, I started to really dig into music of all styles and generations, not just what was popular on the radio. This was still a few years before the Web, so there weren't that many people to talk to about it, other than my friends. Still, there were lots of great things to discover about music in the local library, and it was great fun to seek out other writers (mainly rock music critics) who felt the same way about music that I did. People like Lester Bangs, Dave Marsh, and Greil Marcus had been writing for a long time about the importance of popular music and what it could mean to the lives of the people who listened to it. More interesting to me, because I always loved to write, was that these critics were also having fun with the idea of the record review. Sometimes they would write about the music, but other times they would use the music as an excuse to write about whatever they felt like, be it relationships they were in, the state of the world, you name it. This was cool stuff, reading about the music you were listening to.

Music has remained a central part of my life. With a 45-minute commute to work, I have lots of time to listen to my favorite CDs. That kind of commute would drive some people crazy, but I love it because it gives me time to rock out on my way to and from work. I've even built into my morning routine a few minutes to peruse through my CD collection (which now totals well over 1,000 individual discs) and pick out just the right discs to match my mood for the day.

So, given what I've written here, it probably shouldn't surprise you that when I got interested in blogging, I knew very quickly that I wanted to focus my blog on music. Rather than have just straight postings of my personal experiences, I decided to theme my postings around how life can be interpreted and analyzed through music. In the process, I also wanted to turn other people on to the same writers and ideas that interested me when I first started to listen and think about music seriously. Thanks to the Web, I can place links to my favorite rock critics' Web sites on my blog, as well as links to other music-related sites.

In reflecting back on the previous sections of this chapter, then, I can answer the issues presented so far in the following way:

◆ **Why am I blogging?** Given my interest in music and technology, it should be fairly obvious that blogging is a great way to merge these two topics. I can use my interest in and experience with technology to develop my blog, and my interest in music and writing to make my blog an interesting one to read.

◆ **How will I "wield my blog power" wisely?** I decided early on that I didn't want my postings to be cryptic or overly personal. Basically, I wanted to share my love of music with as many people as possible, and along the way get my readers to think about music in ways they might not have originally considered.

◆ **What is my "blog voice"?** Too often, people who write about music or literature come across as big snobs. After reading about five minutes of their stuff, it becomes pretty clear they are more interested in showing off what deep thinkers they are than writing anything interesting, let alone getting their readers excited about new ideas. With that in mind, I didn't want to "dumb down" my blog postings. At the same time, however, I didn't want to make my postings so cryptic or intellectual that no one would be able to understand what I was saying. I decided to keep my tone personal. And instead of having my postings read like term papers, I've framed my interest in music around trying to make sense of my everyday life experiences, as well as just posting ideas about the music I am listening to at any given moment.

 Music is a huge part of many teenagers' lives. It's been said that the music you listen to and really like when you are in your teens and early twenties is music that will stick with you your entire life. You might want to read the rest of this chapter with that in mind. It's not so much that I'm trying to convince you to make your blog all about music; rather, you should think of something that is important to you. If you do, you will have far less trouble expressing your ideas about it, and you will have a lot more fun with it, too. Chances are good that if you develop your blog around something you like, you will continue to gain a great deal of enjoyment and satisfaction from it, both now and well into the future. As an example, the band Led Zeppelin means as much to me now (perhaps more, in some ways) as it did when I was 15, hearing it for the first time blasting from my bedroom stereo.

Organizing Your Ideas

After I decided I wanted to focus on music for my blog, I started to think about all the different music-related things I was interested in. Here's the list I came up with:

◆ Listening to music, especially in my car on the way to and from work

◆ Reading music criticism

◆ Integrating rock 'n' roll into the English classes I teach and showing my students how to use music to better understand the stuff they read, and vice versa

◆ Reading about the history of rock 'n' roll and how it has helped shape the culture of the world over the past 50 years

◆ Going to concerts

◆ Thinking and writing about how music affects me

◆ Writing my own music reviews

◆ Supporting the Rock and Roll Hall of Fame (located in Cleveland, Ohio)

That is a pretty big list, with lots of room in each category for smaller, more specific subcategories. Rather than categorize things too much, though, I decided to work around these general headings. I kept this list in mind as I started to post to my blog. As you will see in more detail in Chapter 12 and when you visit my blog, I try to talk about as many of these categories as possible in my postings.

note In addition to organizing your ideas in a list like the one I've built here, it is worthwhile to think about blogs and other Web sites that you might want to link to. For example, if I was posting something about music criticism, I might link directly to that critic's Web site, a collection of the critic's writings on the Web, comments by other writers about the critic's work, and so on. Don't forget to take full and absolute advantage of linking from your blog, because links give you a great way to expand your voice and give deeper meaning to what you are writing about.

tip Another advantage of organizing your ideas in a list like I've done here is that it can be a great way to generate new ideas for your blog postings. Instead of sitting down at your computer to try to make an interesting posting to your blog out of thin air, you can refer to your list. Although the topics I've picked are pretty general, they are still more specific than if I'd listed "music" as an interest and the purpose of my blog.

When I go into detail in Chapter 12 about how I developed my blog, you will see how you can use your own organized list to help plan your blog. You certainly don't have to do any of this to start a blog, but I think you'll find it a great help, not just in organizing your ideas, but in thinking about your ideas, too. A great deal of the fun of blogging is the thinking you do before you write even one word.

This sort of gets back to my interest in music, but it's relevant to talk about here, too. When I first started to seriously listen to and collect music, I would sit for hours in my room just listening to the music and thinking about what was going on in my life, important decisions I was making, problems I was having… you name it. I spent time talking about all these things with my friends and parents, but there was a great satisfaction in just taking time to think to myself, to work through ideas in my head before I shared them with anyone else.

As you start to develop your blog (more on this in Chapter 10), there's a good chance you will have the same experiences I'm describing here. You will probably find yourself thinking as much about your postings as you do writing them. Again, one of the great benefits of blogging is that it can help you get things straight in your head. Then, when you make postings on your blog, you give a new voice to all the time you spent thinking about those things, and other people can read and comment back to you about them.

What else can I say that I haven't already said time and time again in this book? Blogging is just a cool, fun, fascinating thing to do. Still interested? Good. Keep reading. You are just about ready to start building your blog.

DATE: WEDNESDAY, SEPTEMBER 24TH

MOOD: BUMMED BORDERING ON FANTABULOUS!

TOPIC: COLD WEATHER BITES (SORT OF)

You know what really bites? I'll tell you: the winter. I took my dog Stryder out for his morning walk, and man—I about froze to death! I mean, it's only September, but you can tell the winter is coming. Then on the way to school, I noticed that the rain from the night before had really knocked a lot of the leaves off the trees and that "winter gloom" look is really starting to turn things gray and ugly.

But I have to say there is a certain magical feeling to the winter, too. Ever since I was a little kid, I've always really enjoyed the fall and early winter. There is just something about the changing of the seasons and how everything just sort of turns in on itself and everybody gets ready for the long, dark months. Sure, there are the holidays and everything, but everyone I know gets depressed, too. You know, another year has come and gone, and all that crap.

What does this have to do with anything? I have no idea, really, other than when I was out walking Stryder and thinking about how long it would be until summer vacation, I also had my iPod with me. I was listening to this great old song my brother gave me. It's by this guy named Van Morrison, and the name of the song is "Moondance." The lyrics are pretty cool: "It's a marvelous night for a moondance/With the stars up above in your eyes/A fantabulous night to make romance/'neath the cover of October skies." I love that word "fantabulous"—can't get it out of my head.

So I was walking through the very cold morning listening to this song, and I started to think that maybe the fall isn't so bad. I was thinking about that homecoming dance again and the person I would really like to take. And then I started to think that about how much this person would really like this "Moondance" song because she is so into the whole classic rock thing. In fact, I'm sure she knows the song.

I then had such a lame thought that I'm still laughing to myself about it. You know in the movies, especially those about teenagers and "first date" experiences and all that stuff, where they try to come up with new lines about how to ask someone out? Well, because "Moondance" is a song that I am sure the person I have in mind knows, I could use it as a way of asking her to the dance. Now, this is really stupid, but I actually thought about using a line like this: "Hey, ****, you know the homecoming dance is coming up. Would you be interested in a fantabulous night of romance 'neath the cover of October skies?" Man, I am still laughing at what an idiot I can be. I mean, could you imagine how stupid I would sound if I used a line like that?

But "Moondance" is a great song, there's a special magic to the fall, and I really like this person. The dance is just a few weeks away. Does it all add up? Maybe...

Summary

This chapter was a final "idea" chapter before we get into building your blog. Prior to starting any project, it's good to have a plan, and blogs are no exception. In addition to helping you organize your existing ideas, taking some time to plan can generate new ideas. After you see your ideas on paper, you will often see connections to new ideas or connections between existing ideas that you never previously imagined. There are several preplanning topics you should consider, which were the focus of the first three chapters of this book. From thinking about why blogging interests you to deciding how best to express your individuality through your unique voice, you can refer to those chapters to help you develop a stronger framework from which to build your blog. To close this chapter, I talked about the planning process for my own blog. I also showed you my list of organized topics that I put together before I started development of my blog. This list helped me with general organization, but it's also a useful reference tool in its own right so that when I sit down to make a posting, I have the topics to help organize my thoughts, and to help me generate new things to write about.

We've come to the end of Part One of our blogging experience. It's my hope that you have some great ideas for your own blog in terms of what you want to say and how you want to say it. The rest of this book explores the process of getting your blog online and shows you two full-featured blog examples.

Chapter 6

Choosing Your Blog Hosting Service

Okay, we've spent five chapters talking why to blog, the benefits and fun of blogging, the advanced features of blogging, and how to plan for a blog. Yep, we've talked about nearly everything except for one critical topic: how to build your blog!

Well, I'm happy to tell you that the time has finally come to pick your blog hosting service and to develop your blog. The next few chapters are going to take you through a step-by-step process of selecting, building, and publishing your blog. Although it might seem like a complicated process, the good news is that it is in fact very easy, and—in many cases—won't cost you a dime.

This process has been broken down into four parts, each corresponding to this chapter and the next three:

- ◆ **Chapter 6, "Choosing Your Blog Hosting Service."** This short chapter gives you an overview of the different blogging tools and hosting providers you can use to get your voice published on the Web.

- ◆ **Chapters 7 and 8, "Building Your Blog, Parts I and II."** After you decide on a blogging service, you can start creating your blog. These chapters focus on Lycos Angelfire, which is one of most popular blog hosting services for teenagers. It also happens to be the service I use to host my blog!

- ◆ **Chapter 9, "Advanced Blog Design."** If you've done any work with basic HTML or Web design, there's a good chance you've used a Web editing tool like Microsoft FrontPage. Many blog hosting services allow you to use these tools so that you can bring a tremendous amount of power and design to your blog. This chapter provides you with a mini overview of how to use Microsoft FrontPage to build and enhance your blog.

Did you catch that line I wrote about how many blog hosting services are free? Did you read it and think, "Whoa, wait a minute—does it actually cost money to blog?" In most cases, blogging is free. Many of the hosting services allow you to blog at no charge; however, for a small fee (usually a monthly charge), you can add extended functionality to your blog. We'll talk more about these issues later in this chapter. Obviously, though, use caution when signing up for any kind of service that charges you (monthly or otherwise), and be sure you have your parent's permission to do so, especially if those charges are going to be applied to one of their credit cards!

What to Consider with a Hosting Service

Before you decide on a hosting service for your blog, ask yourself and the hosting service several questions to be sure you are picking the best service for your individual blogging needs. Although not every hosting service is going to be able to meet every criterion, you will find that several hosting services are reputable, feature rich, and—in many cases—free. So, as you begin to explore hosting services, don't feel trapped into using one particular service—you have lots of choices! Here are some questions to consider:

◆ **Is there a fee?** Probably the first question you should ask yourself is the most basic one: "What does it cost?" The vast majority of hosting services offer some type of free service; however, the really cool functionality of these services usually comes with the premium (pay) services.

◆ **How much space do I get?** If the main content of your blog is just going to be text, then basic storage—usually in the realm of 20 MB—is going to be plenty. But if you start to add different types of content to your blog, such as sound or video, or you keep your blog for an extended number of years and all this textual content starts to add up, you will want more space. Most hosting services allow you to upgrade your storage requirements, and many have different tiers of available storage, depending on how much you pay each month.

◆ **What is bandwidth, and why should I worry about it?** *Bandwidth* describes how much signal can go through an access line at one time. The more bandwidth you have, the more signal you can transfer in and out. Like storage, bandwidth probably isn't going to be a big issue for you unless you begin to have video/audio streams from your blog or you happen to have an incredibly popular blog, with thousands of people accessing it on a daily basis. Many hosting services give you unlimited bandwidth because it's not an issue for the majority of bloggers.

◆ **How can I post to my blog?** Ideally, you want to be able to post to your blog in the easiest fashion possible. That is, you don't want to mess with complex codes or programming just to get your latest news posted to your blog. Again, most hosting services provide you with some method of easy posting, be it through a Web interface (that is, a Web form you load in your browser and on which you type in your posting) or by use of a Web editing application like FrontPage. As with most of the other options, though, different hosting services give you different levels of functionality in how you can post, or they charge you for the use of a tool like FrontPage. Generally speaking, though, nearly all of the hosting services let you post to your blog through an online form.

◆ **Can I get my own domain name?** A domain name is how your blog is accessed. For example, the domain name for my blog is http://www. my-15minutes.com. Depending on the hosting service you choose—particularly if you choose a premium service—you can pick your own domain name instead of having the hosting service automatically select a domain name for you. For example, if you were hosting your blog on the ABC Blog Hosting Service and you were using their free service, the address (domain name) of your blog might be http://www.abc-bloghosting.com/users/blogs/teenblogs/coolblog.htm. If you used their premium service, you might get to pick your own domain name, such as http://www.coolblog.com. Obviously, there's a big difference between the two domains and the amount of typing you need to do to access the blog.

◆ **What are the "community" or interactive features of the service?** The great fun of having a blog, of course, is being able to hear what other people have to say about your thoughts and experiences. To facilitate this discussion, hosting providers give you different tools to stay in touch and organize these online discussions between you and your readers. Features like threaded discussions (that is, where one topic is given its own unique space within your blog so that it can remain separate from other topic discussions), the ability to search user profiles, and so on are "community" features that hosting services treat in different ways. As you'll see later in this chapter, this sense of community plays a part in the overall style of different hosting services. (See the "LiveJournal" section later in this chapter for more on this issue.)

◆ **What special content features does the service offer?** You know how annoying pop-up advertisements can be when you are surfing the Web? Imagine having to deal with these ads when you're trying to read a blog. If you were just mildly interested in the blog, you might get frustrated and move on to another "pop-up free" blog if these ads became too annoying. Many hosting services allow you to have "pop-up free" blogs, but this is usually available only through a premium service.

◆ **What kinds of security features are provided?** Although a great deal of the fun and excitement of keeping a blog is sharing your voice with a potentially worldwide audience, you might not want everyone in the world reading your blog. Many hosting services provide ways to limit who can read certain parts of your blog, along with other content/security features.

◆ **What is the "teen focus" of the hosting service?** You will see in the descriptions of the hosting services in this chapter that some have more of a teen focus than others. (Compare Angelfire to Weblogger to see what I mean.) Because you are reading this book, there is a good chance you are a teenager and want to host your blog with a service that focuses on teen issues and has a large number of teens as part of its blog community. Take some time to review the style and tone of the service and see if it caters to your overall tastes and interests.

◆ **How reliable is the hosting service?** If you go to the time and trouble of posting to your blog and keeping it current, you want to be sure that it is accessible so that others can read it. Although there are always issues with technology and no service can promise a 100% uptime in terms of accessibility, some services do a better job at this than others. Do a little research on each one, and see how often you have trouble accessing a blog that is hosted by that service. Pick different times of the day or night to access the blog, and if you consistently have problems accessing it, that hosting service might be having difficulty meeting the demands of its users. Be aware, though, that the evening hours are the most popular time to be online for the majority of users (bloggers or otherwise), so access time will generally be a bit slower at 10:00 p.m. than at 10:00 a.m.!

 The information about each of the following hosting services is current at the time of this writing; however, you should check out the actual hosting service sites for current pricing, among other things.

*Blog*Spot and Blogger*

Web URL—http://www.blogger.com/blogspot-admin/
Basic Service—Free
Storage—Unlimited
Premium Service—N/A

If you look at Figure 6.1, you will notice the text that reads, "Blog*Spot is the turn-key hosting service for Blogger," which is shown in Figure 6.2.

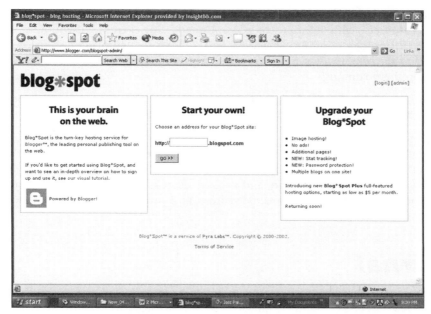

FIGURE 6.1 *The Blog*Spot home page, offering the "turn-key" solution for Blogger.*

FIGURE 6.2 *The Blogger home page. Build your blog here, and then use Blog*Spot to place it on the Web.*

Huh? What is a "turn-key" service? Traditionally, this means that the service provides you—the customer—with solutions to all your needs. For example, if you have a business and a technology company is selling you a "turn-key computer solution," that would mean the company is selling you the computers along with all the support you need to keep them running.

Blog*Spot is the "turn-key" solution for Blogger, in that Blog*Spot takes the blog you develop with Blogger and actually makes it live and accessible on the Web.

Compared to several of the other blog hosting services, Blog*Spot and Blogger are not excessively feature rich, but—like most blog services—they are easy to use. Although you can make a new posting to your blog in different ways (you can do it through your Web browser or e-mail), the security and account features are slim to nonexistent. For example, you can't limit access to specific visitors, and you can't prevent specific visitors from viewing your blog.

LiveJournal

Web URL—http://www.livejournal.com/
Basic Service—Free
Storage—Unlimited
Premium Service—$25/year

LiveJournal prides itself on being a true community of users, and as such, its focus is on communication. Although fancy templates and graphics are features of many blog hosting services, this isn't really the case with LiveJournal. As you can see in Figure 6.3, the emphasis is very much on creating a network of friends.

Like the other blog hosting services described in this chapter, if you choose to upgrade to the LiveJournal premium service, you will have access to a significant number of additional features. Figure 6.4 is a good example of the difference between free and premium services available on LiveJournal.

If you read through the documentation and FAQs (Frequently Asked Questions, as shown in Figure 6.3), you will quickly notice that LiveJournal really is all about community. The service puts great emphasis on taking care of its users and even has a "social contract" where they promise (among other things) to stay advertisement free and to never send spam e-mail. Although some of this might give the site service more of a serious tone than your average teen blogger might like, if you are serious about your blogging, you might find LiveJournal very appealing.

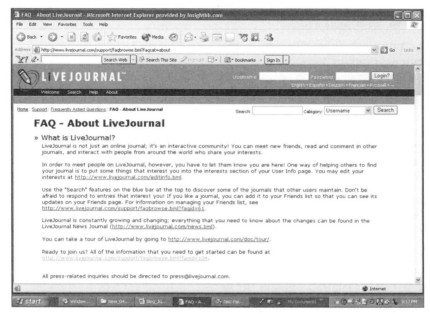

FIGURE 6.3 *Developing a friends list—so that others know who you are and what you are about—is a critical component of blogging on LiveJournal.*

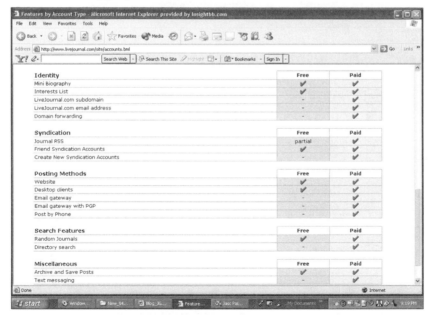

FIGURE 6.4 *For a small yearly fee, you can have access to a significant number of additional blogging features on LiveJournal.*

Angelfire

Web URL—http://www.angelfire.lycos.com
Basic Service—Free
Storage—Varies, depending on service selected
Premium Service—$4.95–$14.95/month

One of the most popular teen blogging hosting services is Angelfire, provided through the Lycos network. Although there is a free hosting option, Angelfire also provides a range of premium service options, ranging from $4.95–$14.95 per month. Figure 6.5 illustrates these various service plans and briefly describes the differences between them.

Aside from being feature rich, the Angelfire service is very much oriented toward teens. Figures 6.6 and 6.7 illustrate the teen focus of Angelfire. As of this writing, there are more than 183 pages of teen blogs listed on Angelfire!

I use Angelfire to host my own personal blog and have found the features under the "Argon" subscription plan (shown in Figure 6.5) easy to use and functional, including the use of Microsoft FrontPage to edit my blog.

I'll discuss Angelfire in greater detail in Chapters 7–9, where I illustrate the entire blog building and hosting process.

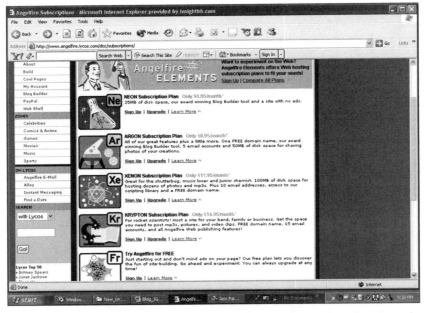

FIGURE 6.5 *Angelfire offers a variety of free and premium hosting plans.*

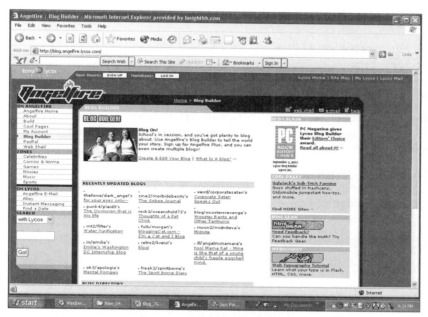

FIGURE 6.6 *Angelfire clearly targets a teen audience with its site and blogging tools.*

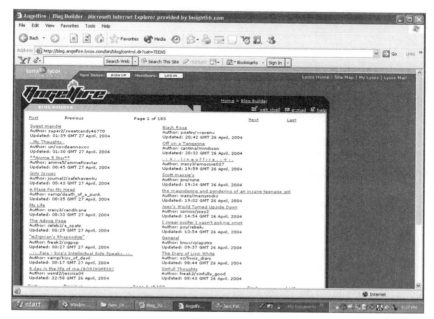

FIGURE 6.7 *Although teen blogs are not the only category on Angelfire, they are certainly the most popular.*

Xanga

Web URL—http://www.xanga.com
Basic Service—Free
Storage—Unlimited Text
Premium Service—$25/year

A solid blog hosting service, Xanga started out as a forum to share music and book reviews. Even today, you can quickly find information on a book or music item of interest through the site.

In addition, Xanga gives you a flexible WYSIWYG (What You See Is What You Get) editor, similar in concept to an application like FrontPage. Figure 6.8 illustrates this editor, available as part of the premium service.

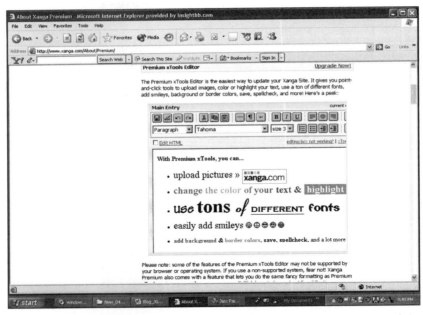

FIGURE 6.8 *The Xanga WYSIWYG interface allows for easy, powerful editing of your blog.*

Weblogger

Web URL—http://www.weblogger.com/
Basic Service—$9.95/month
Storage—Varies depending on service selected
Premium Service—$39.95/month

Although it's probably beyond the budget of most teenagers, I wanted to include a hosting service like Weblogger in the hosting services comparison, just so you can see what is perhaps the more extreme end of serious blog hosting. Figure 6.9 highlights some of the blog themes available at Weblogger.

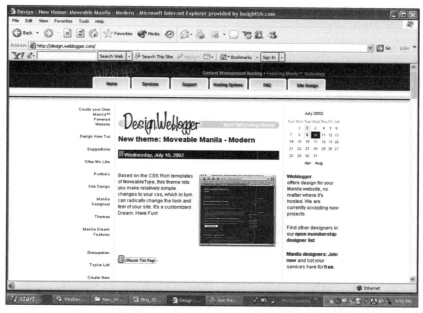

FIGURE 6.9 *One example of the functionally rich design templates available at Weblogger.*

If you compare Weblogger to Angelfire, you can tell (even from the site home pages) that the focus and tone of the two hosting services are different. Undoubtedly, there are teen bloggers on Weblogger, and—undoubtedly—they are good blogs. But generally speaking, and especially if you are just getting interested in blogging, you might take less of a risk money wise (and find more of a teen-focused community) with some of the other hosting services described in this chapter.

tip The hosting services listed in this chapter are in no way meant to be comprehensive; rather, they're meant to give you an idea of some of the more popular services, as well as those that have more of a teen focus. A few other blog hosting services you might want to check out include

◆ Radio UserLand: http://radio.userland.com/

◆ TypePad: http://www.typepad.com/

◆ DiaryLand: http://www.diaryland.com/ (see Figure 6.10)

◆ Easyjournal: http://www.easyjournal.com/default.asp

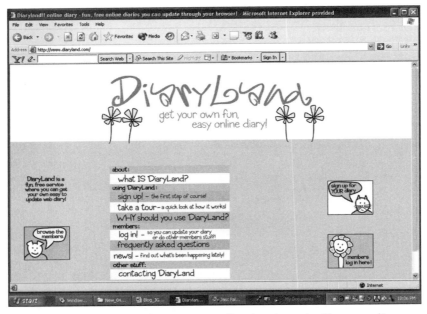

FIGURE 6.10 *DiaryLand (http://www.diaryland.com) offers an ultra-easy, friendly approach to setting up a blog.*

Monday, October 7

Mood: Excited

Topic: Taking a Stand... Maybe?

I was working with Jessica on the yearbook Web site today. Have I mentioned that little project? I wasn't really that interested and didn't think I would have the time to do it, but I thought if anyone was going to comment on the high school experience, I should do it. I mean, I don't claim to be the next "voice of my generation," but I am getting really sick of all these people proclaiming to have all the answers on what it means to be a teenager today. Sure, people have their own opinions and I respect that, but... I'm sorry... just because you listen to what is popular on the radio and because you watch The Real World *does not mean you are in touch with today's turbulent youth. I like some of the stuff on the radio, but I don't want, 50 years from now, people thinking that Britney Spears was the true voice of my generation. No offense, Brit. I suppose you have to deal with your problems just like the rest of us. But I would much rather be remembered as a person and a generation who had more of a—how should I put this?— wide range of interests and tastes. Anyway, I am rambling as usual, but that is what I love about keeping a blog. I can say whatever is on my mind without worrying if all of it makes sense.*

So, Jessica and I were working on the home page for the yearbook Web site, when Mr. Reynolds, the yearbook faculty sponsor, came in and said that the school administration announced it would have the final say as to what the cover of the yearbook looked like. In the past, this was decided and developed by the student yearbook committee and the administration stayed out of it. But this year, because of some parents complaining that least year's cover was not representative enough of the (and I'm quoting here) "challenges overcome by the graduating class," the administration is taking over. Apparently, the administration is going to work with a local design company to come up with a suitable cover for the yearbook.

Now, I wouldn't consider myself very political. I'm not a member of Greenpeace or Amnesty International (not yet at least—Jessica really wants me to sign up). But, go with me here for a minute: The cover of last year's yearbook was of the space shuttle, transposed against a collage of student activity pictures, with the heading, "Reaching for the Stars." If that doesn't express the "challenges overcome by the graduating class," I don't know what does! A lot of us have a feeling that word has gotten out about our planned yearbook cover: a collage featuring—among many things—a few pictures of American soldiers and some political figures (President Bush is in there...) with the phrase "Blowing in the Wind" above it. In case you don't know, that is a reference to an old Bob Dylan song about how the answers to all the world's problems are "blowing in the wind" and can be found if we just open our eyes to see them.

Like I said, I'm not very political, and I think the planned cover is more cool looking than making any big political statement. But obviously lots of other people don't think so. Since I've been keeping a blog, I've started to realize how important it is to let people know what you really think and to practice your right to free speech. I'm thinking about starting a whole thread about the yearbook cover on my blog (I guess by making this posting, I already am), but Jessica thinks I should just drop it. But something doesn't seem right about letting a design company and the administration take over. I can't yet put my finger on how I feel, but I know that I'm going to be writing more about this in my blog postings in the next few weeks.

Summary

This chapter introduced you to a few different blog hosting services and highlighted the major features of each. It also detailed a list of questions you should ask in evaluating any blog hosting service, ranging from how much it costs to how teen oriented the service is.

The next three chapters will take you through a step-by-step process of building a blog, using one of the more popular teen hosting services, Angelfire, as an example. Please keep in mind, however, that even if you don't plan to use Angelfire as your hosting service, the general functionality and issues that I discuss will be the same, regardless of what hosting service you decide on.

Chapter 7

Building Your Blog with Angelfire, Part I

From finding your voice to deciding what to write about, the first six chapters of this book have provided you with lots to think about in terms of what you want your blog to be.

Now is the time to put all those thoughts and ideas into action as you build your blog and bring it to life on the Web in the next three chapters. If you have some experience with building a Web page, you are going to be pleasantly surprised at how easy it is to get your blog up and running. However, even if you've never worked with a single line of HTML, don't worry. Nearly all of the blog hosting services make constructing and publishing your blog a snap. You don't have to be a computer programmer to enjoy blogging.

For my blog hosting provider, I've chosen one of the most popular services around: the Lycos Angelfire service. If you are still unsure which provider is best for your needs, you might want to take another look at Chapter 6. Or, if you are still deciding, you can just follow along over the next three chapters and see how I've constructed my blog with Angelfire.

The next three chapters focus on the nuts and bolts of getting your blog up and running. This chapter in particular looks at the following:

◆ **Registration process on Angelfire.** You can see everything that is involved in this crucial first step and the kind of information you must submit.

◆ **Optional features.** One of these features is having your own specific domain name, which is another way of referencing the address or URL (Uniform Resource Locator) of your blog. We'll look at this and other advanced options in this chapter.

◆ **Initial setup features.** This includes deciding on a template that you can use to customize the appearance of your blog. This is discussed in far greater detail in the next two chapters, but you'll get a preview of it here.

You can think of this chapter, then, as "taking care of the preliminaries," or the critical first steps in building and publishing your blog. The next chapters discuss how to customize your blog's functionality and appearance.

 I chose a pay service to build and publish my blog. Although some blog hosting providers don't charge you a monthly fee, many of the better ones do (well, at least the ones that offer you more functionality). Before you sign up for a hosting plan, be sure to read the fine print and get your parents' permission, especially if you are using one of their credit cards to cover the initial setup charge and ongoing monthly fees.

Signing Up with a Blog Hosting Service

The next three chapters walk you through the process I used to register and start building my blog. Once again, I decided to use the Angelfire hosting service. You might decide to use a different hosting service, but the general concepts and ideas presented here—along with the figures that will illustrate the process—are basically the same across hosting services.

The first step is to sign up for a hosting plan. The following steps illustrate how to do this on Angelfire and present the kind of information you will be asked to provide.

 Things change quickly on the Web, and that goes for pricing plans of blog hosting providers, too. Although the screen shots in this chapter were accurate at the time of this writing, they might have changed by the time this book makes it into your hands.

1. Open your Web browser, and log in to the Angelfire home page located at http://www.angelfire.lycos.com. You are presented with the Angelfire home page, as shown in Figure 7.1.

2. If you click on the Learn More link, you are shown a number of different hosting plans. Figure 7.2 briefly details these plans.

---

tip Do you really need to pay for your blog? That's a good question. It depends to some degree on what you hope to get out of your blog and how you want it to function. Generally speaking, the free hosting plans don't enable you to have your own personal domain name (discussed later in this chapter), and they have limited storage space. And they usually won't block advertisements from appearing around your blog, which can distract from the overall look and feel that you are trying to develop. You can certainly begin your blogging experience with a free hosting plan to see if you like it. Then if you want to add more, you can upgrade to a fee-based plan.

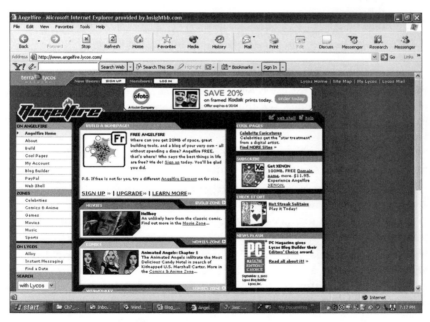

FIGURE 7.1 *The Angelfire home page.*

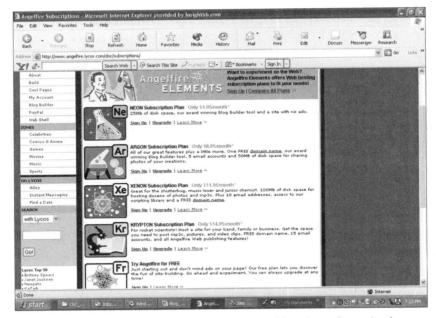

FIGURE 7.2 *You can choose from a variety of hosting plans via the Angelfire site.*

I chose the Argon plan for my blog. Why? Well, as you can see in Figure 7.2, you get 50 MB of storage space, 5 e-mail accounts, and your own free domain name. (My domain name is my-15minutes.com.) If you click on the Compare All Plans link, as shown in Figure 7.2, you can see a more detailed comparison of the feature set for each hosting plan. It's worth noting that the free plan—although limited—offers some strong functionality.

3. You might want to investigate a bit further before signing up, but for the sake of this example and following along in the chapter, let's say that you also want to sign up for the Argon plan. As shown in Figure 7.2, click on the Sign Up link. You're then taken to the hosting plan selection page, as shown in Figure 7.3.

4. Note the asterisk after "Only $8.95/month." A word to the wise guy here: Whenever you see an asterisk after a price, there's some fine print involved. If you scroll to the bottom of this page, you'll see what that fine print is. In this case, it is in regard to additional setup fees, as shown in Figure 7.4.

5. Okay, so 15 bucks isn't a lot of money, but it's still an additional fee that you should be aware of. For the purposes of this example, it's a fee you can live with. Scroll back to the top of this page, where you see the Sign Up link in the Argon plan description, and click on that link. You are presented with step 1 of the registration process, as shown in Figure 7.5.

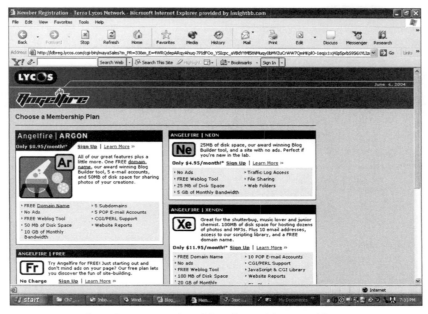

FIGURE 7.3 *Choosing a membership plan with Angelfire.*

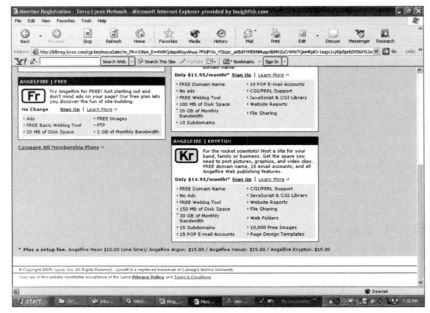

FIGURE 7.4 *As you can see, there are some additional setup fees involved. For the Argon plan, it is a $15.00 fee.*

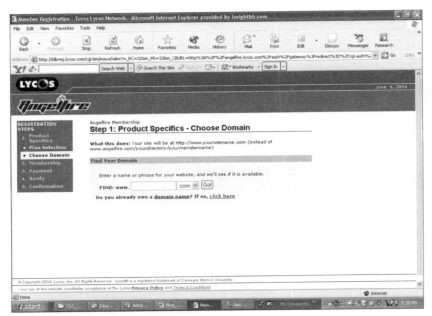

FIGURE 7.5 *A key benefit of the Argon plan is the ability to choose your own domain name, which is step 1 in the registration process.*

6. Remember that the domain name is the address that you and others will enter into your Web browser to load your blog. A good domain name is one that is easy to remember, not too long, and—ideally—catchy or representative of what your blog is all about or a reflection of your personal style. Although many of the best domain names have already been taken, millions of good ones are still available. Just use your imagination. First, try typing the name of my blog domain: my-15minutes. As shown in Figure 7.6, the domain is already taken.

7. You can choose from a list of other naming options. If you want one of these suggested domain names, select it, scroll to the bottom of the page, and click Continue. For this example, imagine that you like all-my-15minutes.com. (I don't like it either, but this is just an example.) Select it, and then scroll to the bottom of the page and click Continue to be presented with the domain name verification screen, as shown in Figure 7.7.

8. After you verify that the domain name is what you want (and spelled as you want, too), click on the Continue button. You're presented with step 2 of the registration process, as shown in Figure 7.8.

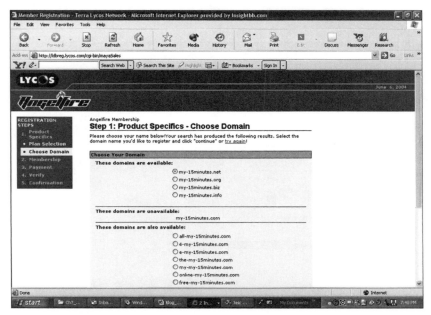

FIGURE 7.6 *Angelfire gives you different naming options if the domain name you want is already taken.*

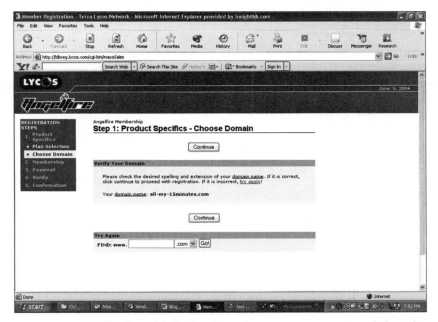

FIGURE 7.7 *Verify that this is the domain name you want and that the spelling is as you want it, too.*

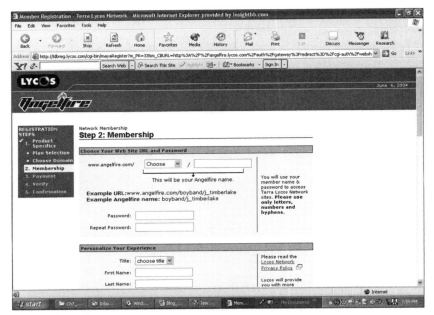

FIGURE 7.8 *Step 2 asks you to select a unique Angelfire name.*

9. From the drop-down list (where it says "Choose" in Figure 7.8), select one of the options. Then, in the name space to the right, type a specific username, something like the first initial of your first name, an underscore, and then your last name (for example, j_gosney, w_becker, r_plant). You also need to provide a unique password. Make sure your password is something that is easy for you remember but hard for others to guess. Figure 7.9 shows a completed username entry. The asterisks in the password field indicate that a password has been entered. (Asterisks appear as you type, for security.)

10. Scroll further down the page, and enter the usual information about yourself (your name, your address, and so on), as shown in Figure 7.10.

Concerned about entering personal information on a Web site? It's good to be concerned. Always use caution when providing any kind of identifying information to a Web site. Be sure to read the Lycos privacy policy (see the link on this page, as shown in Figure 7.10). Or, if you decide to use another hosting provider, familiarize yourself with its privacy policy to make sure the information you provide stays safe and protected and is used only in the ways you want it to be used.

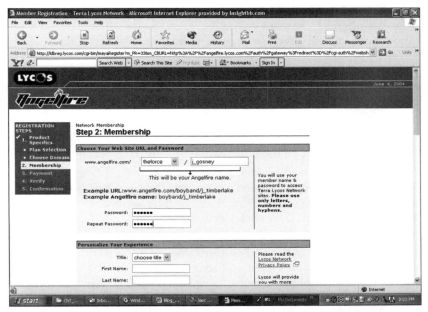

FIGURE 7.9 *Pick a password that is easy for you to remember but hard for others to guess.*

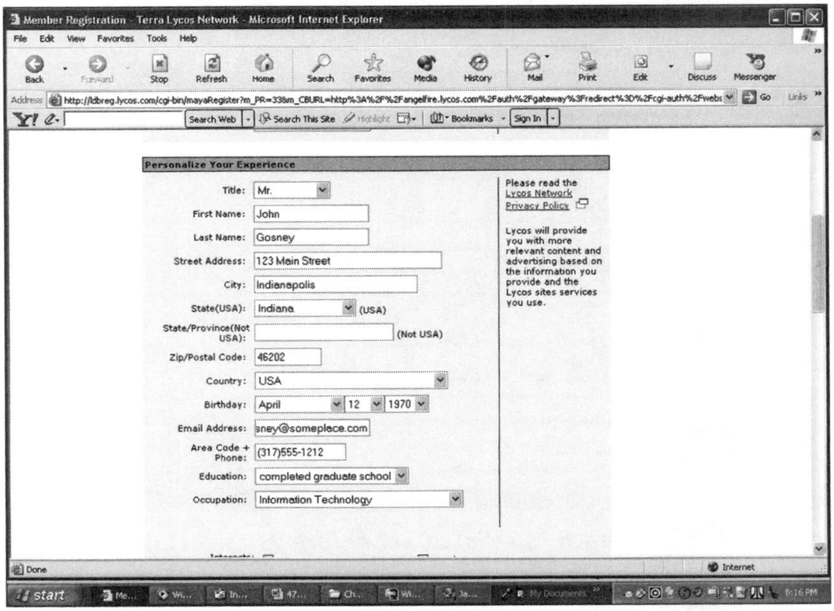

FIGURE 7.10 *Enter the usual information to identify yourself.*

11. The last section of step 2 asks you to check the boxes that indicate your interests and to select whether you want to participate in special offers or receive information about such special offers. Be careful about selecting any of these offers. More than likely, you won't be interested in the offers that show up under the Lycos Registration Offers section (see Figure 7.11). For those options that appear under the Angelfire and Terra Lycos Network Offers section, you might want to leave some of these checked (they primarily represent e-mail alerts and free services), but read through them carefully. Personally, I don't like to receive any of these, so I've unchecked all of them.

12. When you've completed all the information on this page, scroll to the bottom and click Continue to be taken to the main billing page, as shown in Figure 7.12.

13. Again, if you are using your parents' credit card, be sure they're in full agreement and completely understand the charges that will be applied. Complete this information as requested, and then click Continue.

14. On the next few screens, you are asked to confirm all the information you've entered up to this point. After you confirm that everything is correct, you are presented with a confirmation screen and sent a confirmation e-mail that includes a summary of your membership plan.

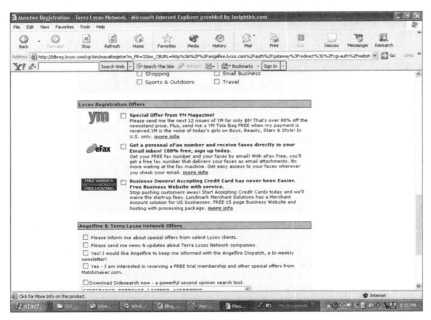

FIGURE 7.11 *Carefully read each "special offer" before you select it.*

FIGURE 7.12 *Enter your credit card information, to which your monthly fees (and initial setup fee) will be charged.*

Accessing Your Blog Account

Now that you have a membership account, it's time to access that account so that you can begin working on your blog.

Again, each hosting provider varies in how it allows you to access your blog, but the steps described in this section should apply across all hosting providers. Every provider gives you a specific username and password, which you'll need to use to log in and access your blog.

note   If the plan you've selected allows you to select your own domain name, know that it might take up to 72 hours for the domain name to propagate throughout the Web. What does that mean? To put it simply, it takes a while for the Web to recognize your specific domain name that's associated with the physical computer it is hosted on. Whenever someone anywhere in the world types in your domain name, this command makes its way to the computer your site is stored on, and your blog is loaded into that person's browser. You can think of the Web as a huge set of phone directories. When a new "phone number" is added (that is, a new domain name), it takes a while to get that "number" listed in all the individual directories.

Here's how to access your blog via Angelfire:

1. First, open your Web browser and navigate to the Angelfire Blog Builder page, located at http://blog.angelfire.lycos.com/, as shown in Figure 7.13.

2. This page probably looks familiar because you've seen it illustrated in previous chapters. The difference is that in this example, you have an account to log in to. At the top of the page, you will see a Members: Log In link. Click on that link to be taken to the login page, as shown in Figure 7.14.

Many Web services (blog hosting providers or otherwise) allow an automatic sign-in feature, and Angelfire is no exception. Note the Sign Me in Automatically check box, as shown in Figure 7.14. Basically, this feature stores your username and password in a special file on the computer you are using, so that the next time you visit, you are logged in automatically without having to enter this information. As a general rule, I never use these features because other people often use the same computer that I do (either at work or at home), and I don't want them accessing my private stuff. Although the automatic sign-in feature is convenient, keep the privacy issue in mind.

FIGURE 7.13 *The Angelfire blog home page, where you can log in to your account and get the latest in blogging news and updates.*

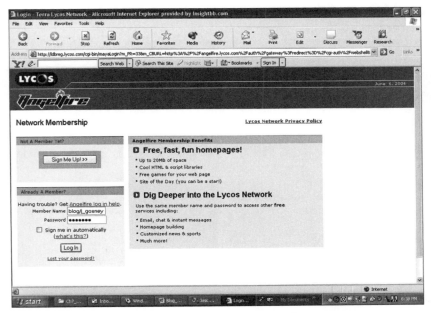

FIGURE 7.14 *Enter your username and password.*

After a few seconds, the Webshell page loads, as shown in Figure 7.15. On Angelfire, this is the main page from which you can access various administrative features of your blog.

3. If you scroll down this page, you will see the different administrative features you have access to. However, most of these features will come into play after you have something on your blog, and you are not quite there yet. What you need to do now is format your blog and set up some general parameters for how it will appear. To do that, you need to access the Blog Builder. Click on the Blog Builder link. You are returned to the page shown in Figure 7.13. After you're there, click on the Create & Edit Your Blog link. The Blog Control Panel appears, as shown in Figure 7.16.

4. Although all these features are discussed in Chapter 8, let's take a quick look at a few of them now to highlight how easy it is to work with the appearance and functionality of your blog. First, click on the Create a New Blog link. A list of blog templates appears, as shown in Figure 7.17.

5. A neat feature of this function is that you can preview what each template looks like. Figure 7.18 shows the preview of the Music template (which I used for my blog), and Figure 7.19 highlights the Movie template. Click a few of the templates now and preview them to see which one you like the best.

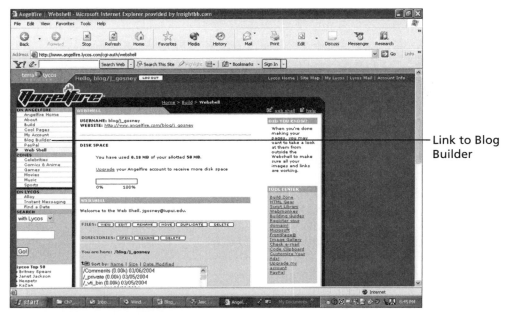

Link to Blog Builder

FIGURE 7.15 *The Webshell page is "command central" for your Angelfire blog.*

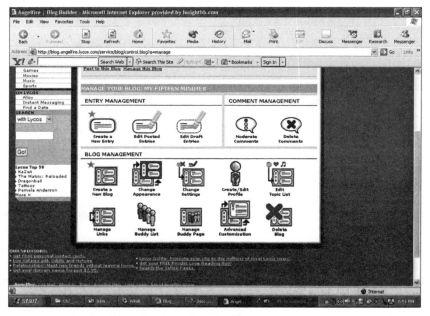

FIGURE 7.16 *The Blog Control Panel offers you easy access to various administrative functions of your blog.*

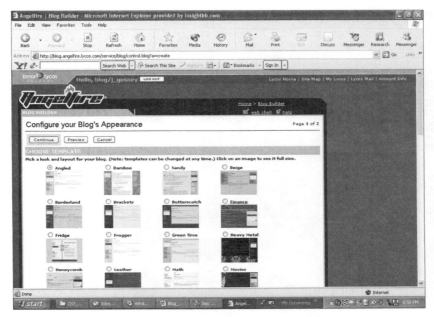

FIGURE 7.17 *Choosing a design template for your blog.*

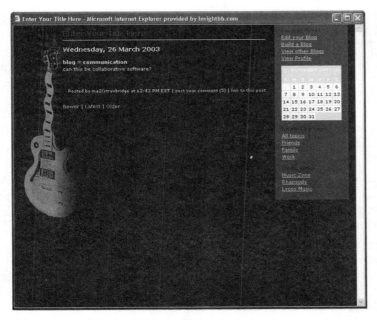

FIGURE 7.18 *The Music template.*

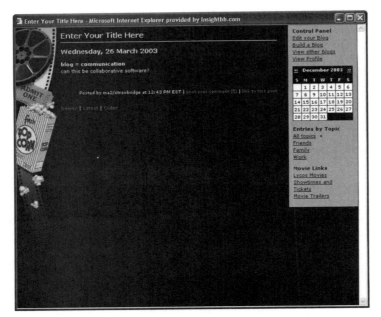

FIGURE 7.19 *The Movies template.*

Your blog's appearance should be a direct reflection of your style and interests. The Angelfire Blog Builder tool gives you lots of options to help you design the blog that best represents you; however, you can also access and design your blog with a Web editing tool like Microsoft FrontPage. (You can do this with Angelfire, as well as many other blog hosting providers.) You'll learn how to do this in Chapter 9.

6. After you've previewed a few of the blog templates, click the Back button on your browser to return to the Blog Control Panel page (as shown in Figure 7.16). Again, even though all the functionality presented here will be discussed in detail in Chapter 8, let's look at one more of the administrative features. Click on the Change Settings link to bring up the Configure Your Blog screen, as shown in Figures 7.20 and 7.21.

These figures highlight the detailed control you can administer over your blog, from who can post comments to what format (simple text, HTML) those comments are made. Again, all this will be described in more detail in the coming chapters, but the important thing to keep in mind is that you should use this kind of specific control to best administer and enjoy your blogging experience.

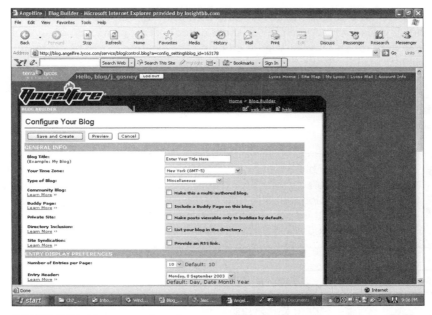

FIGURE 7.20 *You can set various access controls on this page, including who can see your blog and on which Angelfire listings your blog will be posted.*

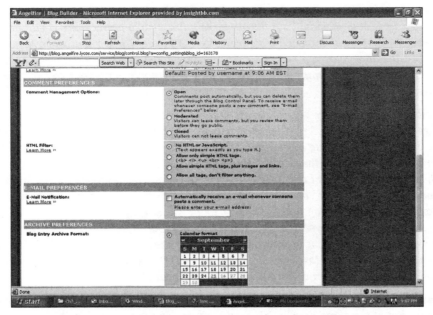

FIGURE 7.21 *Notice here how you can moderate comments posted to your blog or allow comments to be immediately posted without your prior review.*

If you have been following along in real time with this chapter and have actually signed up for a hosting plan with Angelfire (or some other hosting provider), congratulations! You are now very much on your way to enjoying the exciting world of blogging! But, if you are still just reading through all this to get a better idea of what to expect, that's fine, too. The next chapter digs deeper into the specific functionality of an Angelfire blog, and Chapter 9 serves as a general overview of how you can use Microsoft FrontPage to design and administer your blog. There's lots of great stuff just around the corner, so keep reading!

---

 tip   Remember that a blog is, in essence, a Web page. That said, when we get to Chapter 9 and working with FrontPage, you will not only be learning how to use it with your blog, but also how to use it to build general Web pages. FrontPage is not the only such tool, but it is one of the easiest applications to learn and one of the most powerful as well.

THURSDAY, OCTOBER 17

MOOD: CREATIVE

TOPIC: BLOG THE POWER!

If you read my last posting, you know about the "Yearbook Cover Scandal." Well, I'm not sure I would call it a "scandal," but it's got quite a few people pretty upset. I still don't understand why it is raising such a controversy, but I ** do ** know that when someone tells me I can't do something, I want a good reason why. And so far, the reason behind our school administration putting the brakes on our planned yearbook cover is... well... no good reason!

Remember my last posting, where I wrote that the yearbook committee wants to put the phrase "Blowing in the Wind" above the picture collage? Well, I was bored the other day, so I started rummaging through my parent's old record collection, and I found the Bob Dylan album that has that song, "Blowin' in the Wind." I still don't get the appeal of Bob Dylan. I mean, I guess I can appreciate how great of a songwriter he was, but have you heard that guy sing (if you call it singing)? It sounds more like a moose in its final dying moments than singing to me. Anyway, like I was saying, I was really bored, so I dug out the old record player, too, and hooked it up to the basement stereo. If you've never heard an old record, it is an experience. There are so many pops and clicks (from the scratches in the vinyl) that it really distracts from the sound, but at the same time, it sounds good, too. It's sort of hard to explain but worth checking out.

Anyway, I'm listening to that song, and the lyrics really start to hit me. I mean, they are so simple, but at the same time speak so directly to what is going on in the world right now: "How many times must the cannonballs fly/Before they are forever banned/The answer my friend is blowin' in the wind." As I was looking through all the old stuff, I found some newspaper clippings of stories my mom wrote for her college newspaper. Most of them had to do with the Vietnam War, and my mom wrote several opinion articles, arguing against the war. You see, she and my dad were quite the hippies in their day!

As I was reading through her articles and some of the Letters to the Editor responses that her columns generated, it occurred to me that, in a way, this was just like a blog. I started to imagine how those blogs might have been used and if they would have made a difference against the war if they had existed back when my mom and dad were in school. I actually asked my mom about this, and after I spent what seemed like an eternity explaining what a blog is (my mom is great, but she's not really techno-savvy, if you know what I mean), she started to get really excited, telling me that I should definitely use my blog to express my opinion about the yearbook cover. I told her I didn't think I was really a political activist, but she was so passionate about me expressing my opinion that it was hard to tell her no. One cool thing about my mom is that she always encourages me to express my ideas. Like I said, she was a big hippie in her day, so I guess she expects me to be one, too.

I talked to Jessica about using a blog as a way of generating interest about the yearbook cover issue, and she was all over it, of course. She even asked if she could come over and listen to the old Bob Dylan record. I never thought the "dying moose" voice of Bob Dylan would be a way to get Jessica to come over, but whatever works, I guess (just kidding, Bob...). So, it looks like I'm taking more of a political stand on this issue than I thought, and blogging about it in the process. It should be interesting, to say the least...

Summary

This chapter walked you through the process of creating a membership with the Angelfire hosting service. It introduced the general concepts of what a membership implies (including what fees are associated with it) and the types of information that you are required to give. Next, we used our newly created membership to log in to our blog account, and—via the Angelfire Blog Control Panel page—took a quick look at some of the administrative features, including selection of a design template and an overview of the specific access and control features that can be set. The next chapter will delve deeper into these Angelfire-specific features, and Chapter 9 will give you an overview of how to use a Web editing tool like Microsoft FrontPage to design your blog.

Chapter 8

Building Your Blog with Angelfire, Part II

You are getting closer to having a live blog. Actually, if you have been following along through Chapter 7, you already have a blog. Granted, there might not be anything on it, and it might not be much to look at it, but you are definitely on your way.

Again, even if you aren't using Angelfire to host your blog, you can still follow along with the material presented in these chapters. The functionality is generally the same across the different hosting providers, although—in my opinion—Angelfire's functionality and ease of use sets it above much of the competition.

In this chapter, we'll delve further into hosting your blog on Angelfire as we look at the administrative and design features that are available. If you thought Chapter 7 was sort of boring, I apologize. It's a necessary evil to get through that kind of preliminary stuff with any hosting provider. After you sign up for a membership plan, you can really start to enjoy the blogging experience. This chapter is an introduction to that fun.

So, in this second chapter of building your blog, we'll look at the following elements as they specifically relate to Angelfire:

◆ **Blog entry management.** See how you can make new postings to your blog, as well as edit entries you have already made.

◆ **Blog management.** This is the nuts and bolts of how your blog is put together. From design templates to creating and editing your profile, the Angefile Blog Control Panel gives you access to a rich and easy-to-use set of features.

 The functionality presented in this chapter can, in many cases, be achieved by using a program like Microsoft FrontPage. In fact, you might find that you have more control over the look and feel of your blog if you use a program **note** like FrontPage rather than the Angelfire Blog Control Panel. Still, it's a good idea to understand the tools that the hosting provider offers before you move on to using something like FrontPage. You can design a perfectly acceptable and functional blog by using just the hosting provider's tools.

Logging In to Your Blog

I'm guessing that after reading through all the early chapters, you have lots of great ideas and are ready to make some postings to your blog. Well, that time has finally come!

Before you can make a posting, though, you need to log in to your blog. Let's do that now.

1. Open your Web browser to http://blog.angelfire.lycos.com. The Angelfire blog home page opens, as shown in Figure 8.1.

2. Click on the Log In link at the top of the page. Enter your username and password, as shown in Figure 8.2.

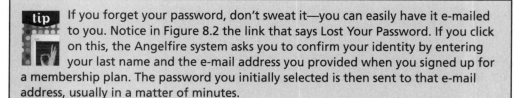 If you forget your password, don't sweat it—you can easily have it e-mailed to you. Notice in Figure 8.2 the link that says Lost Your Password. If you click on this, the Angelfire system asks you to confirm your identity by entering your last name and the e-mail address you provided when you signed up for a membership plan. The password you initially selected is then sent to that e-mail address, usually in a matter of minutes.

3. It was a successful login! Figure 8.3 illustrates the page that appears after your username and password are verified.

Most of the special functions that are highlighted in Figure 8.3 will be discussed in more detail in Chapter 9 when we talk about using FrontPage. However, take a few minutes now to recognize all the useful information that is presented to you here, especially in regard to how much of your allotted space you are using and how you can easily access the files (Web pages, images, sound and video clips, and so on) that will make up your blog.

FIGURE 8.1 *Remember to check this page for news and general updates, as well as using it as your launching point to log in to your blog.*

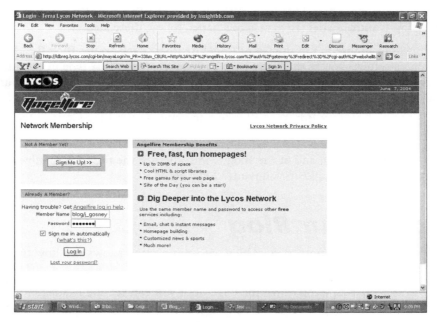

FIGURE 8.2 *Logging in to your blog.*

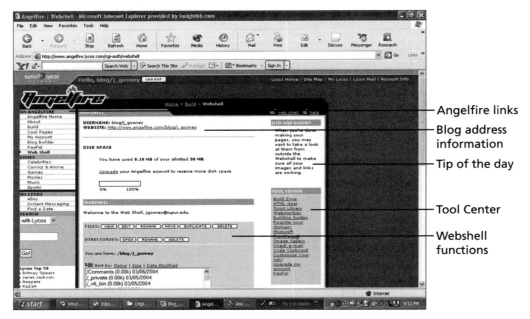

FIGURE 8.3 *From this screen, you can access all types of tools and functions of your blog.*

Now that you are logged in, let's look at the first of the three major functions of the Angelfire Blog Control Panel. To access this panel, follow these steps:

1. As shown in Figure 8.3 in the list of Angelfire links, click on the Blog Builder link. This returns you to the same page you see when you first type in the address http://blog.angelfire.lycos.com/. However, as you can see in Figure 8.4, you are now logged in.

2. Click on the Create & Edit Your Blog link to bring up the Blog Control Panel, as shown in Figure 8.5.

Now that you are logged in and at the Blog Control Panel, the time has *finally* come to make your first blog posting! Are you ready? Let's get to it!

Posting to Your Blog

Angelfire makes it easy to post to your blog, and this section shows you how to do just that.

If it's not already visible, scroll down the page until you can see the Manage Your Blog section and corresponding links (see Figure 8.5). We're going to start the discussion with the Entry Management links.

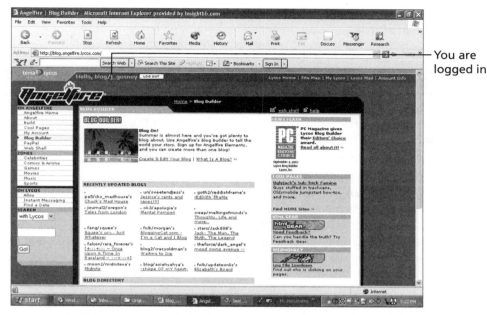

FIGURE 8.4 *This is the same initial page as that shown in Figure 8.1,
but notice that you are now logged in to the site.*

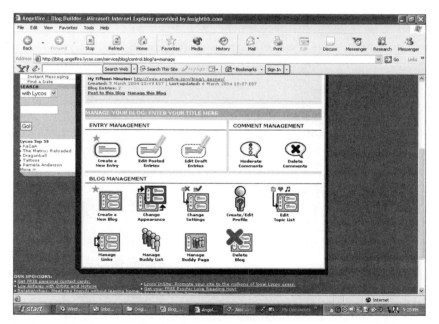

FIGURE 8.5 *The Blog Control Panel, offering you easy access to all
kinds of neat administrative features.*

I'm actually jumping the gun a bit here by having you make your first posting. You still need to decide on some preliminary issues (like a design template, for example), but I want to get you blogging first.

1. Click on the Create a New Entry link, as shown in Figure 8.5. You are taken to the Create a New Blog Entry screen, as shown in Figure 8.6.

2. Although this form is fairly self-explanatory, let's go through each item to make sure you understand what it's all about:

   ◆ **Title.** You can title your posting, which is useful if your initial post generates related comments. When this happens, the title helps you identify the first (and subsequent) postings from other topic postings on your blog.

   ◆ **Mood.** Sometimes when you sit down to make a posting to your blog, you will be happy, but other days, you might feel down in the dumps. The Mood line allows you to identify how you are feeling, which helps to give additional meaning to your posting. If you click on the drop-down menu, you will see a long listing of possible moods you can select from, as shown in Figure 8.7.

   You can also choose your mood from a set of emoticons, as shown in Figure 8.8. I use emoticons in moderation, because it's not always clear what some of

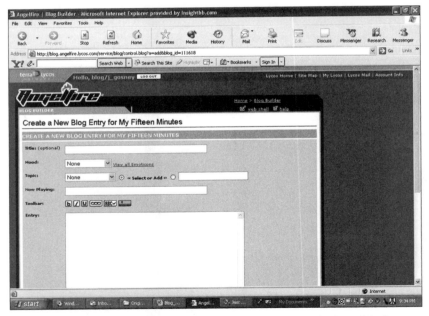

FIGURE 8.6 *Making a new posting is as easy as completing this form.*

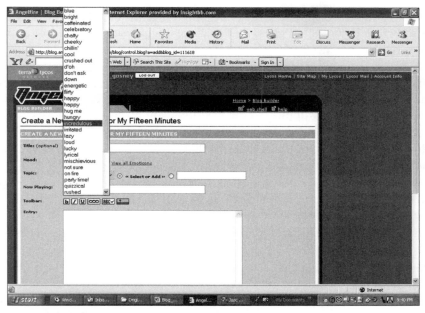

FIGURE 8.7 *What kind of mood are you in? Take your pick!*

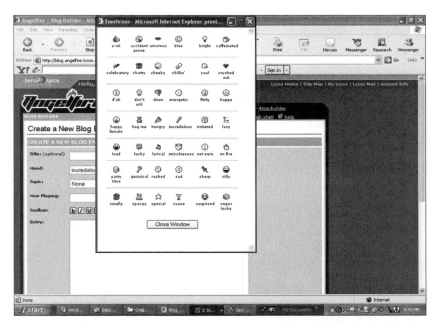

FIGURE 8.8 *Emoticons are fun, but use them in moderation to make sure what you have to say comes through clearly to your readers.*

them are supposed to represent. For example, see the emoticon for "spacey," as shown in Figure 8.8. I guess that creature is supposed to represent a space alien (and so you get "spacey"), but like I said, it can get a little confusing.

◆ **Topic.** What is the general topic of your posting? Are you ranting about the amount of homework you have for the weekend? Or maybe you want to comment on the new Lenny Kravitz CD? Use this field to enter a topic. Notice that you can add new topics, so the next time you make a posting about that topic, it is included in the drop-down list.

◆ **Now Playing.** You can use this field to link to sound or video files. We'll look at this and related topics in more detail in Chapter 9.

◆ **Toolbar.** The toolbar lets you perform some basic editing on your posting, including bolding and underlining text, as well as adding a hyperlink. You'll see the toolbar functionality illustrated in more detail in Chapter 9.

◆ **Entry.** This one's self-explanatory. It's the place where you type in what you have to say.

◆ **Post This Entry as HTML.** You might have to scroll down the page a bit to see this check box and the following options (see Figure 8.9). The Post This Entry as HTML check box allows you to use the Entry space to enter special HTML tags to add new levels of appearance and functionality to your posting. Leave this box unchecked for now. We'll discuss this feature in the next chapter.

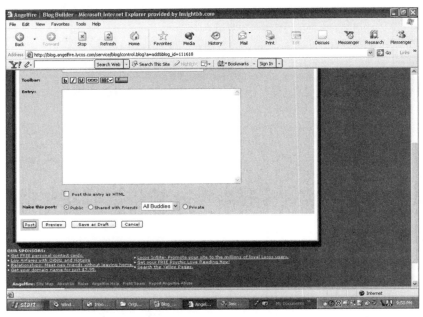

FIGURE 8.9 *The bottom set of options on the Create a New Blog Entry screen.*

◆ **Make This Post.** You can choose from these options to determine whom you want your post to be visible to. This option defaults to Public, which means that anyone who accesses your blog can view the post. However, you can also restrict your postings to your buddy list, or you can make them private. We'll talk more about these different types of visitors to your blog—and why you might want to change your postings from the default Public option—later in this chapter.

◆ **Post, Preview, Save as Draft, Cancel.** The final options on this screen are self-explanatory. You can post your entry, preview it first, save it for later, or cancel it altogether.

3. Figure 8.10 shows a completed blog entry form. If you are following along on your Angelfire blog, go ahead and create your own first posting now.

4. If you click the Preview button (as shown in Figure 8.9), a separate preview window appears, as shown in Figure 8.11.

 tip Definitely take advantage of the Preview option. It allows you to proofread your postings and make sure you have them just the way you want before you take them live for others to see.

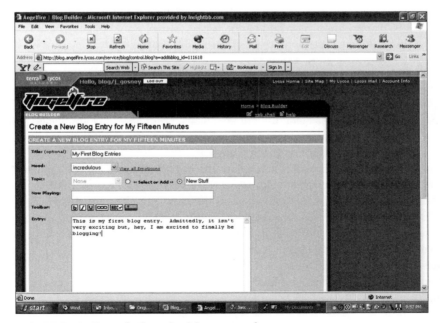

FIGURE 8.10 *Completing the blog entry form.*

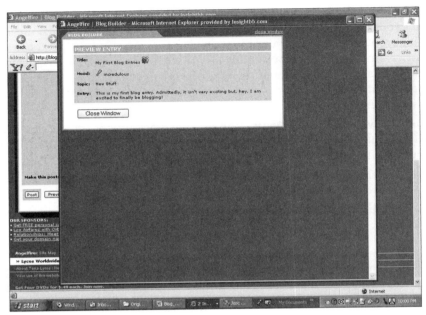

FIGURE 8.11 *Previewing your blog posting.*

5. When you have your entry as you like it, click on the Post button, as shown in Figure 8.9. You are then returned to the Blog Control Panel page, where you can, among other things, edit the previous postings you have made. Because we just made a posting, let's look at how we can edit those postings now.

As you get more involved in blogging, you are going to come across some flat-out cool blogs. From how they are designed to what they have to say, the really fun part about blogging is viewing and reading other people's stuff. You might be wondering, after working through the previous steps, how your simple posting could ever compete with the really great blogs you will discover. Well, don't worry. By reading this book, you are learning all you need to know to make a great blog. The point of this chapter is to introduce you to the basics of managing your blog. The next chapter shows more of the cool stuff, in terms of how to add images, music, and video files to your blog, and how to format your text to make it more interesting than just the plain text you see illustrated in Figure 8.11. You'll learn how to use the toolbar presented in the Create a New Blog Entry form, as well as how to use an application like FrontPage to make your blog come alive. Be patient—the really cool stuff is just around the corner.

Editing Previous Blog Postings

The great thing about blogging as compared to a traditional journal or diary is not just that other people can read and comment on your ideas, but that you can easily change what you have posted previously. That's the focus of this section.

Imagine that you want to go back and make some changes to the simple posting you made earlier. How do you do it? It's easy:

1. After you clicked the Post link on the Create a New Blog Entry form, you were returned to the Blog Control Panel. To edit this entry, click now on the Edit Posted Entries link, as shown in Figure 8.5. This brings up the Edit Posted Entries screen, as shown in Figure 8.12.

 tip Notice that you can use the Jump To function (see Figure 8.12) to quickly jump to a specific day's postings. Also notice that you can delete an individual posting by clicking on the Delete This Post link.

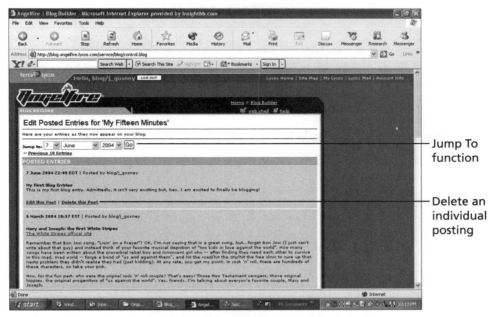

Jump To function

Delete an individual posting

FIGURE 8.12 *You can easily access your previous blog postings from this screen.*

2. You should see the posting you just made (as well as others, if you in fact made more postings). Find a posting that you want to edit, and click on the Edit This Post link for that posting. Doing so brings up nearly the same screen as the initial Create a New Blog Entry form, except that it is filled in with the information you entered originally. Figure 8.13 illustrates this editing screen for the posting I made in the earlier section.

3. When you are finished with your edits, scroll to the bottom of the page to be presented with the same final options (Post/Preview/Save as Draft/Cancel).

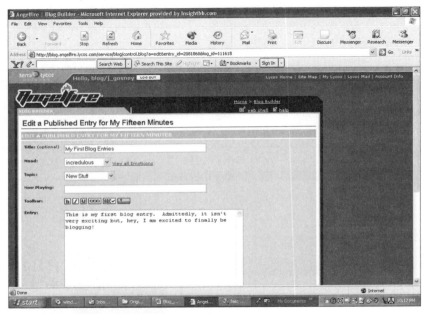

FIGURE 8.13 *Edit your posting in the same way that you make a new posting.*

Once again, you should be back at the Blog Control Panel.

As you can see, making and editing postings is easy. Although you can add more advanced functionality to your postings (more in Chapter 9), the basic functionality is easy to master.

Now that you have made some postings, you probably want to make your blog layout as attractive and functional as possible. You want to give your blog its own style, and you might want to specify who can view your blog postings. You can find all this functionality under the Blog Management section of the Blog Control Panel. We'll discuss much of it in the sections that follow.

Managing Your Blog

So you've made a posting or two to your new blog, and you're feeling pretty proud of yourself. And as well you should: You are now a full-fledged member of the exciting world of blogging!

But from reading Chapters 1–4, you have a whole list of ideas and creative ways to present them in terms of the style of your blog. The rest of this chapter examines how you can use the Blog Control Panel to add this style to your blog. In the process, we'll preview the advanced design and style attributes you can see with an application like FrontPage, which you'll learn more about in Chapter 9.

Changing Your Blog's Appearance

As you saw in Chapter 7, Angelfire gives you a nice selection of predefined design templates from which to choose. These templates are quite varied and highlight a variety of flavors you can give your blog.

Let's go through how you can select one of these design templates for your blog:

1. From the Blog Control Panel (see Figure 8.5), click on the Change Appearance link. Your screen then appears like Figure 8.14.

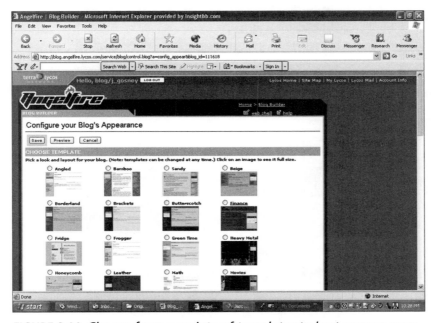

FIGURE 8.14 *Choose from a variety of templates to best express your unique style.*

> **tip** Pay special attention to the small text in Figure 8.14: "Templates can be changed at any time." In other words, don't feel trapped by a particular design: If you don't like the template you chose, you can change it at any time without losing the rest of your blog information (postings, files, and so on).

2. We'll discuss this in Chapter 9, but you should scroll down this page to see the wide variety of additional style options you can set. Figure 8.15 illustrates these settings, many of which have to do with background colors, text colors, and so on.

   Many of these options will be discussed in Chapter 9. For now, though, just be aware that these options are available.

3. Select one of the templates, and then click the Save button, as shown in Figure 8.14. The template is applied to your blog so that all your postings (and other material you have entered) are formatted within the style parameters of the template. We'll preview your blog in a few moments, after we set some more features by using the Control Panel.

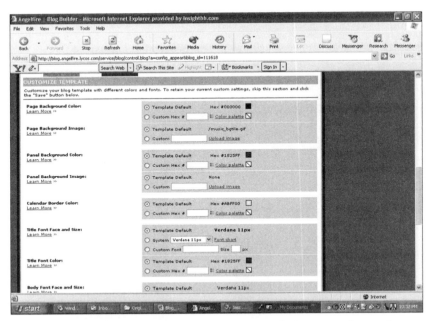

FIGURE 8.15 *You can further customize your design template using these options.*

Changing General Blog Settings

You can apply more general settings to your blog, from setting your time zone to setting preferences for how you want to handle comments that your readers post:

1. On the Blog Control Panel screen, click the Change Settings icon. Your screen then appears like Figure 8.16.

2. Scroll through this page to quickly view the different types of settings you can apply to your blog. Many of these are self-explanatory, whereas others involve working with HTML and other advanced design settings, which are illustrated in Chapter 9. I do want you to look at the Comment Preferences section, so scroll there now, as shown in Figure 8.17.

3. As you can see in Figure 8.17, you have three options for handling comments:

   ◆ **Open.** Visitors can automatically post comments, but you can delete them later. Also, you can receive an e-mail whenever a posting is made to your blog.

   ◆ **Moderated.** Visitors can leave comments, but you review them before they're published.

   ◆ **Closed.** No visitor comments are allowed.

   By selecting one of these options in conjunction with your buddy list or customized list of those who have access, you can add a high level of administration and security to how your blog is both viewed and commented upon. As with all the options here, select one of the three comment preferences.

FIGURE 8.16 *Updating general blog settings.*

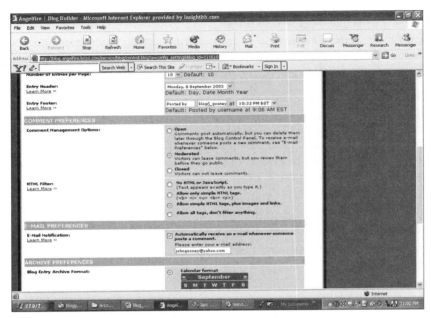

FIGURE 8.17 *You can determine how to handle comments to your blog by setting specific comment preferences.*

 You might remember from Chapter 2 that I talked about finding your own voice and style but doing so in a way that allows as many people as possible to read and comment on your ideas. Although it's certainly your prerogative to design your blog the way you like—including who can read your blog—you might want to consider allowing either an open or moderated option instead of closing it entirely. Why? Again, the real fun of blogging is receiving new ideas and comments on your ideas. Given that the Web is, after all, the *World* Wide Web, if you close your blog to all but a select few readers, you are severely limiting yourself from getting a worldwide viewpoint on your ideas. Okay, so maybe you won't get many international readers of your blog, but the amazing thing about the Web is that you just never know who will be reading what you write. So why not leave the door open—if just for a little while to experiment—and see who comes knocking?

4. Before you leave this page, take some time to view all the options and change a few from their default settings. Click on the Preview button to see how the changes will affect the appearance of your site. When you are finished, click on the Save and Create button at the top of the page to save your changes and be returned to the Blog Control Panel.

Editing Your Blog Profile

Who are you? What are your interests? What is your bio? You can enter this information—and make it visible to visitors of your blog—through the Create/Edit Profile link
on the Blog Control Panel.

 Throughout this book, I've mentioned that you should use caution when
providing personal information, especially if it clearly identifies where you
live or other specific contact information. The same holds true for
completing your profile. Although many people spill their e-guts on the
Web, it is generally not a good idea to give out too much personal information.
Letting people know your interests is one thing; letting them know your home
phone number is another matter entirely. Keep this in mind when completing your
blog profile. Be cool, and play it safe when providing personal information.

1. On the Blog Control Panel screen, click on the Create/Edit Profile link. Your
   screen appears like that shown in Figure 8.18.

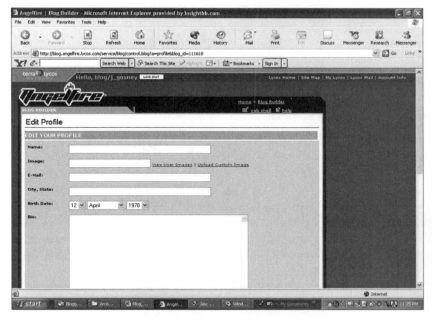

FIGURE 8.18 *Tell visitors about yourself by setting your profile.*

2. Like the Create a New Blog Entry screen (see Figure 8.6), the fields here are self-explanatory. However, note the Image field and the option to select a user image or upload a custom image. If you click on the View User Images link, you'll be presented with a selection of icons to graphically represent yourself, as shown in Figure 8.19.

You can also upload a custom picture of yourself by clicking on the Upload Custom Image link. When you do, a screen appears (see Figure 8.20) asking you to navigate to where the file is stored on your computer, select it, and then upload it to the Angelfire servers.

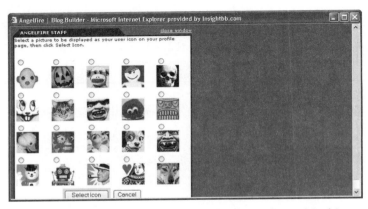

FIGURE 8.19 *You can pick from a selection of graphical icons to best represent who you are.*

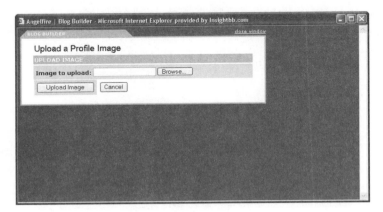

FIGURE 8.20 *Upload a custom image of yourself to include with your profile.*

3. Scrolling further down this page, you can also post your general bio (such as where you were born), as well as your interests. When you have your profile as you like it, scroll to the bottom of the page and click on the Save and Post link to make it active.

As with other information you enter, your profile can be updated at any time.

note

Advanced Customization Features

Other features within the Blog Management section of the Control Panel screen are worth exploring (as we'll do in Chapter 9), but I want to preview a final option here: the Advanced Customization link.

By clicking on this link, you are presented with a list of templates for the pages that compose the major functionality of your blog. Figure 8.21 highlights this advanced customization listing.

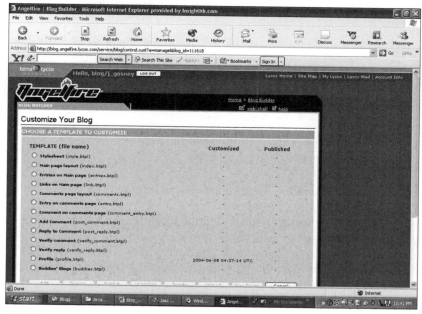

FIGURE 8.21 *You can specifically customize the appearance of the major functional links on your blog through this page.*

Although a full discussion of this advanced customization is best left to Chapter 9, I want to show you the level of control that you have with your Angelfire-hosted blog. If you select one of the templates and then click the Edit link, you'll see what I mean. Let's do this now:

1. From the Customize Your Blog screen (see Figure 8.21), select the Add Comment template.

2. Next, click on the Edit button to bring up the edit page for this particular template. Your screen appears like Figure 8.22.

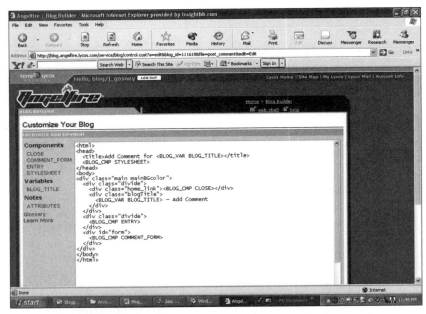

FIGURE 8.22 *You can edit the HTML code behind these template pages to give them an even more customized, personal look and feel.*

Don't worry about understanding what you see in this figure. The important thing to realize is that you can further customize how these pages appear by changing their HTML. As I've mentioned, Angelfire allows you to configure and work with HTML to bring added design capabilities to your blog. (A prime example of this is the toolbar that is available when you make a new posting.) If you have built Web pages in the past and know HTML, you should experiment with this ability to customize your blog. Even better, if you have used an application like FrontPage to build or edit Web pages, you can also use it on your blog. As you will see in Chapter 9, Angelfire allows you to use FrontPage and the FrontPage extensions to author or edit your blog, which brings a whole new level of functionality to the way you interact with your blog.

However, if all this code scares or just plain bores you, fear not: You don't have to worry about any of it to have a great blog. But if you are even just a little interested, check it out and read through Chapter 9. It's not difficult to work with this stuff, and you'll be amazed at the cool things you can bring to your blog by customizing it at this level.

 Microsoft FrontPage is an incredibly popular application. That said, many blog hosting providers allow you to use FrontPage to design and edit your blog, so this is by no means a feature that is specific to Angelfire.

Deleting Your Blog

Before we leave this chapter, I want to bring to your attention one final icon on the Blog Control Panel: the Delete Your Blog icon.

If you click on this icon, your blog won't be deleted automatically, but you'll receive a warning message, as shown in Figure 8.23. Heed this warning. When the blog is gone, it's gone forever. Consider yourself warned!

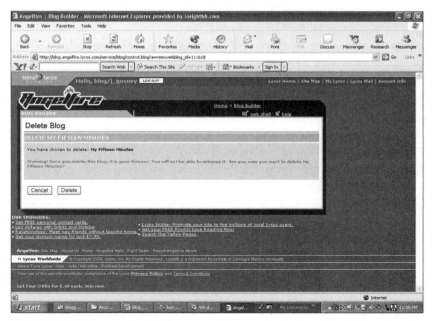

FIGURE 8.23 *Be careful when you click on the Delete Your Blog icon!*

SATURDAY, NOVEMBER 2

MOOD: SPOOKY

TOPIC: THE CONTINUING SAGA OF SATURDAY NIGHTS

As I sit here two days after Halloween, typing this before I head out for Kickstart's annual costume party, I can't help but add my humble thoughts to the inevitable question all teenagers face:

What is the real meaning of Saturday night?

I used to worry about this night. I mean, I would actually start to sweat at the thought of staying home, especially if my parents were gone. Now, you might think that having them gone would be better than having them home, but I would think to myself, "Wow, even my parents have something to do on Saturday night. What's my problem?" These types of thoughts were not healthy, but I had them. And I had them quite often.

But now with my trusted blog, I always have something to do on Saturday night, right? I mean, when all else fails, I can grab a Mountain Dew (or several Mountain Dews) and spend the evening updating my blog, hitting a few chat rooms, and doing the whole online thing. However, the thought sometimes occurs to me: Does spending a Saturday night locked up in my room with my computer make me a total geek?

That's a good question. In junior high, spending Saturday night at home by myself was something just short of a prison sentence. But now that I'm older and wiser (ha!), I realize that spending a little time alone isn't so bad. I mean, a lot goes on during the week, and I can use Saturday night to get my head straight and in the process update my blog.

Still, the thought prevails: Millions (right, millions?) of other teenagers are out partying it up, living in the real world—not the online world—and don't need Saturday evening to put themselves back together from a long week. In fact, they are probably spending Saturday night in an effort to become more broken apart (so to speak).

I asked my brother about this and whether it gets any better in college. He laughed and said he almost always has someone to do something with on the weekends, or he's so behind from a week of classes that he needs to spend the night studying. Studying on a Saturday night? Maybe college isn't as fun as it sounds.

So, bringing this post full-circle: I do have plans for this particular Saturday night, and, at least for tonight, I will leave the blogging to other tortured souls. But as I head out to see what the night will throw my way, I will be thinking of all the blogs that will be updated across the world tonight, and wondering if somewhere, in one of those millions of postings, the real answer to the meaning of Saturday night is being written, just waiting for me to discover. But instead, I am dressing up in a giant egg costume to actually be seen in public. Life is strange...

Summary

This chapter continued where Chapter 7 left off. In Chapter 7, you got started with a membership plan, and in this chapter, you began exploring the administrative and basic customization features available to you as you build your blog. You learned how to make and edit a simple posting. You also were introduced to a variety of useful and powerful blog administrative features, from setting a design template to getting a preview of how to customize your blog by working directly with the underlying HTML. The next chapter expands on many of these subjects, and also shows you how you can use an application like FrontPage to bring even more power and customization to your blogging experience.

Chapter 9

Advanced Blog Design with Microsoft FrontPage

Chapter 8 had several references to using Microsoft FrontPage to further enhance your blog design. Although it is certainly not a requirement to use an application like FrontPage as you design and maintain your blog, it can be a benefit to do so. Why? Remember that a blog resides on the Web and has HTML (Hypertext Markup Language) as its underlying structure. Although you don't have to know anything about HTML to work with your blog—most hosting providers take care of this for you—the simple fact is that you can do much more with your blog if you do know HTML.

The good news is that learning a fair amount of HTML isn't complicated at all. And if you use FrontPage, it becomes even easier because so much of the programming aspect of working with HTML is automated. Maybe you'll have to work with HTML as part of a school assignment. Just consider working with a blog as yet another fun way to get a jump start on some homework!

This chapter is not meant to teach you everything there is to know about FrontPage, but it does give you a comprehensive introduction. This chapter will

◆ Discuss the concept of FrontPage extensions and how to determine if your blog hosting provider supports them

◆ Provide a general introduction to the larger functionality of FrontPage, with a focus on how you can use it to make working with your blog more fun

◆ Examine how working with FrontPage can help you learn HTML and how you can apply that knowledge to working with some of the content editing features that your blog hosting provider might provide

> **note** I chose to use Angelfire to host my blog, so the illustrations in this chapter will again highlight Angelfire and how it can be used in conjunction with FrontPage. However, the ability to work with FrontPage is in no way unique to Angelfire. In fact, the majority of hosting providers (blog, Web, or otherwise) allow the integration of FrontPage. If you're interested in working with FrontPage but not in using Angelfire, still read this chapter because there is much you can learn from it.

Enabling FrontPage to Work with Your Blog

Before we go any further with this discussion, you need to understand two important points:

1. FrontPage has its own unique set of features that provide all kinds of cool functionality without your needing to understand any kind of programming. These features are enabled by the use of the FrontPage extensions, which are a special set of programs that run on the hosting provider's server.

2. Even if your hosting provider doesn't utilize the FrontPage extensions, you can still use FrontPage to help you learn HTML and use it on your blog. As you'll see in this chapter, if you know HTML, you can use it to add all kinds of additional designs and features to your blog. The cool thing about FrontPage is that it automates HTML. That means if you want to add a neatly formatted table of information to your blog, you can use the FrontPage interface to draw the table and then just cut and paste the HTML that is behind that table into your blog. When you do this, the table automatically appears in your blog without your having to understand the HTML that is used to create it.

If the previous points confuse you, don't worry. The great functionality that is being described here will become clearer as you start working with FrontPage. FrontPage can help you with your blog, and it's fun to use, too!

tip Many blog hosting providers—even the free ones—allow you to utilize FrontPage.

 note This chapter has been written to correspond to FrontPage 2003. However, even if you are using an older version of the application, much of the functionality will be the same. The way you access the menu options and the appearance of some of the windows might be a bit different, though.

Most blog hosting providers give you direct and easy access to enabling your blog to work with the FrontPage extensions. The following example illustrates how to FrontPage-enable and access your blog with Angelfire:

1. The best hosting providers have a conspicuous Help link, and Angelfire is no exception. Click on this link, as shown in Figure 9.1.

2. When you click on this link, you are presented with a comprehensive listing of help topics. Click on the Microsoft FrontPage link, as shown in Figure 9.2.

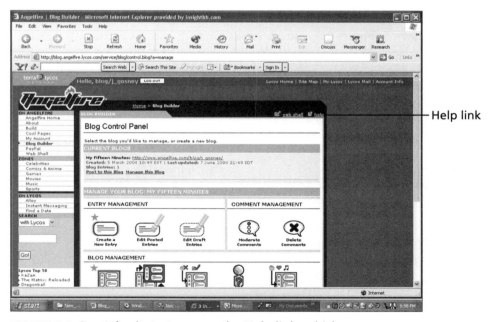

Help link

FIGURE 9.1 *Don't hesitate to access the Help link, which can answer many of your questions.*

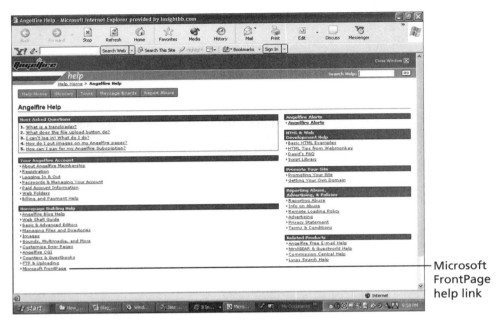

Microsoft
FrontPage
help link

FIGURE 9.2 *The best hosting providers have excellent online help pages, and Angelfire is no exception.*

3. As shown in Figure 9.3, you are presented with a list of Frequently Asked Questions (FAQs) about using FrontPage with your Angelfire blog. Note the second question, "What are Microsoft FrontPage server extensions and how do I use them here?"

4. Click on that question to see a detailed answer, as shown in Figure 9.4. As you'll read more about in just a few moments, you need to enable the FrontPage extensions on your blog to make those extensions (and thus, special FrontPage functionality) work.

5. As you can see in Figure 9.4, you need to use the special Enabler feature to enable the FrontPage extensions. Click on this link, which brings you to the main FrontPage enabler screen, as illustrated in Figure 9.5.

---

note Although the figures shown here are specific to Angelfire, most hosting providers provide this type of "one-click" method of enabling the FrontPage extensions. The best place to get more information is the online help of your specific hosting provider.

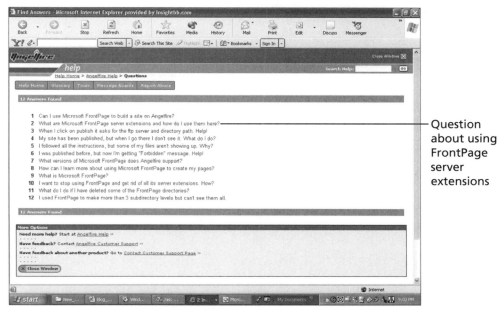

Question about using FrontPage server extensions

FIGURE 9.3 *Depending on the topic (in this case, FrontPage), a detailed list of questions appears.*

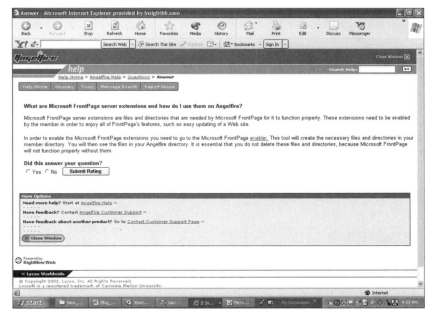

FIGURE 9.4 *You need to enable the FrontPage server extensions as a first step in integrating FrontPage with your blog.*

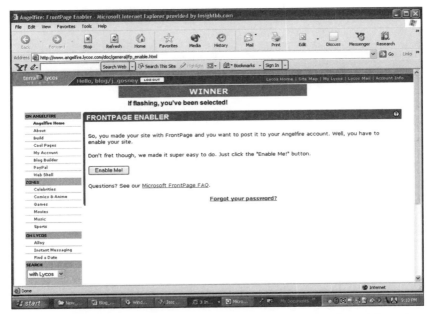

FIGURE 9.5 *Angelfire gives you a "one-click" method of enabling the FrontPage extensions.*

6. Click on the Enable Me button, as shown in Figure 9.5. After a brief moment, you are presented with what appear to be some pretty complicated-looking instructions, as shown in Figure 9.6.

7. Although Figure 9.6 might look complicated, it's really just giving you detailed instructions for how to access your blog (as it resides on your hosting provider's Web server) through FrontPage. So, let's do that. I'm assuming that you have FrontPage installed on your computer, so open it now. If you are using FrontPage 2003, your screen will appear like Figure 9.7. However, if you are using an older version, the functionality explained here will work the same way.

> Note in Figure 9.6 that Angelfire doesn't support versions of FrontPage earlier than the 2000 version. At the time of this writing, FrontPage 2000 was three versions behind the current (FrontPage 2003) version, so chances are good that you have one of the versions that will work. Most blog hosting providers require you to have at least FrontPage 2000 or later—this is not specific to Angelfire.

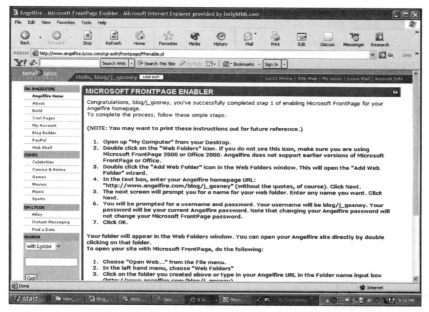

FIGURE 9.6 *This looks complicated. Fear not, though; it's easy to understand.*

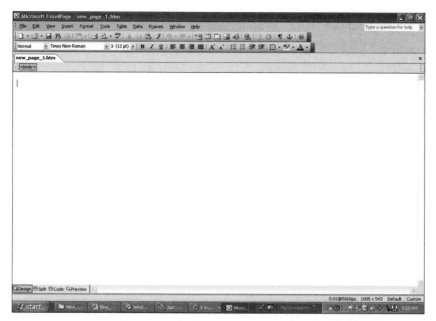

FIGURE 9.7 *Depending on which version of FrontPage you are using, the opening screen might appear slightly different from what you see here.*

8. You now want to access your blog—as it resides on the hosting provider's server—through FrontPage. To do this, you first need to request that your blog be opened in FrontPage, and then you need to provide your username and password (you received these when you first established your blog) to open it. From the FrontPage File menu, select Open Site, as shown in Figure 9.8.

9. You are now presented with the Open Site dialog box. When you enabled FrontPage to work with your blog, you were given a special URL for when you wanted to access your blog in this way. For my blog, the access URL is http://www.angelfire.com/blog/j_gosney. (This address is shown in Figure 9.6.) Enter this address into the Site Name field, as shown in Figure 9.9.

10. Click Open. You are then prompted to enter your username and password, as shown in Figure 9.10. These are the username and password that were given to you when you signed up for a membership plan.

 Note the check box in Figure 9.10 to remember your password. Use this with caution: Although checking this box can be convenient so that you don't have to enter your password every time you access your blog through FrontPage, it can also give someone else who uses your computer easy access to personal information on your blog.

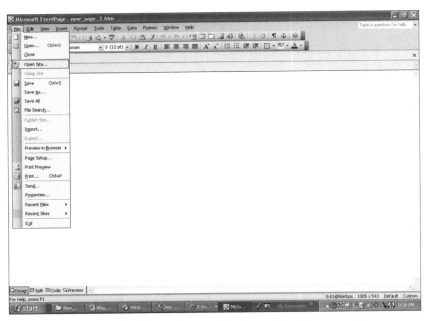

FIGURE 9.8 *Select the Open Site option from the File menu in FrontPage.*

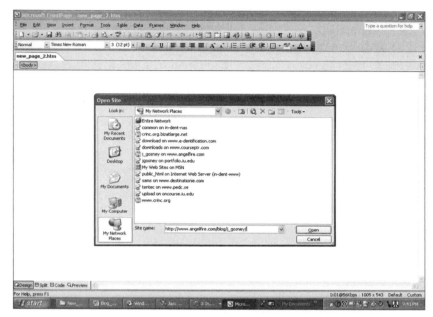

FIGURE 9.9 *Use your special access URL to open your blog in FrontPage.*

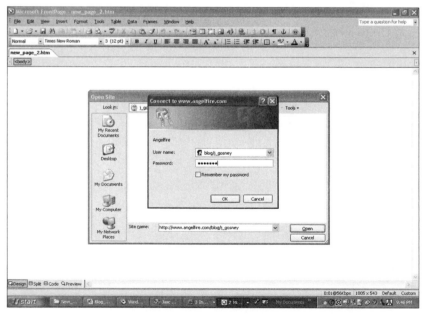

FIGURE 9.10 *Enter your username and password.*

11. Click OK. Assuming you've entered your username and password correctly, you are then presented with a window that looks like Figure 9.11. This is a listing of the folder directories as they currently exist on your blog.

12. At this point, you can either click on the individual folders to access the files contained within (and in turn use FrontPage to edit them) or just click the Open button to see your entire blog file structure in FrontPage's folder list view, as shown in Figure 9.12.

Enabling FrontPage to work with your blog is easy. You just need to go through a few initial steps. After you enable your blog for FrontPage, you don't have to go through those steps again. From then on, you just open FrontPage and complete steps 8–11.

If you are going to read on in the chapter now, leave FrontPage open and stay connected to your blog. If you're going to take a break, close FrontPage to disconnect from your blog.

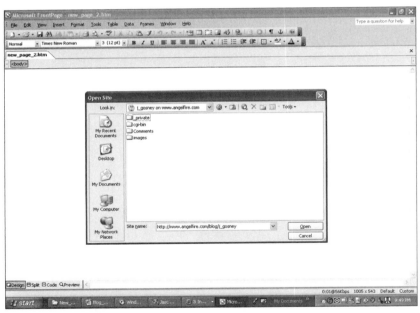

FIGURE 9.11 *Success! You are connected to your blog through FrontPage.*

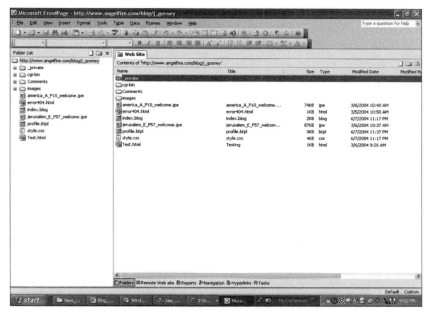

FIGURE 9.12 *Aside from added functionality, FrontPage makes it easy to visualize all the files that make up your blog.*

A FrontPage Overview

As I said earlier, this chapter won't provide a discussion of every feature to be found in FrontPage. Although FrontPage is easy to use, it's rich in functionality, and a lot could be discussed. This chapter focuses on the highlights, with special emphasis on how you can use FrontPage to make your blogging more efficient and fun.

> **tip**
>
> You could write a book on all the cool stuff to be found in FrontPage. As a matter of fact, many books have been written on just that topic. One good one you might want to consider is *Microsoft FrontPage Fast & Easy*.
>
> For a good reference on HTML in general, check out *HTML Professional Projects*. This book also contains a detailed chapter on how to use FrontPage when working with Web projects of varying complexity.

The following sections briefly describe the main menu headings in FrontPage 2003 and what you can find under each. Remember that if you're using an earlier version of FrontPage, most of this will still apply—it will look just a little different in your version.

The File Menu

If you have worked with any of the other Microsoft applications (such as Word or Excel), you are familiar with the File menu. In fact, one of the great things about FrontPage is that even though you use it to work with Web-related projects, the interface is similar to Microsoft Word. I told you earlier that you can draw a table, format text, and so on, and FrontPage will generate the underlying HTML for you so that you can cut and paste that HTML into your blog. You will see this functionality and much more illustrated in these sections.

Getting back to the File menu, let's take a quick look at what it contains. Figure 9.13 illustrates the File menu in FrontPage 2003.

You've already used the File menu's Open Site function to access your blog. You can think of the File menu as the launching point for much of the work you do in FrontPage, including opening and closing your blog, creating a new page, accessing recent files you've worked with, and so on. This menu is pretty self-explanatory, so let's move on to the Edit menu.

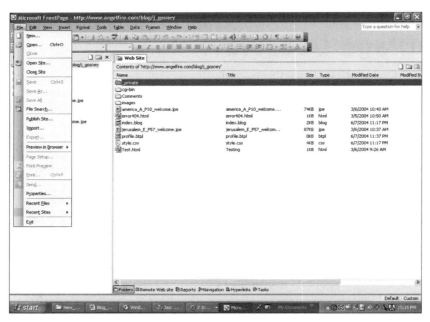

FIGURE 9.13 *The FrontPage 2003 File menu.*

The Edit Menu

If the File menu was self-explanatory, the Edit menu is even more so. Most of the options found here can be found in other Windows applications. Figure 9.14 highlights the Edit menu.

There are a few FrontPage-specific features here (such as the check-in/check-out listings), but they aren't specific to blogging, so I won't discuss them.

FrontPage 2003: The View Menu

Admittedly, the File and Edit menus are pretty boring. The View menu is more interesting, though. Figure 9.15 illustrates the View menu and some FrontPage-specific terminology that you should be familiar with.

Basically, the first several options in the View menu give you various ways of working with the FrontPage interface. Depending on which view you are in, you will see your Web site (or in this case, your blog) presented in different ways. As your blog grows—and in turn, the number of files that make up your blog increases—the different views can help you to organize your blog. For example, Figure 9.16 highlights the Reports view, which gives you a snapshot of information about your blog files.

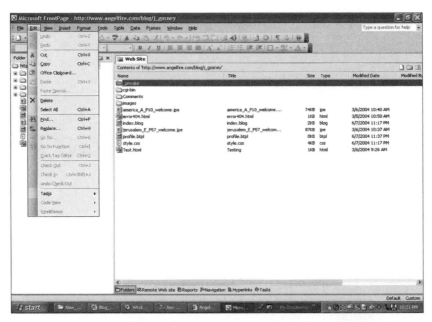

FIGURE 9.14 *Most of these functions can be found in other Windows applications.*

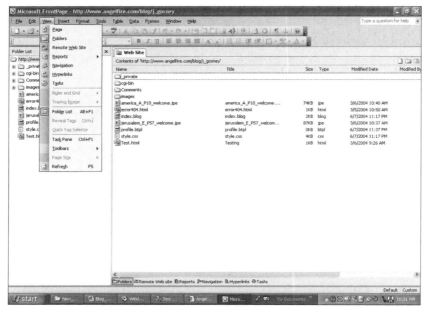

FIGURE 9.15 *You can view your files in different ways via the View menu.*

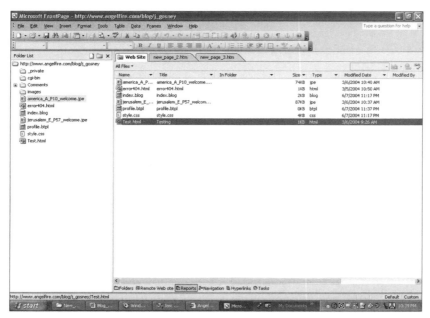

FIGURE 9.16 *The Reports view shows you critical information such as file size, location, and last modification date.*

The Insert, Format, and Tools Menus

These three menus offer you more of the nuts-and-bolts functionality than the other FrontPage menus. They also present you with functionality you can find in other Windows applications.

The Insert menu gives you options for quickly locating and inserting files into your pages. Figure 9.17 highlights the Insert menu and its Picture submenu.

The Format menu gives you access to the usual text formatting (fonts, bullets and numbering, and so on) but also presents functionality that is specific to the Web, such as page transitions and style sheets. You'll see some of these functions demonstrated later in this chapter. Figure 9.18 illustrates the FrontPage Format menu.

The Tools menu contains a few items that you'll want to use quite often (the spell check and thesaurus), as well as those you might never touch (the Macro functionality). Figure 9.19 shows the Tools menu. Note that those two most frequently used options— spelling and thesaurus—are at the top.

Don't be afraid to dig around in these menus and see what you can find. Experiment with the great functionality that is possible with these menus but that is beyond the scope of this single chapter on FrontPage.

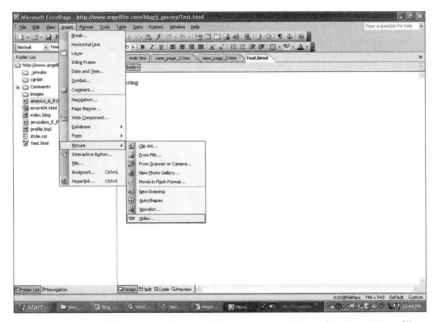

FIGURE 9.17 *The Picture submenu gives you options for inserting files ranging from clip art to video.*

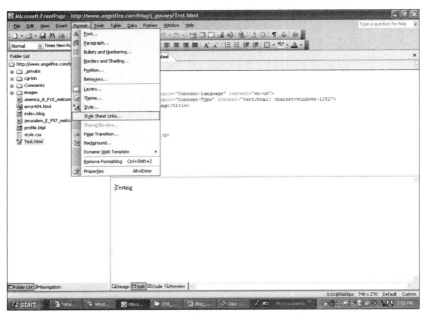

FIGURE 9.18 *The Format menu has standard text formatting options, as well as those specific to the Web.*

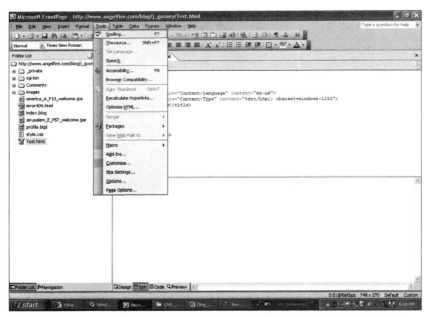

FIGURE 9.19 *The all-important spell check function is found under the Tools menu.*

The Table and Frames Menus

By far, two of the most useful menus in FrontPage are the Table and Frames menus. As you design the visual content and general layout of your blog, you'll find the functionality contained in these menus incredibly useful. The following two sections describe the Table and Frames menus in more detail.

A quick note about frames: If you don't know what they are or if they confuse you, don't worry about it. Many of the blog templates have a kind of "frame" approach anyway, as they segment the content into specific areas of the screen. You can get the same type of visual design by using tables. The choice is up to you.

 What about the Data menu? I'm skipping over it because it extends beyond the scope of our discussion. If you really want to learn more about the options presented in the Data menu, check out one of the books on FrontPage listed earlier in this chapter.

Working with Tables

Let's talk about the Table menu first. Figure 9.20 shows all the table-specific functionality and tools that can be found there.

As you might have guessed, the Table menu is used to insert tables into your Web pages. Why would you want to use the Table menu? That question really strikes at the heart of why you should use an HTML editor like FrontPage. As you'll see, this same question can be asked when talking about frames.

Although there is something to be said for learning how to code HTML by hand, I don't see a great advantage to it. Even when you're working with an application like FrontPage, you'll need to learn some things about HTML, but you will save yourself a tremendous amount of time by using FrontPage rather than trying to code by hand.

To illustrate this, let's work through an example in FrontPage:

1. If it's not already, open FrontPage on your computer. For this example, you don't have to access your blog.
2. From the File menu, select New, and then in the dialog box that appears, select Blank Page. Your screen should look similar to Figure 9.21.

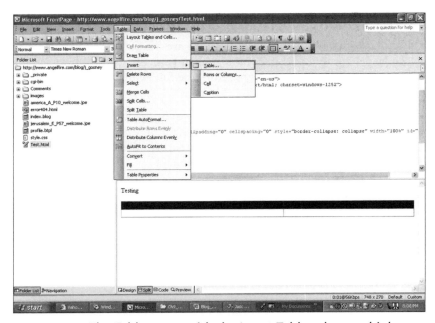

FIGURE 9.20 *The Table menu with the Insert Table submenu high-lighted.*

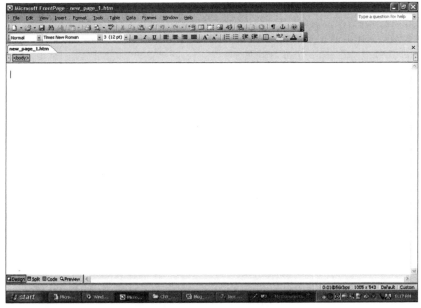

FIGURE 9.21 *A new, blank page in FrontPage.*

3. From the Table menu, select Insert, Table (as you saw in Figure 9.20). A dialog box appears, similar to that in Figure 9.22.

4. For this example, change both the Rows and Columns values to 4. Also, change the Cell Padding and Cell Spacing values to 1.

5. Click OK. FrontPage automatically creates the table based on the values you entered, as shown in Figure 9.23.

6. To get an idea of the amount of time that FrontPage saves you, click on the Code tab at the bottom of your screen. Your screen should look like Figure 9.24.

7. What you see in Figure 9.24 represents quite a few lines of HTML. If you were building this table by hand, you would have to write all of this out yourself, but FrontPage did it in seconds. As you develop more complicated tables, you will start to see why using FrontPage makes more sense than struggling to do this yourself.

8. You could save this page and work on it more later, but because it really doesn't represent anything, go ahead and select File, Close. In the dialog box that asks if you want to save the page, click No. Leave FrontPage open, though, because you're going to work through another example in just a second.

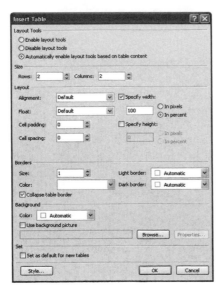

FIGURE 9.22 *You can quickly set various parameters of your table here.*

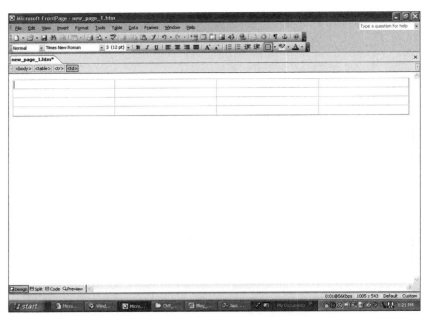

FIGURE 9.23 *You've just created your first table!*

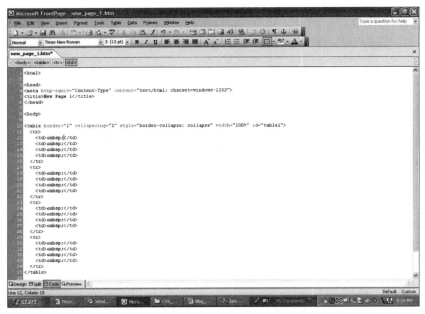

FIGURE 9.24 *FrontPage automatically created this HTML for you.*

Working with Frames

What are frames? Web pages that utilize frames can be thought of as two or more individual Web pages that open together as one page. Frames are useful for keeping some content on the screen at all times in one frame while content in another page can change in another frame. For example, you might have a list of links that you always want to have onscreen so that when you click on a specific link, the page associated with that link loads in the other frame but the list of links remains visible. A picture says a thousand words on a subject like frames, so read on and things will become clearer.

 As I've said many times in this chapter, there is much more to know about FrontPage and HTML than what I am going to present. We just don't have the space to go through everything. Although HTML is a component of blogging, you don't have to know anything about HTML to blog. Don't be afraid to experiment with FrontPage and its features.

Let's go through a quick example of working with frames:

1. With FrontPage open, select New from the File menu. Then, in the dialog box that appears, select More Page Templates so that your screen looks like Figure 9.25.

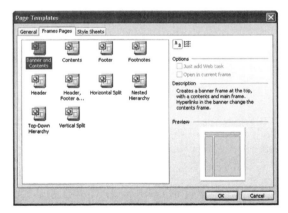

FIGURE 9.25 *FrontPage allows you to create your pages from a variety of page templates.*

> In FrontPage 2000, this wizard opens if you select File, New Page. There is no More Page Templates selection, but you will see three tabs (General, Frames Pages, and Style Sheets) with options to choose from.
>
> **note**

2. Click on the Frames Pages tab. Select the Banner and Contents option, and then click OK. FrontPage will probably open in code view, so your screen will look like Figure 9.26. If it does not, click on the Code tab at the bottom of the screen.

3. It's not necessary to understand the HTML right now. Just know that FrontPage is generating the code to build your frame pages automatically. Click on the Design tab at the bottom of the FrontPage window so that your screen looks like Figure 9.27.

4. Click on the New Page button for each frame. (That is, click this button three times.) When you do, each frame turns white, which designates a blank page.

5. Next, type some text in each frame, as you see in Figure 9.28.

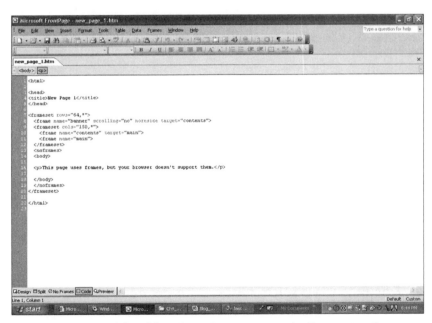

FIGURE 9.26 *As with tables, FrontPage automatically creates the HTML for your frames.*

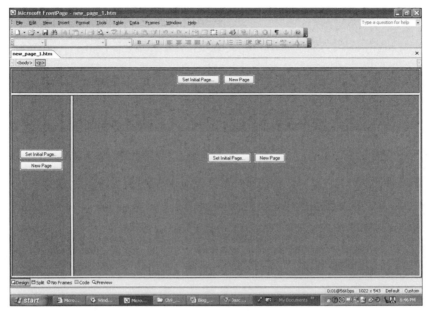

FIGURE 9.27 *FrontPage uses a visual approach to help you build your frame page.*

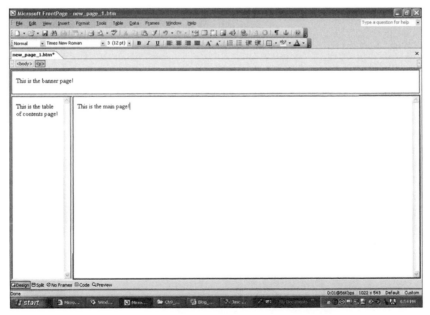

FIGURE 9.28 *Enter this text (or whatever text you like) in each of the three frame pages (or "windows").*

6. Now, click on the Preview tab at the bottom of the FrontPage window so that your screen looks like Figure 9.29. The Preview tab is useful so that you can get a preview of how your Web pages will look when they are live and viewed on a visitor's browser.

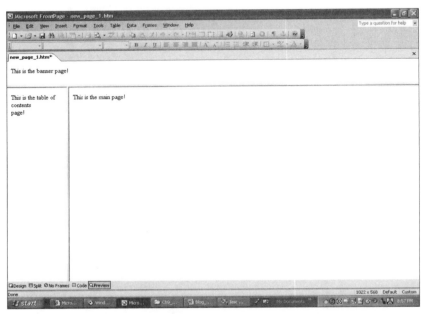

FIGURE 9.29 *The Preview tab lets you see how your frames pages (or any page you design in FrontPage) will look in a Web browser.*

7. Just like the table you created in the previous example, this frame example is pretty lame. But the point here is not to make you a design expert. Rather, I just want to introduce you to the functionality that is present in FrontPage so that, as you work with your own blog and the example blogs in later chapters, you know what is possible. For now, go ahead and select Close from the File menu, and click No when FrontPage asks you if you want to save the frames pages you've just created. You'll need to click No a few times to correspond to each page of the frame that you created (that is, when you clicked New Page three times in step 4).

This brings us to the end of our whirlwind tour of FrontPage. If you are feeling overwhelmed, don't be. FrontPage is a straightforward application to use. It just takes a little time to get used to it. Now let's shift our attention to how you can use FrontPage in conjunction with your blog.

Using FrontPage to Enhance Your Blog Postings

Now that you know how to enable your blog to work with FrontPage and have read about all of its great functionality, let's put two and two together and see how you can use FrontPage to enhance your blogging experience!

I am using Angelfire to host my blog, so the figures presented here are specific to that hosting provider. However, the functionality is going to be the same for any hosting provider, and I will show you how to enhance this functionality by using FrontPage.

Although there is nothing wrong with making simple text postings to your blog, you should consider adding some HTML-based features to your postings, such as these:

◆ **Adding special text formatting.** From bolding and underling text to changing the font style and color, you can do a lot to make your postings look more appealing by changing the overall format of the text.

◆ **Insert hyperlinks into your postings.** Imagine that you've just seen a great movie and are writing about it in a posting. Why not also include a link to the movie's Web site?

◆ **Insert images, audio, video, and other files.** Writing about your dog is one thing. Including a picture of your dog in your posting is something else entirely. Add pictures and other files to your postings to make them more descriptive and interesting.

This section highlights how you can use some basic HTML to work with these features, as well as how to use FrontPage to make simple work out of this HTML.

You might remember from Chapter 8 (in the "Posting to Your Blog" section) that a special toolbar is available to format the text. Now that you have some idea of the benefits of working with HTML and FrontPage, I want to return to that toolbar and show you how you can use it to really make your blog postings come alive:

1. For this example, I have already logged in to my blog on Angelfire. If you are using Angelfire, go ahead and log in to your blog now, too. If you are not using Angelfire, chances are good that your hosting provider will offer similar functionality, so follow along with this example to learn how.

2. Click on the Edit My Blog link, which brings you to the Blog Control Panel page. Under the Entry Management section, click on the Create a New Entry option, as shown in Figure 9.30.

3. The Create a New Blog Entry form appears. Note the toolbar, as shown in Figure 9.31.

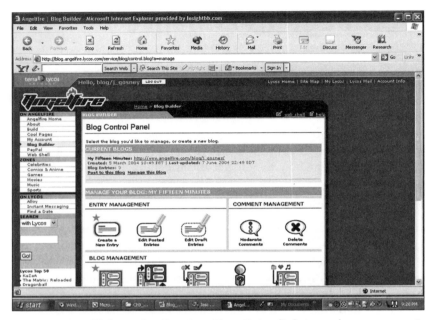

FIGURE 9.30 *Click on the Create a New Entry link to make a new posting to your blog.*

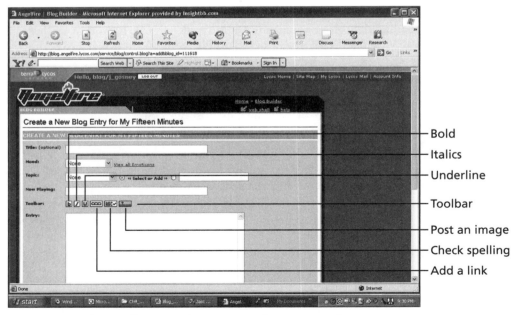

FIGURE 9.31 *The toolbar can give your posting more style.*

4. Figure 9.32 shows the beginning of a posting about the film *The Day After Tomorrow*. Right now, the posting is just simple text, with no formatting or hyperlinks.

5. Compare Figure 9.32 to Figure 9.33. It's a preview of this posting that includes some text formatting as well as a hyperlink. (The text "The Day After Tomorrow" is actually a link to the movie's Web site.)

   As a reader, the formatting effects in this posting are going to be welcomed. For one thing, readers can click on the text "The Day After Tomorrow" to be taken straight to the movie's Web site. Also, the bolding on the word "great" lets the reader know how you (the author) really feel about the special effects in the movie.

6. So how is this formatting done? Let's return to the Create a New Entry form, as shown in Figure 9.30. First, let's start by making the text "The Day After Tomorrow" a hyperlink. If you are following along and typing what you see in the figures, delete the text "The Day After Tomorrow," and then click the Add a Link button on the toolbar to bring up the Link Editor window, as shown in Figure 9.34.

7. Figure 9.34 shows the URL field already completed with the address of the movie's Web site (http://www.thedayaftertomorrow.com). Go ahead and type that in this field, and then click Insert. You are returned to the main posting window. As you can see in Figure 9.35, the HTML for the link has been inserted.

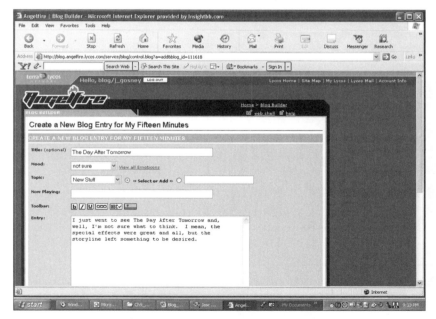

FIGURE 9.32 *A simple text posting with no special formatting.*

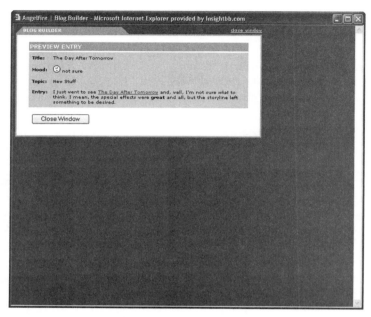

FIGURE 9.33 *Some formatting and a hyperlink add some new life to this posting.*

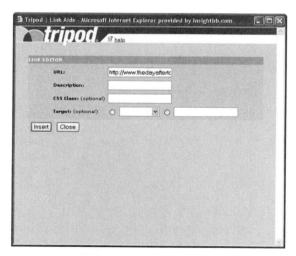

FIGURE 9.34 *You can quickly add a link within your posting by using the Link Editor.*

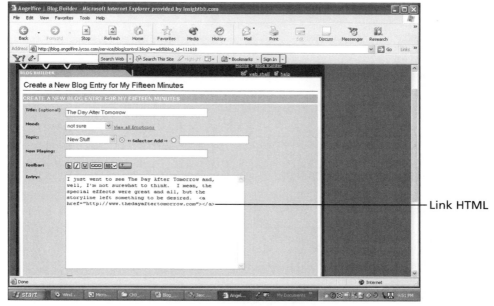
————— Link HTML

FIGURE 9.35 *The link is inserted, but it's in the wrong place in your posting.*

8. Stop the presses! This little example is proof enough why you should consider using an HTML editor like FrontPage. Most online HTML toolbars like the one being illustrated here are clunky at best, and you'll still need to do some work to get the message the way you like it. Let's see how we can accomplish this formatting in FrontPage and then export it to the New Entry form. Open FrontPage on your computer, and select New from the File menu. Then select Blank Page.

9. Type in the following text. Don't worry about formatting.

   I just went to see The Day After Tomorrow and, well, I'm not sure what to think. I mean, the special effects were great and all, but the storyline left something to be desired.

10. First, let's turn the text "The Day After Tomorrow" into a link that points to the movie's Web site. Highlight the movie's title in FrontPage, and then click Insert, Hyperlink. The Insert Hyperlink dialog box appears, as shown in Figure 9.36.

11. As you can see in Figure 9.36, enter the address of the link you want to make (http://www.thedayaftertomorrow.com) and click OK. The text in question becomes blue and underlined, indicating that it is a hyperlink. If you hold your mouse cursor over the text, as in Figure 9.37, you can see the address it is pointing to at the bottom of your screen.

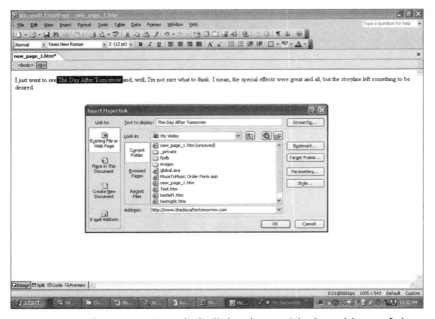

FIGURE 9.36 *The Insert Hyperlink dialog box, with the address of the hyperlink already entered.*

Address of the link you just created

FIGURE 9.37 *The hyperlink is neatly inserted into your text, just where you want it.*

12. Let's change the appearance of the rest of the text. To bold the word "great" as it appears in Figure 9.33, simply highlight it and click on the Bold button on the FrontPage toolbar (indicated by the "B" you see in many of these figures). The other formatting options on the FrontPage toolbars are pretty self-explanatory, so go ahead and play around with formatting the text of this posting any way you want. Maybe you want to change the font size and style of some of the text, or even the font color. Figure 9.38 shows my formatted text.

 tip If you don't see the formatting toolbars in FrontPage, select View, Toolbars, and make sure Formatting is selected.

13. The final step is to export this formatting you've done in FrontPage back into that new entry posting form. Remember, however, that you want to export the HTML behind this text so that all the formatting gets carried over and is properly displayed in your blog posting. To do this, you need to copy the actual HTML code. At the bottom of the FrontPage window, click on the Code tab. Your screen will appear like Figure 9.39.

FIGURE 9.38 *Adding formatting in FrontPage is just like formatting text in Word—easy!*

FIGURE 9.39 *FrontPage has once again generated all the HTML for you automatically.*

14. You are interested in the code between the opening <body> tag and the closing </body> tag. So, as shown in Figure 9.40, highlight the code between these two tags. When it is highlighted, right-click your mouse. From the menu that appears, select Copy. (You can also highlight the text and press Ctrl+C to copy the text.)

15. Return to the Angelfire New Entry posting form (or the new posting form of your hosting provider). Delete any text that is currently in the Entry field, and then paste the HTML you just copied from FrontPage into this entry field, so that your screen looks like Figure 9.41.

16. Note that in Figure 9.41, the Post This Entry as HTML check box is selected. Make sure this box as selected, because it tells the hosting provider to interpret the HTML and display the results. If you don't click this box, the HTML appears, code and all.

17. Click on the Preview button to see how this posting will look.

If you're starting to see the great benefits of working with FrontPage—great! FrontPage can make working on your blog more fun and more powerful. You can still use the tools provided by your hosting provider (such as the Angelfire toolbar, illustrated earlier), but chances are that you can do more—and do it more efficiently—by using FrontPage and then cutting and pasting the auto-generated HTML into your blog entry forms.

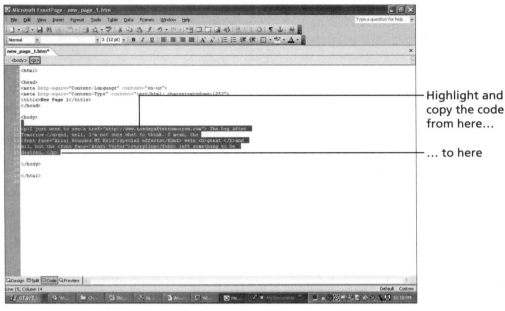

Highlight and copy the code from here...

... to here

FIGURE 9.40 *Highlight the selected code, and then copy it.*

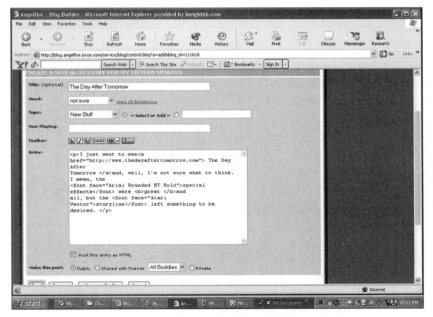

FIGURE 9.41 *You can create better-looking postings faster and more efficiently by using FrontPage.*

Take it easy on the formatting. Excessive formatting can, at best, take away from the meaning of your postings and, at worst, cause your readers to leave your blog.

Advanced Customization of Your Blog Pages

Up to this point, I've shown you how to access your blog via FrontPage and provided you with a brief overview of the functionality contained within FrontPage. You've also seen how you can use FrontPage's ability to automatically create HTML to enhance your blog postings.

If you've read Chapter 8, you know that you can perform more advanced customization to your blog. Specifically, the section "Advanced Customization Features" introduced you to some of these concepts and promised a more complete discussion in Chapter 9. Welcome to that discussion!

A complete discussion of all these features is beyond the scope of this book. However, now that you have been working with FrontPage a while, you should look at these advanced customization features. These features are indeed advanced, but they're not that difficult to understand.

These types of features will differ from one hosting provider to the next, but the terminology used to describe them should remain consistent. In other words, although these examples illustrate an Angelfire blog, you should be able to take what you see here and apply it to your own hosting provider's set of features.

 I know I've said this more than a few times, but it's worth repeating: If you find this stuff too complicated, boring, tedious, or whatever, that's fine. You can add a lot of visual appeal and customization to your blog by accessing **note** these features, but you can certainly have a happy blogging experience without ever touching this stuff.

On the other hand, if you do find this stuff interesting, pick up a book on HTML or FrontPage to help you understand everything you can do with what is described here.

note Depending on your membership plan, some of these advanced customization features might not be available to you.

The following example walks you through some of the advanced customization features available on Angelfire:

1. Log in to your blog. From the Blog Control Panel's Blog Management section, click on Advanced Customization, as shown in Figure 9.43.

2. The Customize Your Blog screen appears, offering you a selection of templates to customize. For this example, we're going to customize the Add Comment template, so select that (see Figure 9.44).

3. After you've selected the Add Comment template, click the Edit button to bring up the customization screen for this specific template, as shown in Figure 9.45.

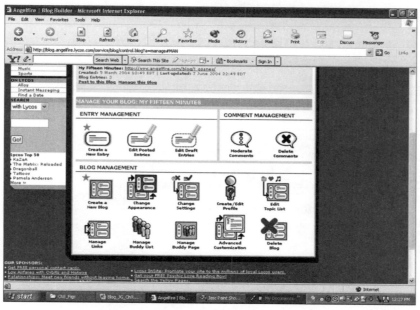

FIGURE 9.43 *The Advanced Customization tab gives you access to specific control features of your blog's appearance.*

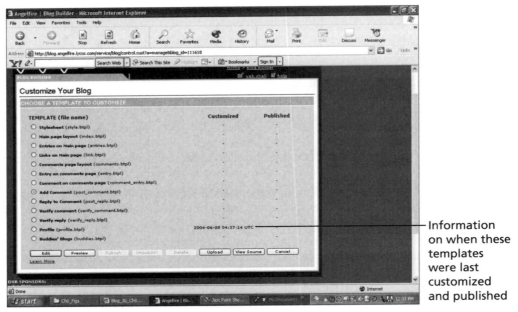

FIGURE 9.44 *Various templates are accessible for your customization.*

Information on when these templates were last customized and published

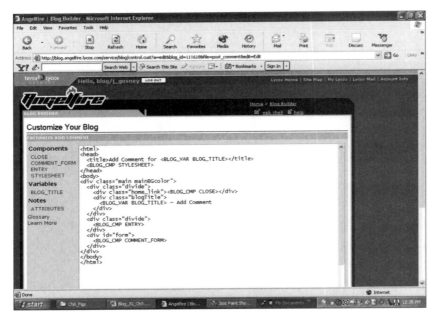

FIGURE 9.45 *Each template allows for similar customization.*

There are a few things you should notice about this screen:

◆ The HTML is readily accessible for you to customize.

◆ The list of configurable components, variables, and attributes is provided, and each is hyperlinked so that if you click on the name, a pop-up window gives you more information about what each one does.

◆ Help and glossary links are provided to give you more detailed information.

tip Don't forget that you can also access many of the pages that make up your blog through FrontPage. After you log in to your blog through FrontPage, you can edit the pages that are currently part of your blog.

4. As the online help suggests, the best way to learn how these customization features work is to experiment with them. For example, if you look at Figure 9.45, you can see the following code:

```
<title>Add Comment for <BLOG_VAR BLOG_TITLE></title>
```

This snippet of HTML tells you that you can provide the title of your blog so that it appears at the top of the Add Comment form. Compare Figures 9.46 and 9.47. Can you spot the difference?

This is a basic example, but it shows you how you can easily change various attributes of your blog's appearance—in this case, the title that appears at the top of the Add Comment form. If you look back at Figure 9.45, you can see how the HTML is marked where there are things you can edit: <BLOG_CMP COMMENT_FORM>, <BLOG_CMP STYLESHEET>, and so on. CMP means components, and VAR means variables.

5. I changed the editable section <BLOG_VAR BLOG_TITLE> to "John Gosney's blog" so that the full title becomes "Add comment for John Gosney's blog." After you make a change on the Add Comment customization screen, click the Save button. This returns you to the main Customize Your Blog screen (see Figure 9.44). The customized information for the Add Comment template changes to today's date. To make your changes live on your blog, click the Publish button on this same screen. The page is refreshed, and your screen should look something like Figure 9.48.

Just customizing a template does not activate changes on your live blog. To make your changes visible, click the Publish button.

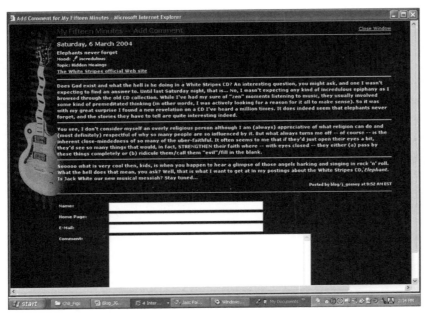

FIGURE 9.46 *The Add Comment form on my blog.*

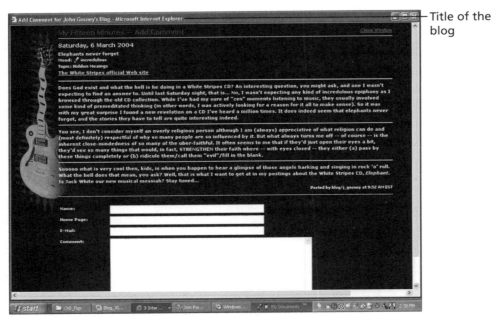

FIGURE 9.47 *The same form after I changed the <TITLE> attribute on the customization page.*

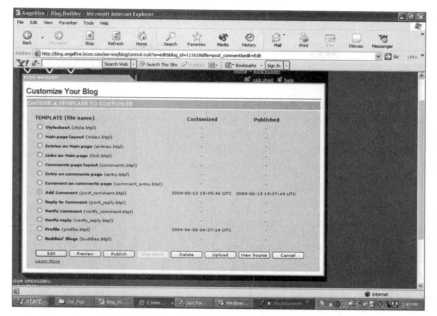

FIGURE 9.48 *You can quickly see the dates and times when you customized and published the different templates that make up your blog.*

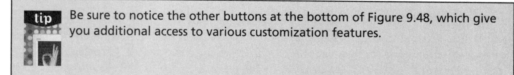

tip Be sure to notice the other buttons at the bottom of Figure 9.48, which give you additional access to various customization features.

Unfortunately, a full explanation of all the customization features presented here is beyond the scope of this book. Once again, if you are really interested in learning more about these types of features, check out the HTML and FrontPage books that are referenced earlier in this chapter.

A Final Note on Customizing Your Blog

Some people think that the best way to learn something is to teach themselves. That's not to discredit the great work of teachers. Rather, it's meant to give you a sense of freedom when working with your blog and to encourage you to experiment. When it comes to blogging—and technology in general—a large part of the fun is digging into the application you are using and discovering things for yourself.

Although this chapter has been written specifically toward blogging with Angelfire, many of the concepts discussed here are common across all blog hosting providers. And, of course, working with FrontPage is not specific to Angelfire. Indeed, you can use FrontPage as a standalone application and then cut and paste the HTML that it generates straight into your blog.

This chapter easily could have been a book in and of itself. Hopefully, what I've presented here will give you some ideas of what is possible with your blog. You will learn more about using these features when you read Chapters 11 and 12, which highlight two sample blogs and discuss how they were created, what advanced design features they employ, and how those advanced features were implemented.

MONDAY, NOVEMBER 11

MOOD: DISAPPOINTED

TOPIC: CORPORATE ROCK STINKS

I've mentioned in other postings how my parents where hippies in their younger days. As such, I've had to listen to many of their Woodstock stories about how great the music scene used to be, about how it all used to be about the music and nothing else, and how today's music is bad. In the past, I have argued against them, saying that the times are different. As far as I can tell, the sixties weren't all they were cracked up to be, and at least some of the music today is good.

Actually, I think quite a bit of today's music is good. You just have to look really hard to find it sometimes and keep your ear to the ground to hear the best stuff. The radio is full of the most commercialized, prefabricated crap imaginable. (Sorry to American Idol *fans, but I just don't see that show as being the best way to find the next great talent.) But I digress...*

Anyway, I went to see one of my favorite bands, The Screaming Lemons, last night. The concert had been hyped for a few weeks as a free show, and the radio spots had quotes from the band members, saying their free show was a direct response to the insanely high (and stupid) prices that some big acts are charging. On the issue of concert ticket prices, I most definitely agree with my parents: When they heard that the Eagles were charging over $100 a ticket for their last reunion tour, they laughed until they cried. They think the Eagles are a great band, but they saw them—when the band was in its prime and releasing all its hits—for $10, and even that might have been considered a bit high. My mom told me the most she ever paid for a concert ticket was to see the final Led Zeppelin tour in 1978, which cost $25 a ticket.

But getting back to my story about the Screaming Lemons concert... Jessica went with me. (No, it wasn't a "date," my inquiring readers. It was a friendly outing, or so it turned out.) Everything was going to be great: a terrific band, a great venue, and free tickets.

It's too bad it didn't turn out that way. First, the lobby was filled with every possible music industry promotion you can imagine, and lots of people (credit card companies, for one annoying example) standing around with booths set up, looking for your business. Clearly, the "free" aspect of this show was being underwritten by the corporate bigwigs, who were obviously hoping to cash in on some new customers waiting for the show to start. And speaking of the show, when it finally did start a mere one-and-a-half hours late, the band spent more time thanking their corporate sponsors than they did playing. And when they did play, it wasn't that great. Finally, to add insult to injury, as we tried to get out of the concert hall, those same promoters were everywhere, trying to hand us leaflets/application forms/you name it about their products or services. "It was like being the only customer at a telemarketer's convention," was how Jessica described it. I couldn't have agreed more.

What has happened to the idea of music for music's sake? Are my parents right in proclaiming that "in their day," music was about the music, and nothing else? Personally, I have a hard time believing that. I mean, think about all the hippies at Woodstock rolling around in mud and rain for three days, while their idols, the musicians, came out and played (and played poorly, if you've seen the movie of that concert) and then split in their private helicopters to a nice, warm, comfortable hotel suite. I'd hardly say it was all about the music even then.

Is it all for nothing? Is there any band that will not sell out to make a quick buck? Or is making money what rock 'n' roll is all about? It's getting harder and harder not to think that way.

Summary

This chapter presented a general overview of the various customization tools for making your blog more personal. It gave specific focus to accessing your blog through FrontPage, assuming that your blog hosting provider supports the required FrontPage extensions. You then saw how to use FrontPage to automatically generate the underlying HTML that makes up your blog, which can save you lots of time and frustration. After a general discussion of the various FrontPage menus and what they contain, the chapter then highlighted how to use FrontPage to enhance your blog postings. The chapter concluded by showing you how to drill down and customize specific elements of your blog.

Chapter 10

The Care and Feeding of Your Blog

So you have a live blog, and you've made a posting or two. You've told all your friends (and yes, maybe even your family), and you've even learned a little HTML so that you can take the best advantage of the customization tools that your hosting provider offers.

Now what?

If you've read the blogging statistics, you know that many blogs are abandoned after a short time, with their owners moving on to other things. The reasons for abandoning a blog are probably as diverse as starting one. Users grow tired of the upkeep, develop other interests, run out of things to say, forget to post. . the list goes on.

Although you should never feel compelled to keep your blog active just for the sake of doing it, you should be able to integrate it into your daily routine so that you can keep it cohabitating peacefully with your other interests.

I'm assuming that if you're still reading this book, you're interested not only in starting a blog but keeping it active as well. This chapter gives you some ideas and general tips for how to do just that, to really "care for and feed" your blog without having it overwhelm your life or—worst case—turn into something that is more of a chore than a fun, interesting activity. So, that said, this short chapter will

◆ Talk about ways to keep your blog active and current so that you are producing something that is as engaging to yourself and other readers as possible.

◆ Examine in more detail the difference between a typical diary and a blog. Remember that a blog can be about anything and doesn't necessarily have to be an online record of your personal life.

Keeping Your Blog Interesting and Engaging

Have you ever read a book, watched a movie, or listened to a CD and thought, "Wow, that is the coolest thing ever! I've got to tell my friends about this!" but then had your excitement shot down because your friends just didn't feel the same way about it as you did?

We've all been in those situations where what we think is awesome, other people think is boring or bad. There's a word I love to use when describing the potential for how people can react, and that word is *capricious*. Don't worry about reaching for the dictionary, because I'll tell you what the word means: unpredictable. There is just no way you can predict how someone is going to react to something, even the people you think you know the best.

What's my point? Well, if you make enough postings to your blog and keep it active for a period of time, chances are good that you are going to get comments from readers who—and I'm putting this nicely—don't agree with what you think. Okay, let's cut to the chase: You might get some really nasty remarks to what you think are the greatest ideas and comments ever produced.

An Engaging Blog: Points to Consider

How do you deal with this type of reaction? You can certainly lash out, or delete the reader's comment from your blog. As owner of your blog, that is certainly your prerogative. But, short of comments that are offensive, you should think twice about removing comments with opinions and ideas that are different from your own. This type of interplay is often what makes a blog interesting. In some radio programs, the host and the audience think the same way. This is all fine and good if you happen to agree with them, but after a while—with everyone agreeing—things get boring. And given that these types of shows rarely take calls voicing the other side's opinion, they can get boring and static quickly. There's just no exchange of ideas, and new and interesting ideas rarely emerge.

You want to avoid having this situation befall your blog. Now, if you've decided to turn your blog into a shrine for your favorite singer, and you're only going to make postings on how great that singer is, that is certainly acceptable. And if you enjoy making those postings, and keeping the blog makes you happy, who am I to say you are doing anything wrong? But think about it: Wouldn't it be just a little bit interesting if someone made a posting and started a discussion about why he thinks your idol is, shall we say, less than talented?

Suppose that you've created such a blog, based around how you think Britney Spears is the greatest singer of all time. What would you do if someone posted a dissenting opinion? Consider the following:

- ◆ **You could invite additional comments on why others think the same way.** Is this person who is writing a differing opinion from you a real nutcase? Is this person the only one who disagrees that Miss Spears is the greatest vocalist ever to grace a CD? Although everyone is entitled to his own opinion, chances are good—especially when we're dealing with someone as controversial as Britney Spears—that you are going to get a few postings from readers who think *you* are the nutcase. Once again, you could react by rudely telling that person he is full of it, or you could delete that posting. Or, you could play a little psychological game and do the unexpected: Ask for more comments from the dissenter. The person certainly wouldn't expect that, especially if asked politely, like this: "Thank you for your comment about how you think Britney Spears is completely tone deaf. I am intrigued by your response and would like to hear more about your ideas." A reply like that would certainly throw that person for a loop!

- ◆ **You could research that person's opinion and reply with a detailed response.** Using the same example, let's say that the reader who thinks Britney is tone deaf happens to think that Tool is the greatest band ever. Instead of making an uneducated response, you could do a little research and maybe borrow a friend's Tool CD, or go to the store and buy one. Then, in your response, you could be more detailed, maybe referencing certain songs and comparing them to your favorite Britney songs, and showing—based on lyrics, style, and so on— why her songs are better.

- ◆ **You could devote an entire section of your blog to an ongoing pro/con discussion.** This last point really gets at how to keep your blog engaging and interesting. If a "Britney Versus the World" blog like this really did exist, wouldn't it be more interesting if it featured this type of discussion, as compared to posting after boring posting about how great she is, without any input from the other side?

If you're reading this and thinking the Britney Blog is just a bit out there, you're probably right. I mean, let's face it: I'm sure there are lots of Britney Spears fans, but I have a feeling that most of you reading this book do not count yourself among them. (I'm guessing more of you are Tool fans.) And you might even be saying to yourself, "Sure, yeah, like that's going to happen on a real blog" in regard to doing research and politely inviting more opinion from some anonymous stranger who has just told you, in no uncertain terms, that the movie/book/singer you like best just happens to suck! Maybe the example given here isn't the most realistic, but the points I'm making here are things you should consider when trying to keep your blog as enticing and engaging as possible to all your potential readers.

Blogging as "The Man on the Street"

What else can you do to make your site engaging? That's a tough question, because no one really knows what will prove popular or engaging to the masses. Take William Hung of *American Idol* fame. If you can explain how in the heck that guy got a record contract (and more interestingly, why thousands of people bought his CD), please drop me a line, because I have a few other small questions for you, like "What's the meaning of life?" and "What numbers do I need to pick to win the lottery?"

No, I'm not suggesting that you devote a blog to William Hung (although I bet there are at least a few of them out there). What I am suggesting is keeping your readers in mind as you develop and post content to your blog.

What exactly does "keeping your readers in mind" mean? You can certainly follow the suggestions in the previous section in regard to making your blog a more open discussion area. But aside from those specific points, as you create and post to your blog, try to look outside of yourself and consider the fact that you are commenting on things that other people have been affected by. Even if you are commenting on your personal experiences, such experiences involve other people. (They went through those experiences with you, after all.) And those people might have a different take on that experience than you do.

A blog can focus on situations or events that are outside of a purely personal frame of reference and that might have a wider appeal to more readers. Thousands of blogs are not online diaries but rather provide a forum for immediate reactions to specific events. Maybe you've heard the phrase "our man on the street" in reference to certain news reporters who go on the scene to get an eyewitness reaction to a specific event. The idea is that such reporting is more realistic and immediate, because it isn't filtered through an editing process or sanitized in any way.

As it turns out, many people think blogs are the new equivalent of the man on the street, because they allow immediate reactions to events by people who witness them directly. Man on the street interviews are popular because they give a sense of reality and truthfulness that an ordinary "from a distance" news report just can't provide.

Imagine that you are researching a report on the Burning Man festival that is held every year in the Nevada desert. What would you consider more realistic and informative: a written essay on the festival by someone from the East Coast who is only responding to what he's read elsewhere about it, or a man on the street report from a guy who actually went to the festival and recorded his experiences with photographs, audio recordings, and interviews with other festival participants? You'd probably think the second was the better reference for your report, because you would be reading about someone who had experienced the festival firsthand.

The next section talks much more about this man on the street concept of blogging, but the larger point to consider here is this: Although writing about personal experiences is a terrific use of your blog, keeping a more generalized "global" point of reference might attract a wider reader base, at least initially.

 Wait a minute. What if the whole point of your blog is to chronicle your experiences? Maybe you're asking yourself, "Hey, didn't you spend a lot of time in the early chapters of this book telling us about how to write about ourselves? So, are you telling us now that this is not a good idea?" There is nothing wrong with thinking of yourself as the only reader of your blog. As has been stated repeatedly throughout this book, if you want to keep a blog as an outlet for your thoughts and experiences (that is, as a true online diary), that's cool. But even if that is the focus of your blog, it can't hurt to suggest to your potential readers that you are interested in what they have to say. That is, after all, one of the great benefits of posting to a forum that is accessible to a worldwide audience. Always leave the proverbial porch light on for those readers who want to comment on what you have to say, wherever in the world they might be.

The Topical Versus Personal Blog

Keeping in mind the man on the street concept of a blog, let's explore a bit further how you can keep your blog engaging both to yourself and to your readers by making it more topical than personal.

Many bloggers think that blogging should be about responding to public events and situations, as opposed to being a diary of personal experiences. Much of this thinking goes back to the idea of the blog as a tool of the common man, or a way of lending a voice to those who would otherwise not have a way of expressing themselves.

There are some interesting things to consider about this point. You might have seen the movie *Pump Up the Volume*, which starred Christian Slater. The movie was released in the early 1990s before the Web as we know and love it today was in existence. A brief summary of the movie goes something like this: A high school teen named Mark (Slater) finds himself transplanted to a Phoenix suburb when his father takes a job there. Although intelligent, Mark is introverted and finds it difficult to talk to people and make new friends. However, Mark has an alter ego who none of his friends or family knows about. In the evenings, locked in the basement of his family home, Mark runs a pirate radio station where he becomes the voice of Hard Harry. Illegally broadcasting over the pirated airwaves of an otherwise quiet and conservative suburbia, Harry spouts the real truth about the high school experience, seeking to expose the viciousness of various cliques and the fraudulence of many teachers and school administrators. Intermixed with this commentary, Harry enlightens his captivated listeners with the best in alternative music and graciously reads fan letters that are sent to an unmarked P.O. box. More than 10 years later, *Pump Up the Volume* is still a pretty decent flick. Although it shows some signs of age, it is no worse than all those John Hughes movies (*Pretty in Pink, The Breakfast Club*) that were so popular in the 1980s.

 note There's actually an Angelfire site devoted to Christian Slater with information on this movie. Check out http://www.angelfire.com/hi2/slaterphobia/ if you're interested.

I'm bringing this movie into the discussion for a few reasons. First, it's interesting to view this movie now—in the age of the Web and blogging—as an alternative to how people might have expressed themselves to the masses before the Web. Actually, if you haven't thought about this point, take a minute to do so: Consider what it was like in the days before the Web. If you wanted to express yourself and make your opinion heard, the best outlet was probably a letter to the editor of your local newspaper. The idea of anyone reaching a potentially global audience was reserved for the elite few—most notably writers and television reporters who had access to large distribution networks. Indeed, the concept of individuals being able to reach out to the world with their ideas is a new one. It's such a revolutionary idea that all of us living today are probably unaware of just how radically different our world is in this regard, as compared to the *Pump Up the Volume* days of pirate radio.

But the other point that is more specific to our discussion of topical versus personal is that, although Mark's character in the film did invariably make comments about his own life, the really interesting thing was that a person living the high school experience could comment on it first-hand (the whole man on the street idea). And, rather than just writing about it in a diary that no one else could read, he commented on those experiences, as they happened, directly to a large audience. The immediacy of the commentary made pirate radio interesting. There was no editorial filtering of the content. It was raw, and it was real.

The days of pirate radio are behind us. There's no need to break the law when you have legal access to a world audience through your blog. Still, the ideas of that movie are interesting to compare to the concept of making your blog more topical—that is, focusing on public events and situations—than personal.

What are some examples of public events and situations that you could make the focus of your blog? I'm using the word "public" loosely here. Public could be as local as your high school; it doesn't have to imply an event that thousands of people are witness to. On the other hand, you could focus your blog on a world event or situation that—even if you are not directly involved in it—is nevertheless something that millions of people are interested in. (A political issue like the situation in the Middle East would be a good example.)

Keeping things on a more manageable level, though, consider the following examples:

◆ You live in a large metropolitan area. Rather than focusing solely on your own experiences, you devote your blog to commenting on major issues and events that occur within the city, from music festivals to local politics.

◆ You live in a small town. You focus on the issues facing your town, turning your blog into a kind of online newspaper where you keep everyone informed of what is going on.

◆ You are a member of your school's student council, and your blog is an open forum for discussion about important issues and events facing your school.

◆ You are a member of one of your school's sport teams, and you decide to use your blog to chronicle your season. Again, rather than focusing only on your personal experiences, your blog is a collection of the stories, opinions, and excitement that surround your season, as collected from your teammates, coaches, parents, and other fans.

The four ideas listed here are just the smallest fraction of the different ways you can focus your blog. The important thing is that they all allow your blog to incorporate the ideas and experiences of others, as well as your own.

Care and Feeding of Your Blog: Other Ideas

I'm guessing that you have all kinds of great ideas for blogging, from personal experiences to recording the thoughts and opinions of others. But there's a central question I haven't really addressed: How do you fit your blog into your busy lifestyle?

As I said earlier, many blogs are abandoned after a short time. In contrast, some people are adamant (almost to the point of obsession) about keeping their blogs up-to-date. As long as these people keep their blogging activities in perspective (you know, they don't forget to eat or sleep), more power to them.

More than likely, you will fall somewhere between those who quickly forget about their blogs and those who decide to make blogging their life. Sometimes you might not feel like making a posting. What should you do when writer's block, procrastination, or lack of interest strike? Try the following ideas:

◆ **Read other blogs.** As I've said before, you can't be a good writer unless you spend time reading. The same holds true for blogging. If you don't spend time reading other blogs, chances are good that you won't produce a strong blog that other people will be interested in reading. So, if you can't think of anything to post to your blog, or you just want to take a break from writing, use that time to find other blogs. You'll not only be giving an audience to what others have to say, but you will undoubtedly develop some new ideas you had never considered, which can be invaluable when you sit down to post to your own blog.

◆ **Spend time doing the things you are blogging about.** That might seem like an obvious statement, but think about it in detail. Let's imagine that the focus of your blog is commenting on the issues of your town. If you never leave your house, you probably don't have anything exciting or interesting to say about the issues you are writing about. Get out and get involved so that you are a knowledgeable resource. This also gets back to the whole man on the street thing. The best blogs provide evidence that the blog authors have spent time away from their computers and in the world they are trying to comment on.

◆ **Add visual or multimedia content to your blog, besides just text-based postings.** Chapter 4 talked about the video blog, or vlog. Moreover, Chapter 9 discussed how you can use Microsoft FrontPage to enhance the design and appearance of your blog. If you don't feel like writing, you can still add multimedia content or graphics design elements to your blog. For example, maybe the focus of your blog is your school's basketball team and their run for a state championship. You could take a voice recorder to the game and capture on-the-scene interviews from other fans, which you could then post to your blog. The Web is a visual and dynamic medium that allows you to do more than just work with text.

◆ **Make your posts short and sweet.** If you've been reading the blogger70 special elements in this book, you've seen that some are short and others go on for several paragraphs. In regard to your own blog, remember that there is no rule for how long your posts have to be. Sometimes a single paragraph can say just as much as a post that goes on and on. If you don't feel like Shakespeare and aren't in the mood to write a book, you can still make a short post. The idea is to keep writing and keep your blog current.

If you capture audio and video and decide to place it on your blog, be sure you consider the feelings of others. Not everyone wants to have his picture or voice on the Web, especially if there is identifying information associated with this content. (For example, let's say you post an audio clip of someone, and instead of keeping it anonymous, you also post that person's name.) When in doubt, clear your content with your subject to make sure that everything is cool before you post something incriminating to your blog.

Audio and video files can get big pretty quickly. If you start to add this type of content to your blog, consider increasing the amount of storage space given to you by your hosting provider. Note, though, that after you go beyond a certain amount of space, most hosting providers charge you for additional storage on their servers.

Blogging is supposed to be fun and interesting, and there are many ways to enjoy the blogging experience without spending all your time writing.

Sunday, November 17

Mood: Reflective

Topic: Reeling in the Year

Here it is, two weeks until Thanksgiving. And you know what that means: Just a few more weeks until Christmas and the end of another year.

I always get a bit depressed at this time of year. Well, maybe not depressed but introspective. I start to think about what is going to happen in the future and all that "where will I be at this time next year" kind of stuff. And, as usual, I look back on the year that is rapidly coming to an end and think about what I've accomplished.

Last night Jessica and I went to see a crummy movie. I thought it was going to set the tone for the whole evening, but it actually turned out to be a great night. After the movie, we went over to her house, ordered a pizza, and spent something like four hours talking about what we hoped would happen next year. We talked about the usual stuff: worrying about our classes, getting ready to take the SAT, wondering what colleges we might want to visit. But instead of making me nervous and worried about the bad things that might happen, it was just a great conversation. I don't know if it was because I was talking to Jessica or because the movie was so bad that it was great to have some intelligent conversation, but... well... it was just a great conversation. Do you ever have conversations like that, where for whatever reason you just click with the person you are talking to, and everything makes sense? That person seems to anticipate what you are going to say next, and you do the same? It was that kind of conversation. I nearly missed my curfew because when I finally looked at my watch, I couldn't believe we had been talking for hours. It felt like we had only been talking for a few minutes. I still had so much more to say.

Tonight I've been sitting here thinking about that conversation. All I can continue to think about is what a great time I have with her, no matter what we are doing. She said something weird again last night, something she had said a few months ago. We were talking about our blogs and how much we both enjoyed posting to them, but I told her that sometimes I can't think of anything to write about. And she said—just like she had said once before—that I should make a posting about what a great couple we could be and then let our friends comment on what they think. She laughed and said that if enough people thought we'd be good together, we should go out on a real date.

So all day, I've been thinking about that. I mean, we talked about a lot of stuff last night, and she is always joking about how she and I spend so much together that people probably think we are going out. But she says it so often. We are reading Hamlet in English class, and there is that great line in there, "Me thinks the lady doth protest too much." I sometimes wonder if she is trying to hide how she really feels about us being together by constantly making jokes about it. I know one thing: I've got six weeks left in the year. By the time midnight on New Year's Eve rolls around, I'm going to know for certain how she really feels.

There's another great line from Hamlet that pretty much sums up all my blog postings about this subject: "My words fly up, my thoughts remain below: Words without thoughts never to heaven go." Yep, it's time to get my thoughts flying with my words and find out just what, exactly, my lady is protesting about!

Summary

This chapter discussed the important issue of how to keep your blog active and engaging, not only to yourself but to your potential readers. In trying to find answers to this dilemma, we considered a fictitious blog that was devoted to Britney Spears. We discussed how such a blog might open itself to dissenting ideas and opinions of others and—in the process—become a more interesting blog than it otherwise would be. This chapter also talked about turning the focus of your blog outward instead of inward so that it considers the opinions and ideas of others instead of just being personal reflections. The man on the street blogs are some of the most interesting and engaging blogs on the Web. The chapter concluded by giving you hints and suggestions for what to do when you just don't feel like writing. From using FrontPage to enhance the design and visual appeal of your blog to adding audio interviews, you can do all kinds of things to stay active in the blogging experience, in addition to writing just text-based postings.

Chapter 11

Blog Example: "In the City"

You've come to the point in your blog journey (well, at least your journey of reading this book!) where a few examples of what we've been talking about might be helpful. That's what this and the next chapter are all about.

For the example in this chapter, I want to turn again to the two popular books that were highlighted in Chapter 2: *The Perks of Being a Wallflower* and *The Catcher in the Rye*. If you've read one or both of these books, think about the main characters and the stories they tell. If they were real people, don't you think they would be interested in keeping a blog? Yep, I think so, too!

But even if you haven't read those books, there is much you can gain from this chapter. Basically, I want to highlight how a blog can be both a place for personal reflection and a way to comment on common experiences. It's that second point that I want to talk about here. It's why I've chosen to call this chapter, and the fictitious blog it represents, "In the City." This blog is a collection of comments and observations about what happens to its writer, a person who lives in a major city and who has a sharp eye for observing what goes on there. Remember, though, that this is a blog, so these observations are not just of the man on the street variety. Rather, they are filtered through the author's own thoughts and opinions.

As you work through this example chapter and the next, you will get an overview of the entire blogging process. You will

◆ Step inside the blogger's mind and see how he developed his ideas.

◆ Examine how the blog was put together in terms of its design and style.

◆ Look at how the blogger integrates his blog into his life, or to use the title of Chapter 10, how he cares for and feeds it. This care and feeding will be particularly interesting when you compare the blog example in this chapter to the one in Chapter 12.

Developing the "In the City" Blog

For this example, imagine that the blog you are going to read is real and that the blogger is a real person. But, as they say in the movies, "any similarity to any person, living or dead, is entirely coincidental!" In other words, none of this is real, but I have tried to make it realistic to highlight all the ideas you've been reading about in this book.

With that said, I'd like to introduce you to Jason Carter. Jason is a 16-year-old who has lived in Indianapolis, Indiana his entire life. Jason knows the city well, and like many of his friends, he's active and interested in what is happening in the city, from art festivals to the city's well-known professional sports teams.

As part of a creative writing assignment last semester, Jason was asked to keep a writer's journal. Basically, he was supposed to record his thoughts and experiences in this journal every day so that some of these ideas could inspire good material for the two short stories he would have to write as part of his final grade. His teacher didn't put restrictions on what students should write about in these journals.

After a few weeks of writing in his journal, Jason discovered that he was spending as much time talking about his journal postings with other people as he was actually writing them down. He also realized that many of these conversations with his friends were generating ideas of their own, so he began recording these new ideas in his journal. Jason didn't really mind this "double entry" of information, but he wished his friends could write directly in his journal so that he wouldn't have to go back and write it himself. He was forgetting a lot of what his friends had said or running out of time to write the ideas down.

One day, Jason was reading the newspaper when he saw a short article on blogging. He had never heard the term before, but because he was interested in technology, he thought the idea of a blog sounded interesting. Later that night, he spent some time on the Web reading more about blogs and visiting a few to see what the fuss was all about. It didn't take long for Jason to realize that a blog was the perfect answer to the problem he was having with recording everything in his journal. If he turned his class journal into a blog, his friends could comment on his postings whenever they wanted, and he would be able to capture all their great ideas because *they* would be writing them down, not him! Better still, because the blog was online, Jason could access and write in it from home, during study hour in the library, at lunch, or anyplace else he wanted. And when he told his teacher about the idea, she quickly agreed to let him keep a blog in place of his written journal. She even gave him some extra credit points for his creativity.

Having been given the green light from his teacher, Jason decided to begin keeping a blog. But before he could begin, he had to take care of a few things:

1. He needed to find a hosting provider for his blog. After doing some research, he decided to use Angelfire because it had a variety of blogs, many of which were by fellow teen authors.

2. He needed to think through how his blog was going to be organized. Although his blog was going to take the place of his writer's journal, he knew that—because it would be open for other people to comment on—he wanted to write about things that would interest both himself and his potential readers. With that in mind, he decided that in addition to making the blog a place where he could record his thoughts, he would also use it to comment on what he thought about the events and issues surrounding Indianapolis.

3. The final step was to put the blog online and maintain it.

You can think of the individual sections of this chapter as detailed commentary on each of these three points. As you read through this chapter, you will see an example of how a blog comes into existence from the "what am I going to write about?"/planning stage to the "care and feeding"/making postings phase.

For the rest of this chapter, let's follow Jason's experiences and see how his blog was developed and brought online.

"In the City" Blog: Organization and Planning

Jason is a fan of reading, not just for school assignments but for his own pleasure, too. He was asked to read *The Catcher in the Rye* recently for an assignment, and he loved the character of Holden Caulfield. One particular aspect that Jason really liked was that Holden (like Jason) seemed most comfortable and at home in a large city. (The book, in many ways, is a description of Holden's thoughts and experiences as he spends a long weekend alone in New York City.)

Not long after finishing *Catcher*, Jason saw a special on MTV that made reference to a book that was similar to Holden and his adventures: *The Perks of Being a Wallflower*. Jason quickly checked out the book from the library and enjoyed it almost as much as *Catcher*. The teenage protagonist in that book is also confronted with some difficult life issues.

In first thinking about his blog, Jason kept drifting back to these books. A central question kept popping into this head: What if the two characters in these books had access to blogging? Given that both books are composed of numerous chapters that are mini stories in themselves, it's easy to imagine these chapters as blog postings.

In talking about these books with his friends and thinking about his own blog, Jason became intrigued with the idea of how his life might be captured and written about in a similar fashion. Jason decided to organize his own blog much like these two books. Although he wanted the blog postings to be ongoing, he also really liked the idea of having postings and related content that told a story in and of themselves. The postings would describe a problem or issue, offer discussion on it, and then come to some kind of resolution.

The first concern, then, was what these postings would be about. Jason was going to post to his blog about whatever he happened to be thinking about or experiencing. After all, this freeform "no rules" way of writing was what his initial paper-based journal was to be all about. Jason really liked the idea of being able to just write down whatever he was thinking, without having to worry that it conformed to some "main idea."

On the other hand, Jason liked the idea of using his blog to comment on specific events and issues that he and others were experiencing. He thought that having a place to comment on these events would encourage others to make comments. Jason hoped that these community discussions would yield him all kinds of cool ideas that he otherwise would never have thought of. And it would all be happening on a blog he was maintaining and authoring!

One night, Jason came up with four specific issues and events to write about on his blog that he thought would be of interest to a large number of people. This is the list he came up with:

◆ **Music/Art Festivals.** Jason is a big fan of music, and Indianapolis is host to several music and art festivals. Jason thought that postings devoted to these festivals would be a great way of hearing others' opinions about the state of the arts in the city.

◆ **Politics 'n' Stuff.** This year is a presidential election year. Although Jason is too young to vote, he and many of his friends are interested in the political scene and how the politicians speak (or don't speak) to the dreams and concerns of young people. Jason wants to provide a forum for himself and other teenagers to talk about what they think of the presidential candidates.

◆ **Colts/Pacers.** Jason is a big sports fan, and Indianapolis has two major sports teams (Colts and Pacers) that Jason follows. His family has season tickets to the Colts, and they often go to Pacers games, too. Given that these events draw tens of thousands of people over the course of a season, Jason thought that various sports postings would be a cool way to gather the opinions of others.

◆ **At the Movies.** When he isn't going to music festivals, thinking about politics, or watching the big game, Jason likes to catch a movie. Movies, too, are something that others are interested in and can relate to. As a result, Jason decided to include a movie review section on his blog.

Now that you understand the organization and planning of Jason's blog, let's look at how he decided to design and publish it on Angelfire. Then we'll wrap up the chapter with a discussion of how the blog met Jason's expectations as both an online journal and a way of allowing him to be the man on the street for various events and issues happening in the city where he lives.

"In the City" Blog: Designing and Publishing

As was mentioned earlier, Jason did some research of the different blog hosting providers and decided to get a membership with Angelfire for his "In the City" blog.

> **tip** For a review and extended discussion of several hosting providers, refer to Chapter 6. For specific information on establishing a membership with Angelfire, see Chapters 7 and 8.

> **note** As I said in Chapters 7–8, even if you aren't using Angelfire, you can learn quite a bit from the examples that are provided. Remember, too, that the use of FrontPage in this and the next chapter are not specific to Angelfire. Many hosting providers allow the use of FrontPage in conjunction with the blog and Web hosting services they offer.

After Jason had his membership, he began utilizing the various tools on Angelfire to build his blog.

The following is an overview of how Jason initially configured his blog not only for general design (such as the template he decided to use), but also for accommodating the different areas of interest he wanted to post about and get comments on.

1. The first thing Jason needed to decide on was which design template to use for his blog. Figure 11.1 highlights all the different Angelfire templates that Jason had to choose from.

> The numbered steps you are reading here assume that Jason has already signed up for a specific Angelfire membership plan and logged in to this blog account.

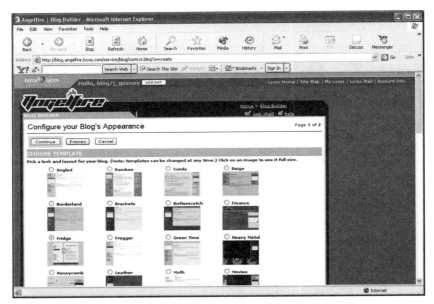

FIGURE 11.1 *Choosing the best design template.*

2. After looking through these templates, Jason found a few that were specific to some of his interests (music and sports). These were cool, but he wanted something that was more generic and applicable to all the issues he wanted to post about. He was worried that if he used the music template (see Figure 11.2), it would give the impression that music was all his blog was about, which wasn't the case. He decided on the fridge template (see Figure 11.3), because it was not specific to any one of his interests, and it gave a cool sense of design to his blog. (Sorry. No pun intended there with the use of the word "cool" and refrigerator!)

3. After Jason decided on the fridge template, he wanted to do some further customization. Specifically, he wanted to change the page background color and the font type and size. Using Angelfire's template customization tools (see Figure 11.4), Jason quickly made these changes.

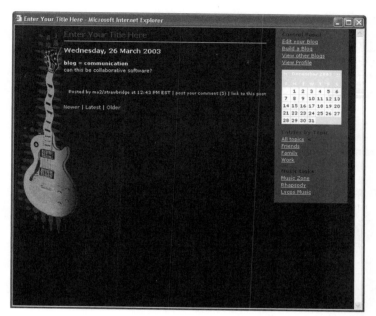

FIGURE 11.2 *Although music is a topic of interest, Jason didn't want to use this design template because it gives too much emphasis just to music.*

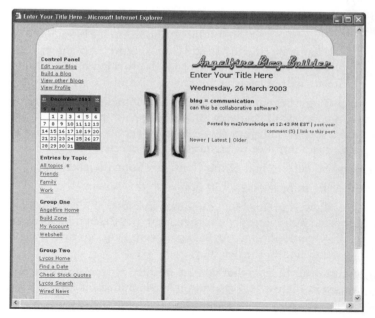

FIGURE 11.3 *Jason decided on the fridge template to give his blog some design flair but not make it specific to one area of interest.*

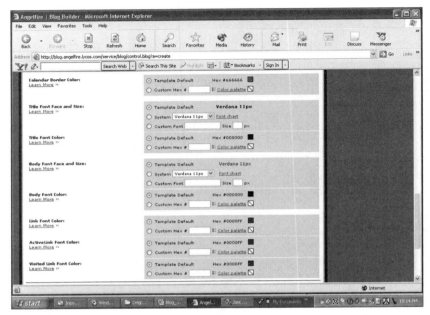

FIGURE 11.4 *To further personalize the template, Jason made some changes to the template background color and some of the fonts.*

4. Next, Jason wanted to configure more of the attributes on his blog, including changing the default template title to "In the City." Figure 11.5 shows the top half of the Configure Your Blog screen, where Jason provided his blog title and assigned other basic attributes, such as the time zone and the type of blog.

   Notice the Type of Blog category. This is a drop-down menu (as shown in Figure 11.6) that contains a variety of category listings. Use this option to have your blog grouped into a specific category on the hosting service. Having your blog properly categorized can improve its chances of being seen by others.

5. Figure 11.7 shows the bottom half of the Configure Your Blog screen.

   Here are a few specific things you should notice on this screen:

   ◆ Open posting is allowed to this blog. As shown in Figure 11.7, reader comments can be posted automatically but then edited or deleted later. You don't have to select the Open option, though. If you want, you can review comments before they are published to the live blog.

   ◆ You can configure your blog so that you are notified whenever a new posting is made. You can see in Figure 11.7 that Jason has included his e-mail address (jacart@someplace.com).

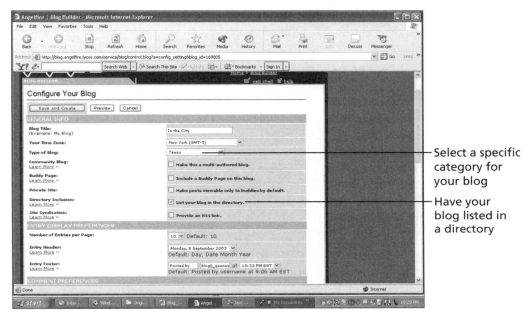

Select a specific category for your blog

Have your blog listed in a directory

FIGURE 11.5 *Assigning basic blog attributes is made easy through this screen.*

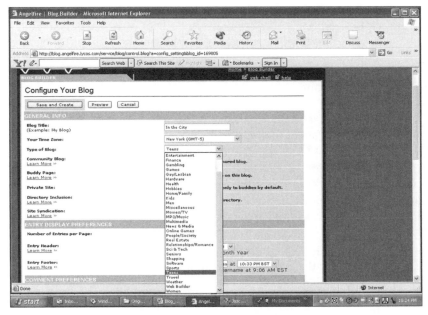

FIGURE 11.6 *Give your blog more publicity by assigning it to a specific category.*

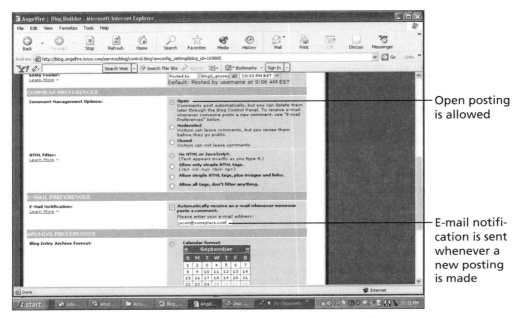

Open posting is allowed

E-mail notification is sent whenever a new posting is made

FIGURE 11.7 *Don't forget to scroll through this page to see all your blog configuration options.*

 I am skipping around a bit here with my description of how Jason built his blog. What is presented here is not a step-by-step how-to list for how to build a blog on Angelfire. For that type of detailed information, refer to Chapters 7–8. The description here just gives you an idea of how Jason took his organization and planning ideas and implemented them on his blog.

6. At this point, Jason wanted to see what his blog looked like because he had selected a template and made some other design and configuration changes. Figure 11.8 shows his blog as it appeared at this early stage, without customization of the side links and without posts.

7. Returning to the Angelfire control and administration pages, Jason wanted to add specific links for his four topic areas. Figure 11.9 shows the Angelfire Topic Editor page.

After you click the Add Topic button, you're presented with a screen that provides a space to enter the topic title. As shown in Figure 11.10, Jason typed "Music/Art Festivals" to correspond to the first of the four special topic areas he wanted to organize on his blog.

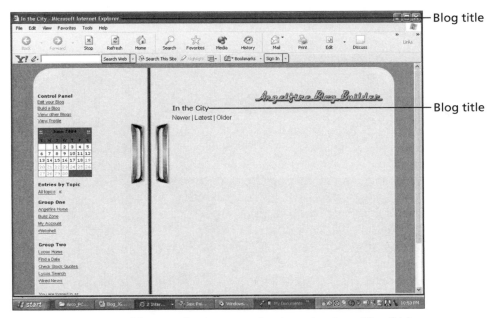

FIGURE 11.8 *Even with some basic customization, the Angelfire fridge template gives Jason's blog a distinctive look.*

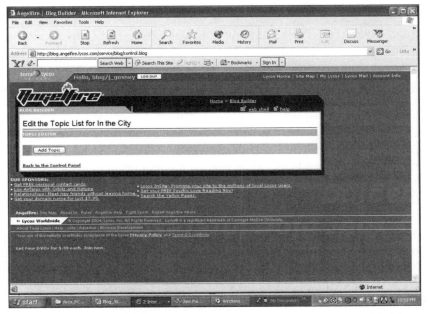

FIGURE 11.9 *Jason wanted to add four specific topic areas to his blog.*

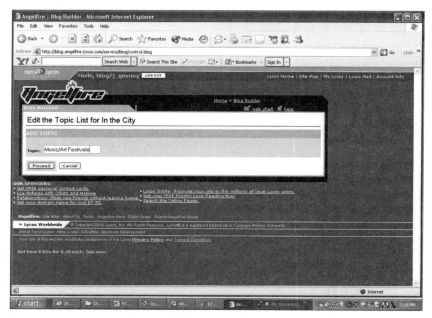

FIGURE 11.10 *Jason entered the specific topic title for each of the four areas.*

After clicking the Proceed button, Jason was brought back to the same screen shown in Figure 11.9. Notice that, as shown in Figure 11.11, the previous topic title that he entered now appears.

8. Jason repeated this process three more times for each of the other major topics he wanted to discuss on his blog. When he was done, he loaded the blog into his browser. Under the Entries by Topic section, he could see the four topic titles he had entered.

9. Jason needed to complete his online profile. A detailed profile would allow others to get a better idea of who he—the blog author—was and what his interests were. Figure 11.13 shows the Edit Profile page in the process of being completed by Jason.

10. The last piece of customization Jason wanted to do was to the Group One and Group Two set of links, as shown in Figure 11.14.

These links are provided automatically when a blog is created. Jason wanted to customize them, though. Figure 11.15 shows the Angelfire Manage Links administrative page.

For these links, Jason wanted to list sites that were related to his four topic areas. Figure 11.16 shows a set of links he decided to provide.

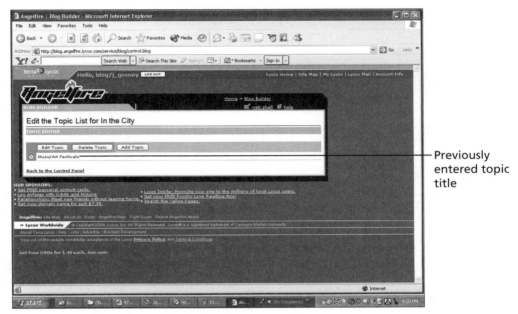

FIGURE 11.11 *Previous topic titles can be reviewed and edited here.*

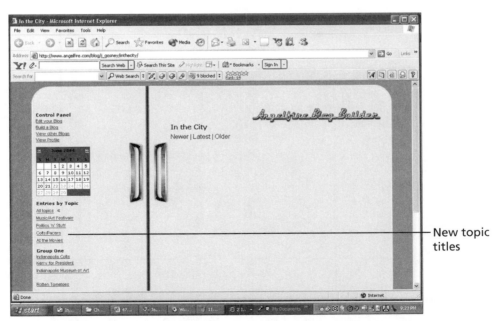

FIGURE 11.12 *Each of the four specific topic areas now appears on the blog.*

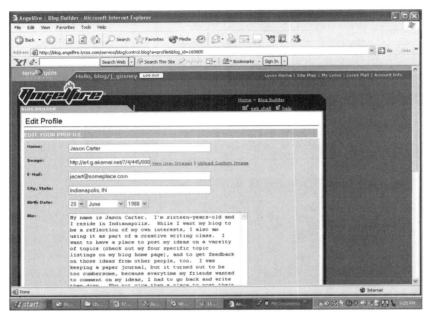

FIGURE 11.13 *A well-developed bio can be a great way to attract other like-minded readers.*

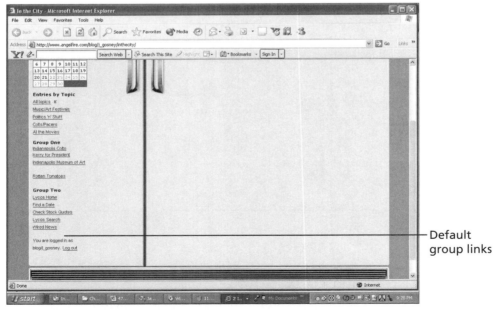

FIGURE 11.14 *Use customized links to give your readers easy access to other related content.*

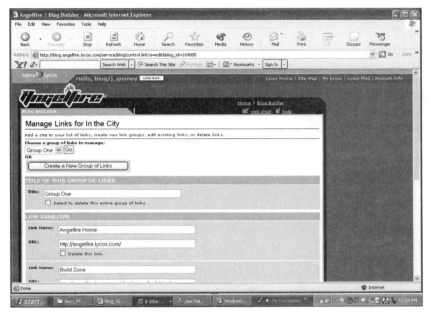

FIGURE 11.15 *The default group links can be changed easily from this page.*

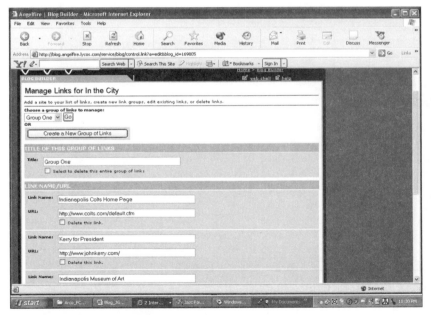

FIGURE 11.16 *Adding links to related content is an easy and effective way to expand the ideas you are presenting on your blog.*

Here are a few things to note about this feature:

◆ Don't confuse the links with the topic areas described earlier. Topics are designed to give organization to the postings that are made to the blog and to make it easier for the blog author and readers to find sets of postings that are related to a specific topic. A group of links point to external Web sites that are a reflection of the interests and focus of the blog.

◆ As you can see in Figure 11.16, if you click on the Create a New Group of Links button, you are presented with additional fields where you can enter descriptions or URLs of links you want to include. The number of links you can provide on your blog is unlimited.

Figure 11.17 shows a customized set of Group One links, as entered in Figure 11.16.

 tip The group links don't have to point just to external sites. For example, you could have a link called Video From the Art Festival that points to an actual video file that you've uploaded to the server.

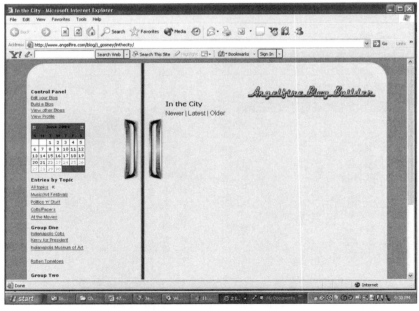

FIGURE 11.17 *Customized links to external sites give a sense of the broader interests of the blog author.*

Jason built his blog utilizing the Angelfire online tools. The blog example in Chapter 12 highlights how you can use FrontPage to build and administer your blog.

note

"In the City" Blog: Care and Feeding

Jason had several different areas of interest for his blog. You might think keeping his blog up and running would take a lot of his time.

In reality, this wasn't the case. Although Jason did make several postings to his blog as part of his journal assignment for his creative writing class, he often posted to just one topic area (such as sports or politics) at a time and made short, "to the point" postings. He liked to use open-ended questions ("What did you think of the festival?" or "I thought the movie was the best of the director's career. Do you agree?") to get his readers to respond. From a short posting, a longer discussion often resulted as readers responded to each other's comments. Jason could monitor these comments and gather ideas that he might never have thought about had he not been keeping a blog.

Jason used his blog to fulfill a school assignment, which is a great idea. But maybe you don't want your blog to be associated with school, because then it won't be fun. That is certainly a valid point. After all, you probably have more than enough homework to keep you busy, so why add one more thing to the list? But don't just ignore the possibility that, like Jason, you could find something you enjoy (your blog) to help make an otherwise boring task (your homework) more fun and interesting. Because blogging is becoming increasingly popular, and because teenagers are some of the most—if not *the* most—active bloggers, keep your eyes open (and talk to your teachers) about the possibility of using your blog to help you complete some of your assignments. Don't forget, too, that your blog might not just help you in your writing or English classes. Many classes will ask you to keep a journal. Because you are writing stuff anyway, why not post your ideas to your blog and see what others think about them?

Jason spent as much time reading other blogs as he did posting to his own. Remember Chapter 4, when we talked about the importance of being a critical reader? This remains true, especially in Jason's case, where he was using his blog to try to generate new ideas for his creative writing class. And because Jason had four topic areas that covered such a wide range of interests, it made sense for him to read as much as he could to stay current on all the issues swirling around these ideas. But again, he often focused on just one topic area at a time. For example, when football season started—and especially near the playoffs—Jason spent more time on the sports topic because it was more timely and more people were talking about it.

Finally, because Jason was interested in blogging about what was going on in Indianapolis, he liked to take the man on the street approach to many of his postings. For Jason, this meant getting out and experiencing as much of the city as he could and then writing about those experiences on his blog. But his postings were not just his personal reflections on the events he experienced. Rather, Jason often incorporated interviews from people he talked to at these events, so his postings reflected a more comprehensive view of the event and not just what he thought.

Of course, there's nothing wrong with having a blog that is a reflection of just your own thoughts, but if you can incorporate what others think—or at least invite their opinions—it will expand your voice and make your blog even more interesting and engaging. We talked a lot about this idea in Chapter 10, but even in the first four chapters of the book, where you read about strategies and techniques to find your voice, you were encouraged to leave the door open to hear what others had so say. Readership of your blog is not limited to just your friends. You are publishing on the World Wide Web, after all. Don't sell yourself short on the potential global readership of your blog.

 **teen talk** Don't underestimate this idea of getting out and experiencing the things you write about. The best writers have firsthand experience with their topics. Get away from your computer and actually experience those things you are writing about! I know that sounds obvious, but your life is busy. There's homework, after-school activities, and hanging out with your friends. Just keep an eye and ear open to the special moments that make it cool to hang out with your friends, go to concerts, go to games, and so on. Then, when you make postings to your blog about these experiences, you'll have all you need to make your postings interesting.

THURSDAY, NOVEMBER 28

MOOD: HUNGRY!

TOPIC: THANKSGIVING

Ah, Thanksgiving. That annual celebration when everyone gets together to eat until they are sick and then verbalize the flaws of the other loved ones gathered around the table. I'm not sure why everyone gets into fights on Thanksgiving. Maybe it's because you always seem to hurt the ones you love the most. Actually, my family always has a great time on Thanksgiving. My cousins from New Mexico often fly in for the holiday, and we have a great time hanging out and eating way too much. Plus, it's a four-day weekend, which is always a great thing.

But this year was different. My grandmother has been sick for the past few months, and we've all been worried about her. This year, as I was talking to her after dinner, it became clear to me that this might be the last Thanksgiving she spends with us. I know, I know... It's sort of a depressing subject matter for a posting, but life isn't all fun and games.

The funny thing is that although I thought I was going to be really depressed thinking about my grandmother not being around, she and I actually had a great time. She started telling me all these incredible stories of my father when he was young. On Thanksgiving afternoon, before dinner, they would always go for a walk in the woods that ran behind their house looking for the best Christmas tree they could find. Then, the next day, my dad and my grandfather would go back out, chop down the tree, and bring it to the house, where they'd spend the whole weekend decorating it and getting ready for the Christmas season. I couldn't believe people actually did that—you know, go out in the woods and find their own Christmas tree. The only hunting I do for the tree is trying to remember where we packed it (artificial tree, you know) and all the decorations. Anyway, it was really cool to imagine them going out in the crisp fall afternoon with flashlights, laughing and singing songs, and trying to find the best tree. I wish we did more stuff like that as a family, but I know everyone is busy (me included).

We usually put up our Christmas tree on Thanksgiving night. I'm looking forward to it. In fact, as soon as I finish this post, I'm going downstairs to help the family decorate it. But this year, as I put each limb on the artificial tree, I'm going to think about my grandmother, smiling and waving to my grandfather and dad as they headed out into the woods to find the best tree. And I know she will be thinking the same thing. But instead of making me sad, wondering if she will be here next year, I know that she's given me a happy memory that will last my entire life. I'll never forget this Thanksgiving and the stories my grandmother told me. Pretty cool...

Summary

This chapter focused on the fictitious "In the City" blog kept by Jason Carter, a fictitious teenager who lives in Indianapolis, Indiana. For his blog, Jason wanted to focus on four specific topic areas: music/art, sports, politics, and movies. Jason also wanted to incorporate comments from others into his blog. Given that he was using his blog to fulfill an assignment for a creative writing class, Jason could use the comments that people posted to his blog to come up with ideas for his class assignments. He also liked to get out and experience things in Indianapolis. That way, he could post to his blog from a man on the street perspective, making his blog more engaging to readers.

Chapter 12

Blog Example: "My Fifteen Minutes"

Well, you've made it to the last chapter. I won't say that I've saved the best for last, because that would be quite conceited of me, given that this chapter is about the genesis and development of my own blog, which I've named "My Fifteen Minutes." In case you're wondering what the significance of that title is, it is actually paying homage to the famous pop artist Andy Warhol, who did most of his work in the mid to late twentieth century. Warhol believed that everyone would be famous for 15 minutes. That saying is a great fit for a blog. With the Internet, everyone really can become famous, because it is so easy to publish to a worldwide audience. So, that's the significance of my blog title.

But enough of the title. My blog is about the one thing I have enjoyed my entire life: music. From old-time country to the hardest of heavy metal, there is little music I don't enjoy. I mentioned in another chapter that I have a CD collection that grows every day. It's more than 1,100 as of last count. Although that probably isn't that great of a number these days—with so many people having access to music via traditional stores as well as the Web—I am proud of the diversity of my collection. As I write this, I have a pile of CDs stacked next to my computer that ranges from Bob Wills and his Texas Playboys (a western swing group famous in the 1940s) to the Doors to Semisonic to Dr. Dre to Duran Duran. Like I said, there's quite a variety!

Aside from just listening to music, my other great passion is talking about music. So, when I decided to start a blog, I knew music would be the focus. This final chapter details how I organized my ideas and implemented them on by blog, www.my-15minutes.com. In this chapter, you will

◆ Get an overview of how I put together ideas for my blog and why I decided to focus on certain music-related issues.

◆ Examine how my blog is put together from a technical perspective. (I host my blog with Angelfire, so much of what you've been reading about in earlier chapters will apply to my blog as well.)

◆ Learn how I care for and feed my blog in the context of my busy life, and learn why posting to my blog is important to me.

Developing the "My Fifteen Minutes" Blog

As I've said before, music has always been a major passion in my life. When my older sisters weren't torturing me (like all good sisters do), they were pretty cool. When I was eight or nine years old, they let me borrow their records and told me the good stuff to listen to. Looking back, this was a tremendous benefit. How would a nine-year-old kid learn about great music any other way? By the time I was 10 or so, I had a decent knowledge of rock 'n' roll. From Led Zeppelin to Billy Joel, I had all the good stuff. Better still, whenever one of my sisters got a new stereo, I would get her old one so that I had a decent system to rock out with.

As I got older, I began to develop my own musical interests and started to seek out stuff on my own. I was in high school in the late 1980s, and, well, let me tell you: It was not a good time for music, at least not until Nirvana came around and blew everyone away. Music in the late 1980s consisted primarily of really awful dance stuff and what we now refer to as the "hair metal" bands like Bon Jovi. Yes, those were the days when Paula Abdul actually was making records and not just judging up-and-coming wannabes on *American Idol*.

Still, there was good stuff to be found if you were willing to look. For example, U2 had just released *The Joshua Tree*, Bruce Springsteen was touring in support of *Born in the U.S.A.* and, of course, there was Prince (one of my favorites) cranking out one great album after the next. And then, when I was a senior in high school, a little band called Guns 'n' Roses released their stunning masterpiece, *Appetite for Destruction*. And, oh yeah, Metallica was never far from me. So, looking back, maybe it wasn't that bad of a time for music. Some of the songs played on the radio were awful, but that has always been the case, hasn't it?

As I started to think about blogging, then, I wanted to try to capture not only my own music history, but also all of the things that I thought about and that were important to me, as they related to music. Specifically, I wanted my blog to focus on the following aspects of music:

◆ First, I wanted it to be a forum where I could record my own personal thoughts and reflections on music and why it's important to me. This is the area of my blog that is most like an online diary.

◆ Second, I wanted to use the power of the blog to allow other people to respond to my ideas.

◆ Finally, I wanted to take the man on the street approach to music and offer a more generalized, comprehensive perspective on various music-related events and issues. For example, I wanted to offer reviews and opinions of books about music, commentary on concerts and music festivals I attend, and—because I teach and am interested in how music can be discussed critically—the deeper meaning of popular music and how it can help explain other subjects, especially poetry and literature.

If you take another look at Chapter 2 in the context of my blog, you might say that I decided to find my voice through my interest in music. I have other interests (such as technology and computers), but music has been, and probably always will be, the one hobby that interests me the most.

Now that you know why I decided to focus my blog around music, let me tell you a little something about how I organized and planned my presentation of all these things on my blog.

"My Fifteen Minutes" Blog: Organization and Planning

I mentioned the three larger themes of my blog in the previous section, but as I was planning it, I needed to decide in what context(s) I was going to discuss those themes.

As I sat down to organize this, I thought about how I am involved personally with music. The following lists the music-related things that I spend the most time doing:

◆ First, I enjoy listening to music and focus a significant part of each day taking pleasure in that. Each night before I hit the sack, I go through my CD collection and pick out three or four discs for the next day. Sometimes I pick three discs from the same band; other times, I pick three wildly divergent CDs. I take my music listening seriously and want to enjoy the time that I have to listen.

◆ Second, I enjoy reading about music almost as much as I do listening to it. I especially like reading autobiographies of famous musicians so that I can learn about how they first got started with music and how their lives changed and developed when they discovered they were going to be professional musicians. I also like reading music criticism. I'm particularly interested in how music can be analyzed from different perspectives. For example, a favorite exercise I like to do in my literature classes is to compare some of the major poems of Sylvia Plath (a poet from the mid-twentieth century) to Eminem, looking for similarities in how they express feelings concerning their relationships with their parents. This type of exercise gives legitimacy to the music of today and helps to clarify what otherwise might be confusing and boring literature.

◆ Finally, I enjoy talking about music with my friends and family. I am lucky because many of the other technicians who work with me are music fans. In fact, three of them are musicians and actively play (or have played) in bands. Dealing with all of the technology-related stuff at the university keeps us busy, but it is great to be able to take a break during the day and talk about some new CD that has just been released or a concert that is coming to town.

To me, music is not a passive activity. In other words, I don't just sit and listen to it, but I actively think about it. Because I spend so much time thinking about it, it made perfect sense that I should make my blog an outlet for all these musical thoughts!

 note You might be thinking to yourself, "Can't he just put on a CD and chill out to it, without analyzing it to death?" That's funny if you're thinking that—I was thinking that, too, as I wrote this. Of course, I do like to put on music and just enjoy it. I don't think about the proverbial meaning of life every time I put on a CD. But I think it's fun to think about the importance of what I'm listening to. Even if I'm just focusing on how a particular song makes me feel or remembering where I was the first time I heard a song, listening to music is an active process for me.

 You might also be wondering if all blogs have to be serious. Admittedly, we've talked about some serious stuff in this book, but if you find that many of your postings are just sort of random thoughts or are funny, that's totally fine! Remember: The only rule of blogging is that it should be something you enjoy doing. So, although my blog is full of some "deeper" thoughts (some would say it's full of something else), there's no reason you can't keep a first-rate blog about your cat. Now, whether anyone would want to read about your cat is a different story. Then again, you should remember to blog first and foremost for yourself. If you blog it, they will come, so don't get too hung up on whether your blog is serious enough or good enough for other people to read.

Now that you know why I'm focusing my blog on music and which music-related topics I want to explore, let's go through the actual creation of my blog from a technical viewpoint.

> **tip** As you read through this chapter, compare it to the blog example you read about in Chapter 11, as well as ideas for your own blog. The point of including these two sample blogs is not to show off or pin down the "right way" to blog. In no way do I claim that my blog is the model blog. On the contrary, many other blogs are better designed and better written than mine. But again, my blog makes me happy, and that is what's most important!

"My Fifteen Minutes" Blog: Designing and Publishing

Like the sample blog in Chapter 11, I chose to host my real-life blog with Angelfire. After reviewing other hosting providers, I thought that Angelfire was best suited for my needs.

The detailed steps of setting up a membership with Angelfire are described in previous chapters, so I won't go through that process again here. That said, keep in mind that there are other steps you need to take to start up a blog like the one I'm showing here on Angelfire. This example—like the one in Chapter 11—is to show you how I was able to express my ideas through the blog design tools available on Angelfire.

> Remember from Chapter 7 that you can assign a specific domain name for your blog. For my blog, the DNS is my-15minutes.com. Just remember that choosing your own domain name usually involves a fee. (For my specific **note** hosting plan on Angelfire, it is included in the monthly charge.)

The following is a general description of how I set up my blog, including some of the choices I made in the design, the larger functionality of the blog, and the links I've included:

1. With the Angelfire service, I had several design templates to choose from. I decided on a music-themed template, as shown in Figure 12.1.

2. After I decided on a template, I needed to assign the basic functional attributes to my blog, including giving it a title, assigning a time zone, and so on. Figure 12.2 highlights the Configure Your Blog page and the settings I chose for my blog.

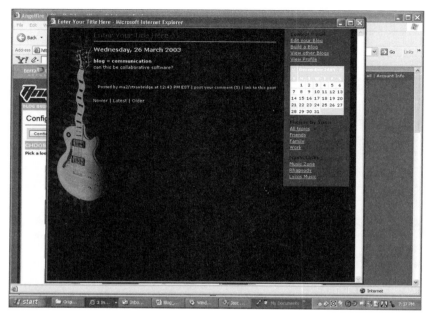

FIGURE 12.1 *Not surprisingly, I chose a music-themed template for my blog.*

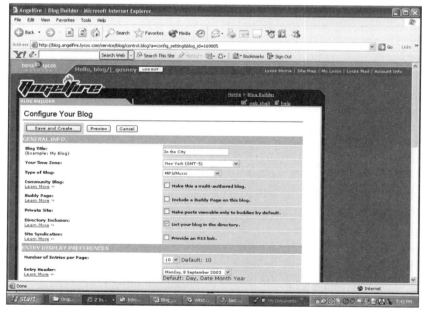

FIGURE 12.2 *Assigning the usual blog parameters, including its title and where it would be listed in the Angelfire blog directory.*

3. Now that I'd worked through these basic setup issues, my blog was ready to go. Let me point out a few specific attributes configured on my blog:

◆ I categorized my blog as a music-related blog so that it would show up in the music section of the blog directory.

◆ Readers are allowed to post comments to my blog, but before those comments are made public, I review them. I am notified via e-mail whenever a new posting is made.

◆ I set up my profile listing general information about who I am and what my interests are so that other readers can learn more about me.

◆ I FrontPage-enabled my blog so that I can access it via FrontPage for easier maintenance and control of the content, as shown in Figure 12.3.

---

tip

You should take advantage of using FrontPage for accessing and working in your blog. Although there are some decent online content editors available with the different hosting providers, none of them comes close to the power and functionality of FrontPage. If you are interested, take another look at Chapter 9, where I detailed the larger functionality of FrontPage and its various tools.

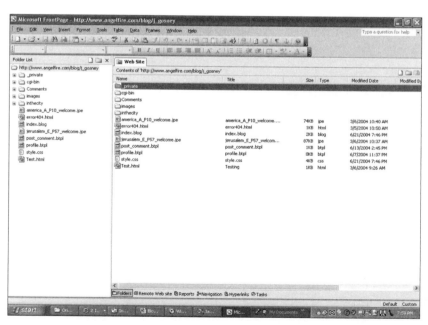

FIGURE 12.3 *Accessing my blog through FrontPage.*

4. After these configuration settings were made, I decided to add a few topic and group links. Figure 12.4 shows the Edit Topic List page for my blog. Remember that you are not limited in the number of potential topics. You should use them to help categorize and organize your content.

5. In addition to topics, you can add groups of links that highlight other blogs, Web sites, or files that are of interest to you and that highlight your content. Figure 12.5 shows my Music Links grouping of links.

6. All in all, the general configuration of my blog as described here only took a few minutes. Figure 12.6 shows the home page of my blog.

   If you scroll down the page a bit, you can see that I've inserted a drawing from the poet William Blake, as shown in Figure 12.7. This graphic—in addition to looking cool—is a hyperlink. (Note the hand icon, indicating that this is a link.) When you click on the picture, you are taken to a Web page related to a discussion of William Blake.

As I've mentioned in other chapters, there is much I could tell you about general Web design and the features that are being implemented on this blog, from basic HTML to cascading style sheets. A discussion of this complexity is beyond the scope of this book, but review Chapter 9, which offers a good overview of FrontPage. Also, take advantage of the online help features that your hosting service provides and, of course, don't forget to search the Web for the hundreds of online tutorials on Web design that can help you as you work with your blog.

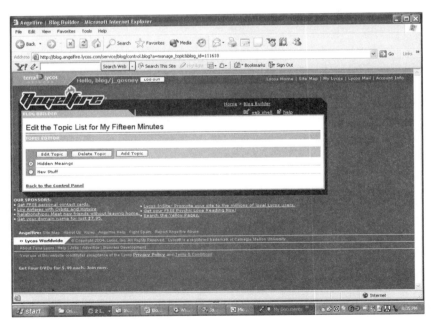

FIGURE 12.4 *Use the topic's functionality to neatly organize your content.*

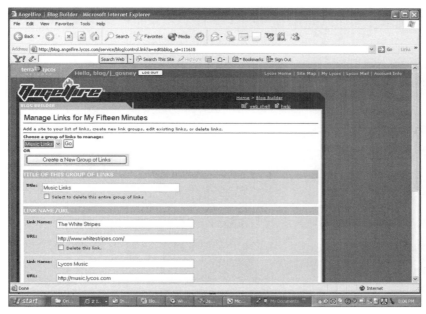

FIGURE 12.5 *Provide links to related sites of interest.*

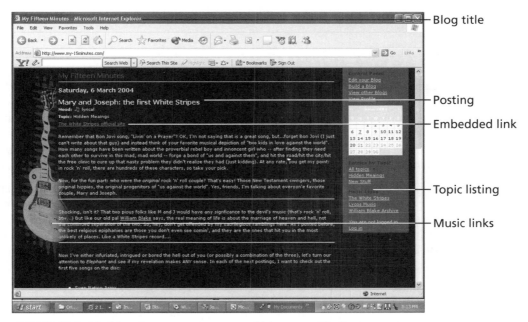

FIGURE 12.6 *My blog incorporates several blog-specific features as well as general Web page and HTML features.*

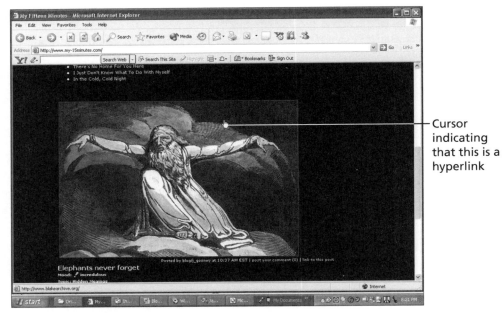

Cursor indicating that this is a hyperlink

FIGURE 12.7 *By utilizing the HTML features of a traditional Web page, you can add all kinds of great content (like images that are hyperlinks) to your blog.*

"My Fifteen Minutes" Blog: Care and Feeding

Not to sound conceited or whiny, but I lead a busy life. In addition to teaching, I manage the technology center for a major school at the university where I work. I also do quite a bit of writing (you probably guessed that part), do freelance Web design, pursue hobbies like music and, of course, spend as much time with my family as possible.

How do I find time to blog? It's not easy. But, as with the Jason Carter blog in Chapter 11, I think the key is to find ways to integrate your blog into your other daily activities so that it's more a part of your life. In the example from Chapter 11, the author used his blog to help fulfill a school assignment. I am looking for ways to incorporate my blog into my teaching. I told you at the beginning of this chapter that I'm interested in the different ways that music can be thought about and experienced.

I'm particularly interested in how music can be used to help explain (and make more interesting) the study of literature. As I write this, it is summer, and I am starting to prepare for the fall semester and the classes I will teach. I'm already thinking about how I can incorporate my blog into that class by having my students read and post to my blog, commenting on the poetry that I am going to ask them to read. Perhaps they will in turn keep their own blogs. The point here is that I'm finding a fun, engaging way to keep my blog active in my daily life.

> **tip** Yes, I've said this a million times in this book, but just be sure that no matter what way you find to integrate your blog, you keep the emphasis on fun. A blog shouldn't be work or something you dread. A blog is a personal thing, and you need to keep it fun and interesting to its most important reader: you!

So, in whatever way you decide to care for and feed your blog, keep it fun, and don't let it become something you stress over. Use your blog as an outlet for expressing yourself and for learning new things via the posting of your readers.

I'd like to end this chapter and book by addressing a question that has been implied several times: What happens if you decide to quit your blog? If blogging stops being fun for you and you're thinking of quitting, let me make one suggestion. Before canceling your hosting plan, take some time off from posting to read other people's blogs and see what they have to say. Your reading might inspire you to think of new ideas, which could allow you to return to your blog with a fresh perspective. Also, many blogs have long lapses between posts, so don't feel guilty if you post only once a month. Just remember that the way you care for and feed your blog is completely up to you. Have fun with it, and enjoy all the freedom that blogging brings to you, even if that means you only post to your blog on an occasional basis.

Friday, December 20

Mood: Exhilaration

Topic: Happy New Year!

Well, I've been making postings to this blog for several months now, and I've talked about a lot of things. One thing has remained consistent, though, and that is my various ramblings about a certain person (Jessica Reynolds, in case you need reminding). From my reminiscing about our times together to my wondering whether she liked me, you are probably tired of hearing about it.

So, let me tell you some interesting news. Now that the year is coming to an end and Jessica is going away for the holidays, I decided to make my move and lay it all on the line by telling her how I really feel about her. My rationale was that if she said shot me down, I could sulk for two weeks over the holiday break and not have to deal with the embarrassment of seeing her in school. Of course, the flip side of that coin was that if she gave me a positive answer, I could bask in that warmth of knowing she felt the same way and take those same two weeks to think about all the different ways I could tell her how much she means to me. (In other words, I'd have to practice a few things to say, so I wouldn't sound like a total dork when the words came out wrong.)

Today was the second to the last day of school before the break. She and I were talking at lunch, and I asked her if she'd have time to come over and study for the exam that our wonderful chemistry teacher decided to give us the day before a major break. A little side note here: Why do some teachers insist on giving exams the day before a major break? Do they get some kind of wicked satisfaction from it? If I ever become a teacher (and the thought has crossed my mind), I've promised myself I will not do that to my students. I mean, maybe teachers have a reason for doing that (so people actually come to school the last day before a break, instead of taking off early to wherever it is they are going), but it seems like pure evil!

Anyway, back to the subject at hand. So after dinner, Jessica came over to study. As we always do when we hang out together, we stopped studying and talked, surfed the Web, read and posted to blogs, and so on. Up to this point, I had restricted access to some postings on my blog to a separate buddy list so that she couldn't read everything that I was posting. She has asked me repeatedly if she could read these secret postings, and I kept telling her no. In thinking back on it, she probably figured out they were about her. I mean, why else wouldn't I let her read them? Anyway, last night, I thought that letting Jessica read those postings would be a great way to let her know how I feel. So I told her, "Okay, Jessica, you can read my secret postings. Start with this posting, and while you are reading it, I'm going downstairs to get us some sodas."

When I came back upstairs with the drinks, I found she had locked herself in my room and wouldn't let me in! When I pounded on the door, yelling at her and telling her that we needed to study, she just yelled back, "Shut up! I'm reading!" Oh man, I thought. What if she is reading all those postings I made about her and cracking up? Or worse, what if she is reading that stuff and getting angry or embarrassed because now she knows how I feel?

After what seemed like forever, she opened the door. She said, "Well, I've read all the postings and all I can say is... " She took a very long pause. Then she slowly got up, walked across the room so that she was standing right in front of me, and said, "All I can say is, why didn't you tell me earlier? Couldn't you take a hint? I felt like I was going to have to hit you over the head with a brick to get you to realize I feel the same way!" And with that, she kissed me (yes, kissed me!) and said she couldn't wait to get back from the holiday and start what she knew was going to be the best year of her life, with me. Talk about a great answer! Wow! And to think I owe it all to my blog! It should be an interesting semester. I hope it turns out to be everything it promises to be.

Blogger70 signing off. Thanks for reading!

Summary

This chapter presented yet another example of a blog (mine!), including the ideas leading up to its development, how it was designed on the hosting provider, and how it is kept current. My blog has a specific focus (music) and tries to incorporate my ideas and thoughts, as well as providing a forum for readers to respond. My blog incorporates several different components to help make it engaging. Finally, my blog makes use of FrontPage so that I can administer it easily and take advantage of the powerful editing tools that the application offers.

Appendix A
Abbreviation Listing

AAMOF, IDK, so TTYL.

Huh? What does that mean? Well, if you were affluent in e-mail/chat-room abbreviation speak, you would quickly recognize that this stands for "As a matter of fact (AAMOF), I don't know (IDK), so talk to you later (TTYL)."

If you are going to spend a significant amount of time posting to blogs, chat rooms, or just regular e-mail, you are inevitably going to need to use and understand these abbreviations. Although the listing provided in this appendix is not meant to be the end-all-be-all (or EABA) listing, it is comprehensive nevertheless. So, if you are reading a posting and you just can't make sense of all the abbreviations, take a look at this appendix, and see if you can find the definition. The capitalization is sometimes a little weird when the abbreviations are spelled out but that's so you can tell what the letters stand for.

 tip Remember, too, that some abbreviations are going to be regional based on the city, state, or even country where the blogger resides, so a 100% comprehensive abbreviation listing is probably not possible. Also, new abbreviations are being invented and put into use every day.

A

A/S/L?—Age/Sex/Location?

A/S?—Age/Sex?

AA—Alcoholics Anonymous

AAMOF—As A Matter Of Fact

Abbr.—Abbreviation

ACK—Acknowledgement

ADN—Any Day Now

AFAIAA—As Far As I Am Aware

AFAIAC—As Far As I Am Concerned

AFAIC—As Far As I'm Concerned

AFAICT—As Far As I Can Tell

AFAIK—As Far As I Know

AFAIR—As Far As I Remember/Recall

AFAIUI—As Far As I Understand It

AFK—Away From the Keyboard

AFL—AbsoFreakinLutely

AISB—As I Said Before; As It Should Be

AISE—As I Said Earlier

AISI—As I See It

AIW—As It Were/Was

AKA—Also Known As

AMAP—As Much/Many As Possible

AMF—Adios, My Friend

ANFAWFOS—And Now, For A Word From Our Sponsor

ANFAWFOWS—And Now, For A Word From Our Web Sponsor

AOB—Any Other Business

AOBTD—Another One Bites The Dust

APAC—All Praise And Credit

ASAP—As Soon As Possible

ATB—All The Best

ATK—At The Keyboard

ATLA—Another Three Letter Acronym

ATM—At The Moment

ATTN—Attention

aVG—AVeraGe

AWCIGO—And Where Can I Get One?

AWGTHTGTATA—Are We Going To Have To Go Through All This/That Again?

AWGTHTGTTA—Are We Going To Have To Go Through This/That Again?

AWHFY—Are We Having Fun Yet?

AYT—Are You There?

B

B/C—Because

B4—Before

B4N—Bye For Now

BAC—By Any Chance

BAD—Broken As Designed

BAK—Back At Keyboard

BBB—Busy Beyond Belief

BBFN—Bye Bye For Now

BBIAB—Be Back In A Bit

BBIAF—Be Back In A Flash

BBIAM—Be Back In A Minute

BBIAS—Be Back In A Sec

BBL—Be Back Later

BBN—Bye Bye Now

BC—Basket Case; Because

BCC—Blind Carbon Copy

BCNU—Be Seein' You

BF—BoyFriend

BFG—Big Friendly Giant

BFMI—Brute Force and Massive Ignorance

BFN—Bye For Now

BIC—Best In Class

BIL—Brother In Law

BION—Believe It Or Not

BITD—Beaten It To Death

BK—Because

BK—Bo Knows

BM—Blonde Moment

BMHATK—Banging My Head Against The Keyboard

BMHATW—Banging My Head Against The Wall

BMOC—Big Man On Campus

BMTA—Brilliant Minds Think Alike

BMTIPG—Brilliant Minds Think In Parallel Gutters

BNF—Big Name Fan

BOC—But Of Course

BOF—Birds Of a Feather

BOHOF—Back Of Hand On Forehead

BOL—Best Of Luck

BOS—Big Orange Switch; Boyfriend Over Shoulder

BOT—Back On Topic

BOTEC—Back Of The Envelope Calculation

BRB—Be Right Back

BRBGP—Be Right Back, Gotta Pee

BRBIGP—Be Right Back, I Gotta Pee

BRO—Brother

Bros.—Brothers

BRS—Big Red Switch

BRT—Be Right There

BS—Bovine manure

BSG—Big Smiling Grin; Broad Sweeping Generalization

BSOD—Blue Screen Of Death

BTA—But Then Again

BTAICBW—But Then Again, I Could Be Wrong

BTAIM—Be That As It May

BTDT—Been There, Done That

BTDTGTTS—Been There, Done That, Got The T-Shirt

BTG—Buck Tooth Green

BTOBD—Be There Or Be Dead

BTOBS—Be There Or Be Square

BTTP—Back To The Point

BTW—By The Way

BTWBO—Be There With Bells On

BWL—Bursting With Laughter

BWQ—Buzz Word Quotient

BY—BusY

BYKT—But You Know/Knew That

BYKTA—But You Know/Knew That Already

BYOB—Bring Your Own Bottle/Booze

C

C&P—Copy & Paste

C/O—Care Of

CADET—Can't Add, Doesn't Even Try

CB—Call Back

CC—Carbon Copy

CCWC—Can't Cook, Won't Cook

CE—Creative Editing

CFD—Call For Discussion

CFV—Call For Votes

CGI—Common Gateway Interface

CHOWUR—See HOW yoU aRe

CHP—California Highway Patrol

CHUR—See How yoU aRe

CIAO—Goodbye

CICO—Coffee In, Coffee Out

CID—Crying In Disgrace

CIO—Cut It Out

Cir.—Circle

CLAB—Crying Like A Baby

CLM—Career Limiting Move

CMF—Count My Fingers!

CMIIW—Correct Me If I'm Wrong

CNP—Continued Next Post

CO—COnference

COD—Cash On Delivery

COTFLGUOAHAHA—Crawling On The Floor, Laughing Guts Out, And Having A Heart Attack

COTN—Coffee/Coke Out The Nose

CP—Chat Post

CPF—Can Pigs Fly

CS—Cop Shop

CSG—Chuckle, Snicker, Grin

CTR—Choose The Right

CTTD—Cute Things They Do

CTTS—Cute Things They Say

CU—See You

CUL—Catch You Later/See You Later

CUL—See yoU Later

CUL8R—See yoU LateR

CWYL—Chat With You Later

CYA—See Ya

CYL—See You Later

D

D&W—Ducking And Weaving

D/L—Download

DAMHIK—Don't Ask Me How I Know

DAMHIK, IJK—Don't Ask Me How I Know, I Just Know

DARFC—Ducking And Running For Cover

DBA—Doing Business As

DBEYR—Don't Believe Everything You Read

DBN—Doing Business—Not

DDD—Direct Distance Dial

DEG—Deliciously Evil Grin

DFM—Don't Flame Me

DFU—Don't Forget Units

DHYB—Don't Hold Your Breath

DIM—Do It Myself

DIY—Do It Yourself

DK—Don't Know

DL—DownLoad

DLG—Devilish Little Grin

DLTBBB—Don't Let The Bed Bugs Bite

DNA—Did Not Answer

DNPM—Darn Near Pissed Myself

DPKOL—Deep Passionate Kiss On the Lips

DQYDJ—Don't Quit Your Day Job

DTOKAB—Drop To One Knee And Bow

DTRT—Do The Right Thing

DTTAH—Don't Try This At Home

DUCWIC—Do YoU See What I See?

DUK—Dead Upon Keyboard

DWIM—Do What I Mean

DWIMNWIS—Do What I Mean, Not What I Say

DWISNWID—Do What I Say, Not What I Do

DWPKOL—Deep, Wet Passionate Kiss On the Lips

DYHWIH—Do You Hear What I Hear

DYSTSOTT—Did You See The Size Of That Thing

DYSWIS—Do You See What I See

E

E2EG—Ear to Ear Grin

EABA—End-All-Be-All

ED—Emotionally Disturbed

EDP—Emotionally Disturbed Person

EIF—Exercise In Futility

ELOL—Evil Laughing Out Loud

EMSG—E-mail Message

EOB—End Of Business

EOD—End Of Discussion

EOL—End Of Lecture

EOT—End Of Thread

EPID—Every Person Is Different

ESOSL—Endless Snorts Of Stupid Laughter

ESP—ESPecially

ETA—Estimated Time of Arrival

F

F2F—Face To Face

FAQ—Frequently Asked Question(s)

FCFS—First Come, First Served

FCOL—For Crying Out Loud

FDROTFL—Falling Down, Rolling On The Floor Laughing

FE—Fatal Error

FICCL—Frankly, I Couldn't Care Less

FIL—Father In Law

FIOFY—Figure It Out For Yourself

FIRST—Forum of Incident Response and Security Teams

FISH—First In, Still Here

FITB—Fill In The Blank

FOAF—Friend Of A Friend

FOAFOAG—Father Of A Friend Of A Girlfriend

FOAG—Father Of A Girlfriend

FOCL—Fell Off Chair Laughing

FOD—Finger Of Death

FOS—Freedom Of Speech

FOT—Full Of Tripe

FOTCL—Falling Off The Chair Laughing

FSD—Fools Seldom Differ

FTASB—Faster Than A Speeding Bullet

FTBOMH—From The Bottom Of My Heart

FTF—Face To Face

FTFM—For The Feeble Minded

FTL—Faster Than Light

FTR—For The Record

FTS—Fixin' To Start

FUD—Fear, Uncertainty, and Doubt

FURTB—Full Up Ready To Burst

FWIW—For What It's Worth

FWY—Freeway

FYA—For Your Amusement

FYI—For Your Information

FYM—For Your Misinformation

G

G—Grin <g>

GA—Go Ahead

GAC—Get A Clue

GAFIA—Get Away From It All

GAL—Get A Life

GBH&K—Great Big Hugs And Kisses

GBH&KB—Great Big Hugs And Kisses Back

GD&R—Grinning, Ducking, And Running

GD&RF—Grinning, Ducking, And Running Fast

GD&RVVF—Grinning, Ducking, And Running Very, Very Fast

GD&W—Grinning, Ducking, And Weaving

GEE—No, GTE

GF—GirlFriend

GFN—Gone For Now

GFR—Grim File Reaper

GG—Gotta Go

GGN—Gotta Go Now

GIF—Graphical Interchange Format

GIGO—Garbage In, Garbage Out; Garbage In, Gospel Out

GIWIST—Gee, I Wish I'd Said That

GJ—Good Job

GJP—Good Job, Partner

GL—Good Luck

GLG—Goofy Little Grin

GLGH—Good Luck and Good Hunting

GMTA—Great Minds Think Alike

GOK—God Only Knows

GOOML—Get Out Of My Life

GOS—Girlfriend Over Shoulder

GOTFIA—Groaning On The Floor In Agony

GOWI—Get On With It

GPF—Go Puke Fast

GR&D—Grinning, Running, And Ducking

GR8—Great

GSH—Good Sense of Humor

GTBOS—Glad To Be Of Service

GTG—Got To Go

GTGN—Got To Go Now

GTP—Got To Pee

GTS—God, That Sucked

GTSU—Glad/Good To See You

H

H&K—Hugs And Kisses

H2—How To

HABO—Have A Better One

HAGN—Have A Good Night

HAGO—Have A Good One

HAK—Hugs And Kisses

HAND—Have A Nice Day

HATM—Howling At The Moon

HB—Honey Bear; HummingBird

HCB—Holy Cow, Batman

HHB—Hello, Honey Bear

HHGTTG—Hitch Hiker's Guide To The Galaxy

HHIS—Hanging Head In Shame

HHO1/2K—Ha Ha, Only Half Kidding

HHOJ—Ha Ha, Only Joking

HHOK—Ha Ha, Only Kidding

HHOS—Ha Ha, Only Serious

HIB__—Have I Been _____

HICA—Here It Comes Again

HIOOC—Help! I'm Out Of Coffee!

HOAS—Hold On A Second

HOMPR—Hang On, Mobile Phone's Ringing

HOPR—Hang On, Phone's Ringing

HOUER—Hanging On yoUr Every WoRd

HOYER—Hanging On Your Every WoRd

HP—Home Page

HSIK—How Should I Know

HSP—Highly Sensitive Person

HTH—Hope This Helps

HUA—Heads Up, Ace

HWY—Highway

I

IAC—In Any Case

IAE—In Any Event

IAGFII—It's All Good Fun, Isn't It

IANAA—I Am Not An Accountant

IANAC—I Am Not A Crook

IANAD—I Am Not A Doctor

IANAL—I Am Not A Lawyer

IANALBIPOOTV—I Am Not A Lawyer, But I Play One On TV

IANYM—In A New York Minute

IANYS—In A New York Second

IAO—I Am Outtahere

IAWC—In A While, Crocodile

IAWTP—I Agree With This Post/Poster

IAY—I Adore You

IAYT—I Adore You, Too [also IAY2]

IB—I'm Back

IBC—Inadequate But Cute

IBCNU—I'll Be Seeing You

IBM—Inadequate But Marketable

IBTD—I Beg To Differ

IC—I See

IC—I See; In Character

ICB—I Care Because

ICBW—I Could Be Wrong

ICCL—I Couldn't Care Less

ICQ—I Seek You [an Internet messaging system]

ICTYBTIHTKY—I Could Tell You, But Then I'd Have To Kill You

ICUR—I See yoU aRe

IDGI—I Don't Get It

IDK—I Don't Know

IDTS—I Don't Think So

IDTT—I'll Drink To That

IE—In Effect

IFABCTE—I Found A Bug, Call The Exterminator

IGP—I Gotta Pee

IHABICNRWTSF—I Hate Abbreviations Because I Can Never Remember What They Stand For

IHTBS—It Has To Be Shown

IHTFP—I Have Truly Found Paradise

IIABDFI—If It Ain't Broke, Don't Fix It

IIRC—If I Recall/Remember Correctly

IITYWIMIWHTKY—If I Tell You What It Means, I Will Have To Kill You

IITYWIMWYBMAD—If I Tell You What It Means, Will You Buy Me A Drink?

IITYWIMWYKM—If I Tell You What It Means, Will You Kiss Me?

IITYWTMWYBMAD—If I Tell You What This Means, Will You Buy Me A Drink?

IITYWTMWYKM—If I Tell You What This Means, Will You Kiss Me?

IITYWTMWYLMA—If I Tell You What This Means, Will You Leave Me Alone?

IIWM—If It Were Me

IJLS—I Just Like Saying

IKWYM—I Know What You Mean

ILI—I Like Ike

ILICISCOMK—I Laughed, I Cried, I Spilled Coffee/Coke On My Keyboard

ILIWAPCT—I Love It When A Plan Comes Together

ILSHIBAMF—I Laughed So Hard I Broke All My Furniture

ILSHIBMS—I Laughed So Hard, I Broke My Stitches

ILU—I Love yoU

ILUT—I Love yoU, Too [also ILU2]

ILY—I Love You

IMAO—In My Arrogant Opinion

IMBO—In My Biased Opinion

IMCDO—In My Conceited, Dogmatic Opinion

IMCO—In My Considered Opinion

IME—In My Experience

IMHO—In My Humble Opinion

IMMOR—I Make My Own Rules

IMNSHO—In My Not So Humble Opinion

IMO—In My Opinion

IMOBO—In My Own Biased Opinion

IMPE—In My Personal/Previous Experience

IMPOV—In My Point Of View

IMS—I Must Say

IMVHO—In My Very Humble Opinion

INGSI—I'm Not Going to Say It

INPO—In No Particular Order

INT—I'll Never Tell

IOU—I Owe You

IOW—In Other Words

IP—Internet Protocol

IRC—Internet Relay Chat

IRL—In Real Life

IRT—In Real Time

ISC—I Stand Corrected

ISO—In Search Of

ISP—Internet Service Provider

ISTM—It Seems To Me

ISTR—I Seem To Remember

IT—Information Technology [a global term for all things having to do with computers]

ITFA—In The Final Analysis

ITMA—It's That Man Again

ITYM—I Think You Mean

IUTHALORFH—I Used To Have A Lot Of Respect For Him/Her

IUTKATS—I Used To Know All That Stuff

IWALU—I Will Always Love yoU

IWALY—I Will Always Love You

IWBNI—It Would Be Nice If

IWIK—I Wish I Knew

IYD—In Your Dreams

IYF—In Your Face

IYF __—Insert Your Favorite _____

IYKWIM—If You Know What I Mean

IYSWIM—If You See What I Mean

J

J/K—Just Kidding

JAM—Just A Moment/Minute

JAO—Just Another Observer

JAS—Just A Second

JFF—Just For Fun

JFTR—Just For The Record

JFYI—Just For Your Information

JIC—Just In Case

JIT—Just In Time

JMHO—Just My Humble Opinion

JMO—Just My Opinion

JMOOC—Just My Opinion, Of Course

JSNM—Just Stark Naked Magic

JSYK—Just So You Know

JTLYK—Just To Let You Know

JTUSK—Just Thought yoU Should Know

JTYMLTK—Just Thought You Might Like To Know

JTYWTK—Just Thought You Wanted To Know

K

KIA—Know It All

KISS—Keep It Simple, Stupid

KMB—Kiss My Butt

KMWIH—Kick Me Where It Hurts

KMYF—Kiss Me, You Fool

KOL—Kiss On Lips

KOS—Kids Over Shoulder

KOTC—Kiss On The Cheek

KOTL—Kiss On The Lips

KOTM—Kook Of The Month

KWIM—Know What I Mean

KYHOOTW—Keep Your Head Out Of The Water

KYHU—Keep Your Head Up

L

L8R—Later

LALL—Live And Let Live

LD—Long Distance

LDTO—Let's Ditch This One

LDTTWA—Let's Do The Time Warp Again

LHM—Lord, Help Me

LHU—Lord, Help Us

LJBF—Let's Just Be Friends

LLAP—Live Long And Prosper

LLTA—Lots and Lots of Thunderous Applause

LMA—Leave Me Alone

LMC—Lost My Connection

LMCOA—Lost My Connection Once Again

LMK—Let Me Know

LOFLOL—Lying On Floor, Laughing Out Loud

LOL—Laughing Out Loud

LOWOTFBTC—Laughing Out, Waving On The Floor, Biting The Carpet

LSFIAB—Like Shooting Fish In A Barrel

LSHHTCMS—Laughed So Hard, Had To Change My Shorts

LSHIH—Laughing So Hard It Hurts

LSHIPMP—Laughing So Hard I Peed My Pants

LSHMBIB—Laughing So Hard My Belly Is Bouncing

LSMIF—Laughing So Much I Farted

LSP—Less Sensitive Person

LTBF—Learn To Be Funny

LTIP—Laughing Till I Puke

LTM—Laughing To Myself

LTMSH—Laughing 'Til My Sides Hurt

LTNS—Long Time, No See

LUSER—Loser USER

LY—Love Ya

LYLAB—Love You Like A Brother

LYLAS—Love You Like A Sister

LYWAMH—Love You With All My Heart

M

MAY—Mad About You

MAYB—Mad About You, Baby

MCIBTY—My Computer Is Better Than Yours

MD—Mailed

MFG—More Friendly Garbage

MHBFY—My Heart Bleeds For You

MHDC—My Hard Drive Crashed

MHM—Members Helping Members

MHOTY—My Hat's Off To You

MING—Mailing

ML—More Later

MMIF—My Mouth Is Full

MNC—Mother Nature Calls

MOF—Matter Of Fact

MOMN—Milk Out My Nose

MORF—Male OR Female

MOS—Member of the Opposite Sex

MOTAS—Member Of The Appropriate Sex

MOTD—Message Of The Day

MOTOS—Member Of The Opposite Sex

MOTSS—Member Of The Same Sex

MPH—Miles Per Hour

MS—More of the Same

MSS—Member of the Same Sex

MT—My Time

MTFBWY—May The Force Be With You

MYOB—Mind Your Own Business

N

N/M—Never Mind

NADM—Never A Dull Moment

NAGI—Not A Good Idea

NAVY—Never Again Volunteer Yourself

NBD—No Big Deal

NBTD—Nothing Better To Do

NCB—Never Change, Baby

NDM—No Disrespect Meant

NGT—Not Gonna Tell

NHOH—Never Heard Of Her/Him

NICBDAT—Nothing Is Certain But Death And Taxes

NIDWTC—No, I Don't Want To Chat

NIH—Not Invented Here

NIMBY—Not In My Back Yard

NIMTO—Not In My Term of Office

NINO—Nothing In, Nothing Out

NIT—Not In Therapy

NM—Never Mind

NMP—Not My Problem

NMS—Not My Style

NMSAA—Not My Style At All

NN—Night Night

NOOTO—Nothing Out Of The Ordinary

NOYB—None Of Your Business

NP—No Problem

NPF—No Problem Found

NPLU—Not People Like Us

NQA—No Questions Asked

NRN—No Reply Necessary

NS—Netscape

NT—No Text

NTG—Not Too Good

NTIBOA—Not That I'm Bitter Or Anything

NTIM—Not That It Matters

NTIMM—Not That It Matters Much

NTL—NoneTheLess/NeverTheLess

NTP—Need To Pee

NYCTMI—Now You Come To Mention It

NYP—Not Your Problem

O

OATUS—On A Totally Unrelated Subject

OAUS—On An Unrelated Subject

OBTW—Oh, By The Way

OD—OverDose

OI—Operator Indisposed

OIC—Oh, I See

OMG—Oh My God

OMIK—Open Mouth, Insert Keyboard

ONNA—Oh No, Not Again

ONNTA—Oh No, Not That/This Again

OO—Over and Out

OOSOOM—Out Of Sight Out Of Mind

OS—Operating System

OT—Off Topic

OT1H—On The One Hand

OTC—Over The Counter

OTD—Out The Door

OTF—On The Floor [mad laughter]

OTL—Out To Lunch

OTOH—On The Other Hand

OTOOH—On The Other, Other Hand

OTSH—On The Same Hand

OTT—Over The Top

OTTOMH—Off The Top Of My Head

OTW—On The Whole

OW—Oh Well

OWTTE—Or Words To That Effect

P

PAW—Parents Are Watching

PCB—Please Call Back

PDA—Public Display of Affection

PDPMEMA—Please Don't Post My E-Mail Address

PDS—Please Don't Shout

PEBCAK—Problem Exists Between Chair And Keyboard

PEST—Please Excuse Slow Typing

PGP—Pretty Good Privacy

PhD—Piled Higher and Deeper

PIMP—Pee In My Pants

PKOC—Passionate Kiss On the Cheek

PKOL—Passionate Kiss On the Lips

PLMK—Please Let Me Know

PLMKO—Please Let Me Know, Okay?

PLOKTA—Press Lots Of Keys To Abort

PLS—Please

PLZ—Please

PMBI—Pardon My Butting In

PMETC—Pardon Me, ETC.

PMF—Pull My Finger

PMFBI—Pardon Me For Butting In

PMFI—Problem Magically Fixed Itself

PMFJI—Pardon Me For Jumping In

PMFJIH—Pardon Me For Jumping In Here

PMJI—Pardon My Jumping In

PMP—Peed My Pants

POAHF—Put On A Happy Face

POS—Parents Over Shoulder

POV—Point Of View

PTB—Powers That Be

PTL—Praise The Lord

PTMM—Please Tell Me More

PTMY—Pleased To Meet You

PTMYA—Pleased To Make Your Acquaintance

R

RAS—Running And Screaming

RBTL—Read Between The Lines

RFT—Request For Thinking

RL—Real Life

RMH—Real Manly Hug

RML—Read My Lips

RMM—Read My Mail

RNA—Ring No Answer

ROFFNAR—Rolling On the Floor For No Apparent Reason

ROFL—Rolling On Floor Laughing

ROFLMHO—Rolling On Floor, Laughing My Head Off

ROFLOL—Rolling On Floor, Laughing Out Loud

ROFLUTS—Rolling On Floor Laughing, Unable To Speak

ROFLWPIMP—Rolling On Floor Laughing While Peeing In My Pants

ROTBA—Reality On The Blink Again

ROTF—Rolling On The Floor

ROTFL—Rolling On The Floor Laughing

ROTFLAS—Rolling On The Floor Laughing And Snorting

ROTFLBTC—Rolling On The Floor Laughing, Biting The Carpet

ROTFLSHISMC—Rolling On The Floor Laughing So Hard I Spilled My Coffee

ROTFLSTCIIHO—Rolling On The Floor Laughing, Scaring The Cat If I Had One

ROTM—Right On The Money

RPG—Role Playing Game

RSN—Real Soon Now

RT—Real Time

RTS—Read The Screen

RUMF—aRe yoU Male or Female?

RUMORF—aRe yoU Male OR Female?

S

SASS—Short Attention Span Society/Syndrome

SCNR—Sorry, Could Not Resist

SEC—SECond [that is, wait a second]

SEP—Somebody Else's Problem

SETE—Smiling Ear To Ear

SFAIAA—So Far As I Am Aware

SFLA—Stupid Four Letter Acronym

SHTSI—Somebody Had To Say It

SIL—Sister In Law

SIT—Stay In Touch

SITD—Still In The Dark

SNR—Signal to Noise Ratio

SO—Significant Other

SOHB—Sense Of Humor Bypass

SOI—Sit On It

SOT—Short Of Time

SOTMG—Short Of Time, Must Go

SOVS—SomeOne Very Special

SRY—Sorry

STS—So To Speak

SUFID—Screwing Up Face In Disgust

SUL—See yoU Later

SUNOILTY—Shut Up, No One Is Listening To You

SUP—what'S UP?

SWAK—Sealed With A Kiss

SWALK—Sealed With A Loving Kiss

SWDYRTW—Since When Do You Rule The Web?

SWL—Screaming With Laughter

SWMBO—She Who Must Be Obeyed

SWYP—So, What's Your Problem?

SYL—See You Later

SYP—Send Your Password

SYT—Sweet Young Thing

SYWWBY—See Ya—Wouldn't Wanna Be Ya

T

TAF—That's All, Folks

TAFL—Take A Flying Leap

TAFN—That's All For Now

TANJ—There Ain't No Justice

TANSTAAFL—There Ain't No Such Thing As A Free Lunch

TAWIS—That Ain't What I Said

TBC—To Be Continued

TBE—To Be Expected

TBYB—Try Before You Buy

TC—Take Care

TCB—Taking Care of Business

TEOTWAWKI—The End Of The World As We Know It

TFN—Thanks For Nothin'

TFS—Three Fingered Salute [Ctrl-Alt-Del]

TFTT—Thanks For The Thought

TGAL—Think Globally, Act Locally

TGIF—Thank God It's Friday

TGTF—Thank God Tomorrow's Friday

TIA—Thanks In Advance

TIATLG—Truly, I Am The Living God

TIC—Tongue In Cheek

TIIC—Those Idiots In Control

TIME—Tears In My Eyes

TIMTOWTDI—There Is More Than One Way To Do It

TINALO—This Is Not A Legal Opinion

TINAR—This Is Not A Recommendation

TINWIS—That Is Not What I Said

TJATAW—Truth, Justice, And The American Way

TLC—Tender Loving Care

TLG—The Living God

TM—Trust Me

TMI—Too Much Information

TMIKTLIU—The More I Know, The Less I Understand

TNOTVS—There's Nothing On TeleVision, So...

TNX—Thanks

TPAE—The Possibilities Are Endless

TPS(S)—This Program Sucks (Severely)

TPTB—The Powers That Be

TRDMC—Tears Running Down My Cheeks

TTBE—That's To Be Expected

TTBOMK—To The Best Of My Knowledge

TTFN—Ta Ta For Now

TTL4N—That's The Lot For Now

TTM—To The Moderator

TTSP—This Too Shall Pass

TTT—That's The Ticket

TTTT—These Things Take Time

TTUL—Talk/Type To yoU Later

TTYL—Talk To You Later

TTYRS—Talk To You Real Soon

TWHAB—This Won't Hurt A Bit

TWIMC—To Whom It May Concern

TWIS—That's What I Said

TWYAS—That's What You All Say

TWYT—That's What You Think

TY—Thank You

TYT—Take Your Time

TYVM—Thank You Very Much

U

UGTBK—yoU've Got To Be Kidding

UOK—yoU OK?

URLCM—yoU aRe weLCoMe

USU—USUally

UTC—Under The Counter

UTT—Under The Table

V

VBG—Very Big Grin

VDPKOL—Very Deep Passionate Kiss On the Lips

VDWPKOL—Very Deep, Wet Passionate Kiss On the Lips

VH—Virtual Hug

VI—Village Idiot

W

W/—With

W/O—WithOut

W8—Wait

W8ING—Waiting

WAEF—When All Else Fails

WALOC—What A Load Of Crap

WAN—Wide Area Network

WB—Welcome Back

WBS—Write Back Soon

WBSP—Write Back Soon, Please

WC—Way Cool

WCAGA—What Comes Around Goes Around

WDYMBT—What Do You Mean By That?

WFM—Works For Me

WIBNIF—Wouldn't It Be Nice IF

WMG—Where's My Glasses

WMMOWS—Wash My Mouth Out With Soap

WOA—Work Of Art

WOM—Word Of Mouth

WOMBAT—Waste Of Money, Brains, And Time

WPKOL—Wet Passionate Kiss On the Lips

WRT—With Regard/Respect To

WSDMU—We Sure Did Miss yoU

WTG—Way To Go (Well Done!)

WTH—What The Heck

WTSDS—Where The Sun Don't Shine

WUC—Why yoU Cry?

WWYC—Write When You Can

WYGIWYG—What You Got Is What You Get

WYGIWYPF—What You Get Is What You Pay For

WYM—What You Mean?

WYP—What's Your Point?

WYSIUWYW—What You See Isn't Usually What You Want

WYSIWYG—What You See Is What You Get

WYSOH—Where's Your Sense Of Humor?

X

XYZ—eXamine Your Zipper

Y

Y2K—The Year 2000

YAABH—You Are A Big Help

YAOTM—Yet Another Off-Topic Message

YBS—You'll Be Sorry

YCIITM—Your Check Is In The Mail

YCLIU—You Can Look It Up

YGBK—You Gotta Be Kiddin'

YGGM—Your Guess is as Good as Mine

YGTBK—You've Got To Be Kidding

YHB___—You Have Been ___

YHBW—You Have Been Warned

YHL—You Have Lost

YHTBT—You Had To Be There

YIAH—Yes, I Am Here

YKWIM—You Know What I Mean

YM—You Mean

YMMV—Your Mileage May Vary

YOYO—You're On Your Own

YOYOW—You Own Your Own Words

YR—Yeah, Right

YT—Yours Truly

YW—You're Welcome

YWSYLS—You Win Some, You Lose Some

YYSSW—Ya, Ya, Sure, Sure, Whatever

Index

F

W–Z